The Collected Courses of the Academy of European Law

VOLUME XXV/3
Freedom of Religion, Secularism, and Human Rights

The Collected Courses of the Academy of European Law
Edited by Professor Nehal Bhuta, Professor Claire Kilpatrick, and Professor Joanne Scott
Assistant Editor: Anny Bremner

Each year the Academy of European Law in Florence, Italy, invites a group of outstanding lecturers to teach at its summer courses on Human Rights law and European Union law.

A 'general course' is given in each of the two fields by a distinguished scholar or practitioner, who examines the field as a whole through a particular thematic, conceptual, or philosophical lens, or looks at a theme in the context of the overall body of law. In addition, a series of 'specialized courses' brings together a group of highly qualified scholars to explore and analyse a specific theme in relation to Human Rights law and EU law.

The Academy's mission, to produce scholarly analyses which are at the cutting edge of the two fields, is achieved through publication of this series, the Collected Courses of the Academy of European Law.

Freedom of Religion, Secularism, and Human Rights

Edited by

NEHAL BHUTA

OXFORD
UNIVERSITY PRESS

OXFORD
UNIVERSITY PRESS

Great Clarendon Street, Oxford, OX2 6DP,
United Kingdom

Oxford University Press is a department of the University of Oxford.
It furthers the University's objective of excellence in research, scholarship,
and education by publishing worldwide. Oxford is a registered trade mark of
Oxford University Press in the UK and in certain other countries

First Edition published in 2019

Published in the United States of America by Oxford University Press
198 Madison Avenue, New York, NY 10016, United States of America

British Library Cataloguing in Publication Data
Data available

Library of Congress Control Number: 2018951256

ISBN 978–0–19–881206–7

Contents

Table of Cases

EUROPEAN COURT OF HUMAN RIGHTS

INTERNATIONAL CASES

India

Malaysia

United States

Notes on Contributors

Timnah Rachel Baker (BA/LLB Monash University and LLM Boston College) is a Research Fellow at the Peter McMullin Centre on Statelessness, Melbourne Law School, and PhD candidate at Sydney Law School. Previously she was a lead researcher on the International Migration Policy and Law Analysis (IMPALA) project.

Rajeev Bhargava is Professor and former Director of the Centre for the Study of Developing Societies (CSDS), New Delhi. He is currently also Director, Parekh Institute of Indian Thought. He is an Honorary fellow at Balliol College, Oxford and a Professorial Fellow at the Institute of Social Justice, Australian Catholic University. He is the author of *Individualism in Social Science* (1992), *What is Political Theory and Why Do We Need It?* (2010), and *The Promise of India's Secular Democracy* (2010). He has also edited books, including *Secularism and its Critics* (1998).

Nehal Bhuta holds the established Chair of Public International Law at the University of Edinburgh. Prior to joining Edinburgh Law School, he held the Chair of Public International Law at the European University Institute in Florence, and was a co-director of the Academy of European Law. He is a member of the editorial boards of the *European Journal of International Law*, the *Journal of International Criminal Justice*, *Constellations*, and *Humanity*. He edits, with Anthony Pagden and Benjamin Straumann, the Oxford University Press series in the History and Theory of International Law.

Nathan J. Brown is Professor of Political Science and International Affairs at George Washington University. He is also non-resident Senior Fellow at the Carnegie Endowment for International Peace. His most recent book is *Arguing Islam after the Revival of Arab Politics* (2017).

Carolyn Evans is Deputy Vice-Chancellor (Graduate) and Harrison Moore Professor of Law at the University of Melbourne. A former Dean of Melbourne Law School, Carolyn's research focuses on human rights, particularly religious freedom and the ways in which it can conflict with other rights, and the role of democratic institutions in protecting rights. In 2010, Carolyn was awarded a Fulbright Senior Scholarship to travel as a Visiting Fellow at American and Emory Universities to examine questions of comparative religious freedom. She is the author of *Religious Freedom under the European Court of Human Rights* (2001) and *Legal Protection of Religious Freedom in Australia* (2012), and co-author of *Australian Bills of Rights: The Law of the Victorian Charter and the ACT Human Rights Act* (2008).

Samuel Moyn is Professor of Law and Professor of History at Yale University. He is the author of several books on European intellectual history and legal history, most recently on the history of human rights. His most recent book is *Not Enough: Human Rights in an Unequal World* (2018).

Winnifred Fallers Sullivan is Professor in the Department of Religious Studies and Affiliated Professor of Law in the Maurer School of Law, Indiana University Bloomington. She studies the intersection of religion and law in the modern period, particularly the phenomenology of modern religion as it is shaped in its encounter with law. She is the author of *The Impossibility of Religious Freedom* (2005); *Prison Religion: Faith-based Reform and the Constitution* (2009);

and *A Ministry of Presence: Chaplaincy, Spiritual Care and the Law* (2014). She is also co-author of *Ekklesia: Three Inquiries in Church and State* (2018) and co-editor of *Politics of Religious Freedom* (2015).

Lorenzo Zucca is Professor in Law & Philosophy at King's College London. His research interests lie in the areas of jurisprudence, constitutional theory, EU constitutional law, and human rights. He is the author of *Constitutional Dilemmas—Conflicts of Fundamental Legal Rights in Europe and the USA* (2007) and *A Secular Europe: Law and Religion in the European Constitutional Landscape* (2012).

1

What Should Freedom of Religion Become?

Nehal Bhuta

1.

'Secularism', 'secularization', and 'freedom of religion' (and/or of conscience)[1] are concepts that are today not only polemical—shaped and deployed in the context of concrete disputations and duelling political projects[2]—but also essentially contested in Gallie's well-known definition.[3] As historical phenomena, secularism and freedom of religion were not co-original, but stood in a dialectical historical relationship. The secularization of the state in the first instance entailed the substitution of a theological judgment with a political one: that the unity presupposed by a political order was now to be found in the unity of public law under an earthly sovereign power pursuing this-worldly peace and prosperity, not in the unity of a religious truth guaranteeing salvation in the next world. As Dumont points out, this is a transformed and transvalued theological structure: the modern state was a 'transformed Church' in so far as the medieval Church after Gregory insisted not on distinct-yet-dependent spiritual and temporal realities, but on a hierarchical spiritual *unity* in which the spiritual took precedence over temporal *functions*.[4] The Gregorian

[1] The author thanks Peter Drahos, Richard Bellamy, Julian Sempill, and participants in the EUI Law Department Faculty Seminar for helpful comments.

[2] Grasping such concepts as polemical is to think of them as 'focused on a specific conflict and … bound to a concrete situation … Words such as state, republic, society, class, as well as sovereignty, constitutional state, absolutism, dictatorship, economic planning, neutral or total state [and I would add secularism and religious freedom—NB] and so on, are incomprehensible if one does not know exactly who is to be affected, combated, refuted or negated by such a term.' C. Schmitt, *The Concept of the Political* (2nd edn, 2007) 30–1. See also Quentin Skinner's reflections on the impulse driving his methods in the history of political thought: 'Our concepts form part of what we bring to the world in our efforts to make sense of it. The shifting conceptualizations to which this process gives rise constitute the very stuff of ideological debate … [I] … assume that we need to treat our normative concepts less as statements about the world than as tools and weapons of ideological debate.' Skinner, 'Retrospect: Studying Rhetoric and Conceptual Change' in Q. Skinner, *Visions of Politics: Volume 1, Regarding Method* (2002) 175, 176–7.

[3] Gallie, 'Essentially Contested Concepts', 56 *Proceedings of the Aristotelian Society, New Series* (1955–1956) 167, 167.

[4] A. Dumont, *Essays on Individualism: Modern Ideology in Anthropological Perspective* (1986) 50–1. Böckenförde of course makes a cognate observation in his famous 1964 essay on 'The Rise of the State as a Process of Secularization', where he argues that the Investiture Controversy resulted in the construction of the Church as 'an autonomous, legally self-constituting, and sacramentally hierarchical institution' to which the emperor—like any other layman—was supposedly subject. But the new *ordo* had as its unintentional by-product the establishment of politics 'as a separate, self-contained realm', 'set free

What Should Freedom of Religion Become?. First Edition. Nehal Bhuta
Published 2019 by Oxford University Press.

Church, with its doctrine of the Pope's infallibility and *plenitudo potestatis*, '*was* the State [in the Middle Ages];... the civil authority was merely the police department of the Church....'[5]

Unity as the *sine qua non* of omnipotence was the *modus* of political authority inherited by the civil state,[6] and for this reason, among others, the Reformation at first inaugurated a thoroughgoing *confessionalization* and forcible *homogenization* of religion within sovereign territories, not the pluralization and toleration of confessional belief: *cuius regio, eius religio* (declared by the 1555 Peace of Augsburg) ratified the seizure of Church property by Protestant princes (the first true instance of 'secularization'—the transfer to earthly power of something previously in the domain of religious authority) and the persecution of non-conforming religious belief.[7] The idea that religious uniformity was necessary for political order and stability remained, in the first decades after the Schism, a point on which 'Roman Catholics, Lutherans, and members of the Reformed Church were in fundamental agreement'.[8] The religious duty of the temporal power was to expel or eliminate seditious heretics and punish non-seditious heretics.[9] At stake in such mutual heretication and persecution were the souls and freedom from sin and death of the religious communities themselves:

> Whether in the form of popular pogroms and riots, the formation of armed religious leagues and militias, or the punishment of heresy in ecclesial or civil courts, confessional violence arose from the fact that the formation of morally regenerated identities through the sacral rites of religious communities was inseparable from the stigmatization and demonization of those polluting identities and communities that threatened these saving rites.[10]

Early modern European secularity, which implies a realm of the political and of rationality distinguishable from the theological,[11] did not emerge upon a foundation of the freedom of the individual or his conscience, or any other philosophical history conjured much later in the name of Enlightenment.[12] Rather, its initial moment of formation rested upon an outgrowth of fanatical religiosity—the heretication of non-conforming beliefs and behaviours, the consequence of which was the intensification of power over community and territory. The paradox (or irony) that the

to pursue its own development as a secular concern'. (New translation of Böckeförde 'Rise of the State as a Process of Secularization' in E.W. Böckenförde, *Law, Religion and Democacy: Selected Writings* (T. Stein and M. Künkler (eds) (forthcoming).)

[5] J.N. Figgis, *Studies of Political Thought from Gerson to Grotius 1414–1625* (1907) 4.

[6] As Dumont puts it compactly: 'The Reformation picks the fruit matured in the Church's lap.' Dumont (n. 4) 59.

[7] Reinhard, 'Reformation, Counter-reformation and the Early Modern State: A Reassessment', 75 *The Catholic Historical Review* (July 1989) 383, 391ff.

[8] Böckenförde (n. 4). See also Figgis, who observes that we 'cannot overestimate the change in men's minds required to produce the ideal of heterogeneity in religion within one state'. Figgis (n. 5) 18.

[9] Hunter, 'Religious Freedom in Early Modern Germany: Theology, Philosophy, and Legal Casuistry', 113 *South Atlantic Quarterly*, (2014) 37, 37.

[10] Ibid. 43 (inline references omitted).

[11] Troper, 'Sovereignty and Laïcité' in S. Mancini and M. Rosenfeld (eds), *Constitutional Secularism in an Age of Religious Revival* (2014) 146.

[12] See Hunter, 'Secularization: The Birth of a Modern Combat Concept', 12 *Modern Intellectual History* (2015) 1.

Reformation 'retarded the secularizing tendency, and made politics more, not less, theological'[13] is inexplicable for those who understand secularity as the consequence of a progressive liberation of reason and conscience from the stifling orthodoxy of Catholicism, commencing with the Lutheran and Calvinist appeal to this-worldly faith and action as the only possible source of salvation—as the progenitor, in other words, of freedom of conscience.

Neither the Catholic Church nor the original Protestant confessions recognized freedom of conscience for others, because as Weber appreciated with his characteristic lack of sentimentality, 'a fully developed church—advancing universalist claims—cannot concede freedom of conscience [unless] ... it finds itself in a minority position and demands something which it cannot grant to others'.[14] The 'genuine early Protestantism'[15] of Lutheranism and Calvinism understood its mission not as relativizing a universal Church under the protection of secular rule, but of re-founding it according to true principles. Troeltsch reminds us that original Protestantism 'never surrendered the thought of the Church itself as the supernatural organ of Salvation', and that it did not see Church and State as 'two distinct organisations, any more than did Catholicism'. The application of uniform religious standards to the whole community, the exclusion of unbelievers and heretics, the principle of intolerance and infallibility, were 'self-evident necessities', and thus, there was 'no direct road leading from Protestant Church-civilization to the modern civilization independent of the church'.[16]

Nonetheless, the intensified domination and homogenization of belief and subjectivity set in motion by confessionalization were essential preconditions for the gradual emergence of a unified realm of public power which was not so much *indifferent* in relation to religion, but unevenly *differentiated* from religious authority even as it inherited and rested upon many of its modes of legitimation and social power.[17] Confessionalization and state-making were closely intertwined, precisely in order to re-establish the foundations for political-theological order in the aftermath of Schism:

> Without doubt, in the long run the [Catholic, Lutheran and Calvinist] churches succeeded in 'confessionalizing' their members to a remarkable extent ...
>
> 'Confessionalization' made an important contribution to the growth of the modern state in Europe. Not that churches intended to do so ... However, they all needed the help of secular authorities ... Early modern state-builders, on the other hand, knew very well that joining the processes of 'Confessionalization' would provide them with three decisive competitive advantages: enforcement of political identity, extension of a monopoly of power, and the disciplining of their subjects. Therefore, it was obvious that a policy of religious toleration

[13] Figgis (n. 5) 18–19. [14] M. Weber, *Economy and Society* (1922/1978) Vol. 2, 1209.

[15] E. Troeltsch, *Protestantism and Progress: The Significance of Protestantism and the Rise of the Modern World* (1912/1958) 35.

[16] Ibid. 41.

[17] Creppell, 'Secularization: Religion and the Roots of Innovation in the Political Sphere' in I. Katznelson and G.S. Jones (eds), *Religion and the Political Imagination* (2010) 23. As Figgis notes: 'Until towards the close of the seventeenth century, the atmosphere of the supporters of popular rights is as theological as that of the upholders of the Divine Right of Kings.' J.N. Figgis, *The Divine Right of King* (2nd edn, 1914) 11.

would not pay at that stage of state-building. Indeed, *tolerant states were powerless states during the first centuries of modern history!*... 'Confessionalization' meant gains of power for the State, because the Church became a part of the State in theory as well as in practice. And if not in theory, as in the Catholic case, then at least in practice! ...

... This alliance of Church and State during the process of 'Confessionalization' reached its culmination in the field of ideas and emotions, where it secured the consent of the subjects to their own subjugation. This had been noticed as early as 1589 by Giovanni Botero: 'No law is more favorable to princes than the Christian one, because it submits to them not only the bodies and means of the subjects, but their souls and consciences, too, and it binds not only the hands, but also the feelings and thoughts.'[18]

Under the banner of *religio vincula societatis* (religion binds society together), confessional church-building enhanced state power by 'establishing new mechanisms of moral regulation and social control'.[19] The peculiar cunning of unreason that characterizes modern European state-formation and secularization is that the intensification of religious discipline and religious conflict laid the foundations for the emergence of public power as representing and materializing the unity essential to the concept of political and social order. The constitution of this unity nonetheless remained deeply entangled with religious authority,[20] which continued as an indispensable (and, at the time, unrivalled) modality for the instauration and imagination of collective being.[21]

The retraction of religion as the primary normative source for the binding of wills in submission to public power would require an alternative *archê* and *telos* for emotional and ideational investment: the this-worldly flourishing of human beings, made *in imago dei*. Whether as a qualified (Catholicism) or an unqualified (Protestantism) *societas perfecta*, the state was consecrated by all confessions as the medium through which human flourishing could be achieved, first and foremost through its achievement of this-worldly civil peace—the practical and effective unity of a people, government, and territory under sovereign power.[22] In the wake of confessionalization came begrudging and reluctant toleration: the sovereign

[18] Reinhard (n. 7) 397, 398, 403 (my emphasis). Footnote to Botero omitted.

[19] P.S. Gorski, *The Disciplinary Revolution and the Rise of the State in Early Modern Europe* (2003) 18. See also D. MacCulloch, *Reformation: Europe's House Divided 1490–1700* (2003) Part III.

[20] As Gorski observes: 'In all these areas—poor-relief, education, and the regulation of sexuality and marriage—cooperation between religious and civil authorities was generally tight. In fact, in most early modern polities, it would have been difficult to draw a clear line between church and state ... such a distinction would be purely anachronistic.' Gorski (n. 19) 19.

[21] M. Gauchet, *The Disenchantment of the World: A Political History of Religion* (1999). The Jesuit counter-reformation theologian de Mariana, for example, asked how, with the loss of religious unity, 'contracts, alliances and covenants among men can be guaranteed?' H.E. Braun, *Juan de Mariana and Early Modern Spanish Political Thought* (2007) 136–9.

[22] As Troeltsch points out, the intensification of conflict after the period of confessionalization accelerated the acceptance of a foundation for absolute state power differentiated from religious unification: 'Three infallible "Churches", unchurching and anathematizing one another, discredited the idea of the Church, for which there is no plural ... Thus Protestantism disintegrates the Christian Church-system and its supernatural foundation, wholly against its will, but by its actual and ever more clearly apparent influence. The plurality of the Churches and their embittered struggle did more than anything else to multiply the "Libertinists and Neutralists", while in France the policy of the Chancellor L'Hôpital, and in the Netherlands that of the Orange Party, and the Pacification of Ghent, tended to the same result.' Troeltsch (n. 15) 54.

without doubt remained Christian, but *raison d'état* did not require that the sovereign decide matters of religious truth and instead should determine which beliefs and kinds of worship were incompatible with loyalty to the sovereign and his public order.[23] His courts might also examine which theological tenets touching upon the maintenance of public order could be deemed *adiaphoric* (indifferent to salvation) and so possibly proscribed as public order necessitated.[24]

This *formal* power and authority to decide upon the content of civil peace and public order as ultimate limits to any substantive system of religious truth, is the essential kernel of the secular as an historical phenomenon.[25]

It presupposes *neither* Enlightenment nor liberalism, both of which remained more than a century away, but Absolutism: the consolidation of a sphere of autonomous political power and judgment, released from allegiance to theological truths and indirect spiritual and earthly powers and propelled relentlessly forwards by exigencies of reason of state. The secularization of the state in this sense went hand-in-hand with the destruction of the medieval 'lawful state' of limited jurisdictions and feudal- and estate-based privileges and competences: answering *quis judicabit* in favour of the sovereign entailed not only the power of decision over the boundaries of the effectiveness of theological judgment, but equally the 'abridging, destroying or absorbing [of] rights previously lodged in other political units: manors, communities, provinces, estates'.[26] The precursor to modern democratic, equal citizenship was equal subjecthood *before* the sovereign, the unbounded competence of which permitted the dissolution or relativization of any intermediate power in the name of reason of state; before subjects could aspire to be *free* and equal, the hierarchical structures of representation and mediation essential to the medieval world-view had to be decisively swept away.[27]

The homogenization and homologation of population, territory, and rule begun under confessionalization—so indispensable to the logic of modern law and

23 Dunn, 'The Claim to Freedom of Conscience: Freedom of Speech, Freedom of Thought, Freedom of Worship?' in J. Dunn, *The History of Political Theory and Other Essays* (1996) 100.

24 See Hunter, 'Religious Freedom in Early Modern Germany' (n. 9); and Hunter, 'English Blasphemy', 4 *Humanity* (2013) 403.

25 Schmitt, 'Die Vollendete Reformation: Bemerkungen und Hinweise Zu Neuen Leviathan-Interpretationen' ('The Reformation Completed') in 4 *Der Staat* (1965) 51–69, translation by Dr Benjamin Schupmann on file with author. Böckenförde (n. 4) (forthcoming).

26 Tilly, 'Reflections on the History of European State-Making' in C. Tilly (ed.), *The Formation of National States in Western Europe* (1975) 3, 37.

27 See, for example, Guido de Ruggiero's observation that 'without the levelling effected by royal absolutism, the regime of privilege ... would never have bridged the gulf that divides privilege from liberty'. G. de Ruggiero, *The History of European Liberalism* (1927/1959) 3–4. In this short sketch for theoretical purposes, I of course do not discuss the sometimes fierce resistance to centralization undertaken by both the aristocratic and clerical estates, which found intellectual expression in various resistance theories concerned with justifying opposition to tyranny. The mitigated success of this resistance is reflected in the highly uneven and varied extent to which *actual* absolutist states succeeded in diminishing the political and economic power of the aristocracy and the estates. See T. Ertman, *Birth of the Leviathan: Building States and Regimes in Early Modern Europe* (1997).

state[28]—accelerated and intensified under the absolutist *polizeistaat*.[29] The governance of souls to the end of the good order and flourishing of the population and territory, becomes an essential part of the purpose of the Christian prince's *ratio status*; in this sense, as Troeltsch noted, the *civilizational* function of the Church ('education, moral order, oversight of food supply, and spiritual and ethical well-being')[30] had been taken up by the state even in Catholic territories, and the pastoral power over the direction and care of souls became a means of the art of government itself.[31] To this end, the state's domain extended to the *subjectification* of the subject himself, not in order to save his soul but to conduce to his 'felicity' as means to the strengthening of the state's utility.[32] Far from becoming a *domaine réservé* in the wake of secularization, the subject's relation to itself—the constitution of its interiority—was intensively problematized as an object and a set of forces to be rationally disciplined and reformed in the furtherance of the political order's stability and prosperity.[33] Early modern natural law theory after Pufendorf and Lipsian neostoicism would provide an essential intellectual bridge between theology, reason of state, and *polizeiwissenschaft* for reforming princes:

> Its aim was to increase the power and efficiency of the state by an acceptance of the central role of force and of the army. At the same time [...] [it] also demanded self-discipline and the extension of the duties of the ruler and the moral education of the army, the officials, and indeed the whole people, to a life of work, frugality, dutifulness and obedience. The result was a general enhancement of social discipline in all spheres of life, and this enhancement produced, in its turn, a change in the ethos of the individual and his self-perception. This change was to play a crucial role in the later development of both modern industrialism and democracy ...[34]

To define the secular abstractly as the 'neutrality' towards religion, or the institutional separation of church and state, or what remains when religion is 'subtracted' from public life, is thus to mistakenly identify specific historical possibilities, deriving from a deeper structuring logic, with the grammar of the language itself; to borrow from Saussure, it is to take a variety of *parole* and believe them to be *langue*. At its most basic, the secular is co-original with the emergence of the political as a sphere of autonomous decision over the constitution and maintenance of a concrete public order in respect of a people and territory; as such it is a constituent element of the process of modern European state formation, with its particularly intrusive types of domination and correlate processes of individualization. As such, secularism is an 'attitude' or 'posture' towards religion maintained by civil authorities which need

[28] For variations on this theme, see N. Elias, *The Civilizing Process* (1939/1978–82) 257–344; Oakeshott, 'The Character of the Modern European State' in M. Oakeshott, *On Human Conduct* (1975) 279; P. Bourdieu, *On the State: Lectures at the College de France, 1989–1992* (2014); M. Foucault, *Security, Territory, Population: Lectures at the College de France, 1977–78* (2004).

[29] M. Raeff, *The Well-Ordered Police State: Social and Institutional Change Through Law in the Germanies and Russia, 1600–1800* (1983); A. Small, *The Cameralists: Pioneers of German Social Polity* (1909).

[30] Troeltsch (n. 15) 62.

[31] Foucault (n. 28) 154–5, 165.

[32] Ibid. 326.

[33] On this, see C. Taylor, *A Secular Age* (2007) Ch. 2; also, Foucault (n. 28).

[34] G. Oestereich, *Neostoicism and the Early Modern State* (1982) 7.

not be neutral[35] but necessarily implying a vantage point of decision 'above' or 'beyond' the obligations of any religious *nomos*.[36] This authoritative power of decision is the *presupposition* of liberal neutrality towards religion—a political philosophical desideratum of the state's posture towards religion that would come much later—but rests in fact on processes of the homogenization of the political (confessionalization, *polizeiwissenschaft*, etc.) that cannot itself be justified by the dictum of neutrality. As Laborde puts it in her trenchant criticism of the Rawlsian prescription of state neutrality towards the Good (epitomized by religion in contemporary liberal thought, and in contrast with the Just, which states may decide upon):

> No theory of neutral justification can justify *this* prerogative—that of adjudicating the boundary problem [between Good and Just, between ethical and moral] in the first place. The prerogative consists in being authorized to define... *where* the boundary between the right and the good lies. Theorists of liberal neutrality tend to assume that the right and the good are self-evident categories of moral reasoning; yet clearly they have evolved historically and are themselves the sites of foundational political disagreement.... The prior identification of which areas of social life are justice-apt [and so amenable to state control]... cannot be made without judgments of substantive, metaphysical, and ontological questions.[37]

To say that the state has the authority to police the line between the Just and the Good is in effect to admit that through a panoply of instances and decisions and prescriptions, the state determines and comes to represent *that substance* which rests *as a condition of intelligibility and condition of possibility for the idea of the state as a unity*. This substance is, of course, historically variable, and as a matter of historical reality has been the carrier of a wide variety of metaphysical and ontological possibilities; but the intelligibility of the prerogative to decide what is essential to the unity of the legal and political order, and what is inessential to it, inevitably has recourse to some operative concept of the substance on which the unity of the state rests.[38] For centuries, as I have labored to show in the foregoing, this operative concept of substance was religious even as the secular power of decision emerged. Indeed, the secular power of decision could not have emerged without the religious, and the distinctive processes and conflicted trajectories (religious settlements and consociations, revolution, counter-revolution and restoration, colonization, to name but a few) through which the secular power of decision completely or partially differentiated itself from this religious substance, were productive of the diverse

[35] Urbinati, 'The Context of Secularism: A Critical Appraisal of the Post-Secular Argument' in S. Mancini and M. Rosenfeld (eds), *Constitutional Secularism in an Age of Religious Revival* (2014) 14.

[36] Bilgrami's formal formulation is helpful here: 'One should be able to characterize secularism (S) independently of whether a polity is authoritarian or liberal in its fundamental orientation ... The point is not to lay down very specific ideals that form a definite list. The point rather is to stress the role of the *priority* such ideals (whatever they may be) will have in *the lexical ordering that forms the heart of the characterization of secularism*.... All the opposition to religion that the characterization in (S) demands is in the notion of lexical ordering that follows the initial starting point in these ideals.' Bilgrami, 'Secularism: Its Content and Context' in A. Stepan and C. Taylor (eds), *Boundaries of Toleration* (2014) 79, 97.

[37] C. Laborde, *Liberalism's Religion* (2017) 109. See also at 160–3.

[38] I take this to be the implication of the famous Böckenförde dictum that, 'the liberal, secularized state draws its life from preconditions it cannot itself guarantee'. Böckenförde (n. 4) (forthcoming).

formations of state-church or state-religion legal and political relationships that characterize Europe. This point of view on the secular also helps us to appreciate the historical specificity and contextual determinacy of the valences and constellations of religious and anti-religious polemics in a given time and place.

Importantly, understanding the secular from this vantage point of state formation and the problem of the non-theological foundations of political unity, allows us to grasp what is shared and what is different in non-Western historical trajectories of secularity and secularization, without rendering such trajectories merely as the incomplete realizations of the liberation of reason from religion or of a failure of political and economic modernization. As Troper points out in his reflection on the 1980 Egyptian constitution's reference to shari'a as a source of legislation, what is at stake is not a 'separation of church and state' but who decides (*quis judicabit*) the meaning and limits of a religious law:[39] precisely the problematic of the constitution of the political and its differentiation from and priority over the religious. What is also made visible in this perspective, is the extent to which the historical trajectory of non-Western formations of the secular are indelibly marked by the experience of state formation under colonial rule and decolonization. In the context of the Middle East, Mahmood observes that colonial state formation 'subjected [religious difference] to a new grid of intelligibility and a form of stratification that is compatible with the rationality of modern political rule.... The colonial state secularized native religious life by instituting the legal division between public and private'[40] but also rendered religion a means through which diverse populations could be governed directly and indirectly by a central territorial authority.[41] In the case of India, colonial administrators notoriously reified and abstracted from the social relationships entailed in the lived practices of religion in order to render the population better enumerated, more legible, and more governable: Hindu/Muslim became categories meaningful in terms of majority/minority, and also became abstract communities 'viewed as giant collective actors, such that an act of an individual or a group of Muslims became to be regarded as an "act of Muslims" as a putative group'.[42] The result was that in colonial, proto-nationalist, and post-colonial politics, religious identity became a political identity pregnant with potential for conflict in the struggle with the colonial power over the control of the state and the constitution of the post-colonial political order. The basic premise of Partition—cynically abetted by the British—was that relative religious uniformity was the most secure foundation for the political unity presupposed by any post-colonial nation-state.[43]

[39] Troper (n. 11) 146ff.

[40] S. Mahmood, *Religious Difference in A Secular Age: A Minority Report* (2016) 62–3.

[41] B. White, *The Emergence of Minorities in the Middle East: The Politics of Community in French Mandate Syria* (2012).

[42] Kaviraj, 'On Thick and Thin Religion: Some Critical Reflections on Secularisation Theory' in I. Katznelson and G.S. Jones (eds), *Religion and the Political Imagination* (2010) 336, 336, 350–2.

[43] This premise of religious identity as a necessary foundation for political unity and thus sovereign power, was similarly visible in the discussions surrounding the drafting of the Malaysian Constitution of 1957: Stilt, 'Contextualizing Constitutional Islam: The Malayan Experience', 13 *International Journal of Constitutional Law* (2015) 407: The clause establishing Islam as a national religion was 'part of a package that connected religion to privilege, language and citizenship. And these four issues were ultimately about loyalty and belonging.' Ibid. 430.

2.

In a 1970 essay on Freedom of Conscience, Böckenförde noted the difficulty of isolating any singular genealogy or identity of this concept.[44] In its early modern usage in Germany, it 'related exclusively to questions of belief and religion', and the Treaties of Westphalia guaranteed a 'restricted and qualified' freedom under which anyone 'may profess the Evangelical Lutheran or Reformed religion or the Roman Catholic religion and nothing may be demanded of such a person that is contrary to the principles of his religion'.[45] The German religious settlement's reluctant acceptance of parity in public law between the three Christian religions and the attendant repudiation of an unlimited *jus reformandi*, gave rise to a constitutional guarantee of 'freedom of belief and conscience' in so far as it entailed a prohibition on compulsion as between the choice of one of the three established religions, and provided it did not manifest itself in modes of worship or kinds of belief that threatened the public peace between believers or the fundamental creedal foundations of the public order.[46] As Troeltsch never tires of pointing out, toleration of religious beliefs beyond these three creeds was never a necessary consequence of the idea of non-compulsion in religion; each creed strongly maintained the necessity of the unity of truth, to be compulsorily protected by the state.[47] Freedom of belief in this sense, leading to toleration as a negative principle, forbade compulsion in religious matters but left no room:

> ... at all for the positive existence of different religious communions alongside one another.... In England, the Long Parliament only granted toleration to the various groups within Calvinistic Protestantism; in order to secure the Christian nature of the State it maintained the Elizabethan legislation which made attendance at public worship compulsory; the only difference was that individuals were now at liberty to choose the religious group with which they desired to worship.[48]

Geuss points out that it was not until the end of the eighteenth century that toleration 'no longer came to be construed as something inherently negative, as a... failure to attack with all one's force something which it would in principle be good to be without, but which it was perhaps too costly fully to suppress'.[49] The Protestant insistence on inner freedom permitted a great deal of compulsion to produce external uniformity on the premise (as somewhat stylized by Geuss) that 'people would be more likely to come freely to accept God in the right way if they were living in a

[44] Ernst-Wolfgang Böckenförde, 'The Basic Right of Freedom of Conscience' in E.-W. Böckenförde, *Law, Religion and Democracy: Selected Writings* (2018) Ch. V, see also Ch. VI (forthcoming).

[45] J.J. Moser, *Von der Teutschen Religionsverfassung* (1773/1967), cited in Böckenförde (n. 44).

[46] Hunter, 'Religious Freedom in Early Modern Germany' (n. 9). Hunter, 'Public Law and the Limits of Philosophy: German Idealism and the Religious Constitution' 44, *Critical Inquiry* (2018) 528.

[47] E. Troeltsch, *The Social Teachings of the Christian Churches*, Volume II (1912/1931/1992) Chs 1–3, but esp. 491–4, 660–1.

[48] Ibid. 671.

[49] R. Geuss, *History and Illusion in Politics* (2001) 80.

religious coherent, homogeneous social world (even if that cohesion was politically produced by coercive means) ...'.[50]

Nonetheless, both Troeltsch and Dumont—following Jellinek—conclude that the early Protestant ideas contained within them the seeds of a more radical but no less theological ideal of freedom of belief and conscience. The principle of a pure religion based on faith and personal conviction alone '*logically* implied the voluntary principle of Church membership'.[51] But the realization of this logical possibility required some real historical actor to articulate and maintain it, in the face of bitter persecution and an overwhelming atmosphere favouring as much religious homogeneity as possible. This historical actor was not a philosopher of secularizing reason, but a fundamentally (and fundamentalist) religious force: the Protestant sectaries. The 'sect-type' of religious movement in Christianity pre-dated the Reformation, characterized by their aspiration to 'personal inward perfection... [and] direct personal fellowship between members of each group'.[52] The theology of the sect-type emphasizes the original ideals of Christianity, a:

> ... direct continuation of the idea of the Gospel... [W]ithin [the sect] there is a full recognition of the value of radical individualism and the idea of love; it is the sect alone which instinctively builds upon its ideal of fellowship and... attains such a strong subjective and inward unity... [T]he sect also maintains the original radicalism of the Christian ideal and its hostility towards the world, and it retains the fundamental demand for personal service... .[53]

The individualism of the sect—inclined towards asceticism and mysticism—'urges towards the direct intercourse of the individual and God;... it replaces the ecclesiastical doctrine of the sacraments by the Primitive Christian doctrine of the Spirit and by "enthusiasm"'.[54]

Unsurprisingly, the Protestant movement in its emphasis on the direct Scriptural sources of God's law and its lack of a universal central hierarchy, provided a rich soil for sect-type movements. These sects sprang forth almost immediately with the beginning of the Reform movement, and—despite vigorous attempts at persecution by territorial Protestant Churches—emphatically rejected any form of compulsion in religious matters not because of a lack of certainty about the absoluteness of Truth but because such Truth could be attained exclusively through an inner spiritual certainty that could never be guaranteed or brought about by an earthly institution. Thus, these sects and movements—Pietism, Puritanism, Congregationalism, Anabaptism and Baptism, Quakers, Presbyterians, and Methodists, to name a few—denied (at least at their origins) any authority of the state over their holy com-

[50] Ibid. 74. Troeltsch's account of the early Protestant Church (Lutheran and Calvinist) strongly accords with Geuss's stylized version of the discourse. Troeltsch writes that despite Luther's early spiritualism and mysticism, which led him to champion toleration initially, the authorities of Wittenberg became increasingly severe towards dissenting Protestant sects (such as Anabaptists) on the grounds that an association based on absolute Truth needs compulsion in order to prevent the undermining of its ability to make men wise unto salvation. Compulsion was not to force inner conviction but to bring about the social and ecclesiastical unity conducive to making this truth accessible to all. Troeltsch, *Social Teaching of the Christian Churches* (n. 47) 492–3.

[51] Troeltsch (n. 47) 491. [52] Ibid. 331. [53] Ibid. 341. [54] Ibid. 342.

munities of belief on the basis of an untouchable and imprescriptible freedom of conscience. The unity of these communities was the unity of their Christian fellowship, and underlying that, the unity of each individual conscience with the Holy Spirit.[55] The Being of God did not require the mediation of earthly institutions, but rather strict practical devotion to the discernment of his Law, which is found within the human conscience and in Nature itself:

> [C]reation places mankind immediately before the task of the realization of its ideal; and this ideal is here presented shorn of the quality of a mystical supernature, which elevates man's nature above itself... In the theology of the sects the idea of law is substituted for the idea of the Church as the Organ of Grace and Redemption, and this conception becomes its essential feature. It is this conception of law which constitutes the essential truth and the objective point of reference for these groups ...'[56]

The 'Pilgrim' communities who would cross the Atlantic to New England were outgrowths of English Congregationalism, carrying with them the ideals that had forced their emigration from England under threat of forfeiture of life and property: the freedom to form independent religious communities, the abolition of state compulsion in religious matters, and the 'exclusion of all forms of heretical religion from the state'.[57] Even here, freedom of conscience and of the church did not mean freedom of any belief whatsoever: they compelled 'no-one to join the Church; but they declined to tolerate the existence of any other Church, and they gave important civic rights to the members of the Church'.[58] As Weber noted tersely, only 'pure sects' such as the Quakers could be advocates of freedom of conscience 'not only for himself but for others' because of their rigorous commitment to the idea that 'no official power can dispense grace to unqualified persons and, hence, all use of political force in religious matters must appear senseless or outright diabolical... [and] because... the [pure] sect just cannot be anything but an absolutely voluntary association if it wants to retain its true religious identity'.[59]

Jellinek's famous and highly influential argument was that it was in the politico-religious communities of the New World, that something approximating a 'human right' to freedom of conscience first appeared in recognizable constitutional form.[60] The foundations of this right derived from the premise that every political association was established on the same basis as the prior religious community: freedom of conscience was the pre-requisite of 'spiritual administration and government in itself and over itself by the common and free consent of the people, independently and immediately under Christ'.[61] The charters of Rhode Island and of Maryland expressly recognized liberty of conscience 'in matters of religion' (Rhode Island, 1647) and to everyone who acknowledged Jesus Christ (Maryland, 1649). The North Carolinian constitution drafted by Locke in 1669 provided for toleration of

[55] See the lengthy and detailed account in ibid. 656–725. [56] Ibid. 346–7.
[57] Ibid. 671. [58] Ibid. 671. [59] Weber (n. 14) 1208.
[60] G. Jellinek, *The Declaration of the Rights of Man and of Citizens: A Contribution to Modern Constitutional History* (1901).
[61] Ibid. 60, citing the petition of Congregationlists to James I, in 1616.

Dissenters, Jews, and heathens.[62] Freedom of belief and religious conscience was not in these charters an inheritance or a grant from a superior authority, but 'inherent in man, that acts of conscience and expressions of religious conviction stand inviolable over against the state as the exercise of a higher right.... The idea of legally establishing inalienable, inherent and sacred rights of the individual is not of political but religious origin.'[63]

The presupposition of this theologically-derived individualism was a two-fold underlying unity of Nature. The first dimension was a unity of the subject in the Truth of Christ's spirit, which through man's conscience would lay hold of and mould the personality towards perfection. This metaphysic of 'absolute Personality... gives to the thought of freedom, of personality, of the autonomous self, a metaphysical background, which has its influence even when it is contested or denied'.[64] The second dimension was a unity of immanent laws governing creation, the Law of God and of Nature; this conception of law as the expression of the Being of God within nature and realized through the intentional application of human will and reason would permit a particular elective affinity between sectarian Protestantism and new economic, social, and political forces.[65] For Charles Taylor, this affinity is at the heart of the historical process driving the emergence of the possibility of a thoroughgoing secularization of self and society, which he calls the 'buffered self' of modern humanism: 'It is no longer a matter of admiring a normative order, in which God has revealed himself through [supernatural] signs and symbols. We rather have to inhabit it as agents of instrumental reason, working the system effectively in order to bring about God's purposes...we have to disenchant the universe...on the high cultural level of science, and [replace] a universe of ordered signs, in which everything has meaning, [with] a silent but beneficent machine.'[66] This 'providential Deism' of the seventeenth and eighteenth centuries becomes an epoch-making phenomenon which eclipsed the earlier emphasis on Grace and supernatural redemption, and instead became a search for God 'in one's own feeling, experience, thought and will',[67] closely connected with an inquiry into the laws upholding the natural order of creation.

God's relation to us comes to be seen as mediated by an impersonal, immanent order...On one level, we have the natural order, the universe, purged of enchantment...operating by universal, unrespondent causal laws. On another level, we have a social order, designed for us, which we have come to discern by reason and establish by constructive activity and discipline....The Law which defines this order, whether as political/constitutional law, or ethical norms, can be expressed in rational codes, which can be grasped quite independent of any special relationship we may establish with God...The human relationships which matter

[62] Jellinek notes sarcastically: 'And so with Locke also liberty of conscience was brought forward as the first and most sacred right, overshadowing all others. This philosopher, who held freedom to be man's inalienable gift from nature, established servitude and slavery under the government he organized without hesitation, but religious toleration he carried through with great energy in this new feudal state.' Ibid. 72.

[63] Ibid. 77. [64] Troeltsch (n. 15) 30. [65] Troeltsch (n. 47) 676.

[66] Taylor (n. 33) 98. [67] Troeltsch (n. 15) 98.

are those prescribed in the codes (e.g. Natural Law, the Utilitarian Principle, the Categorical Imperative).

... Such a purified religion... doesn't need revelation.... The truth is available to calm, dispassionate reason. So the royal road to true religion is right belief. We cannot access it by some relation of devotion which can supposedly yield more intimate insights into the will of God... Rid the world of [superstitions such as cult and sacrifice] and humans will find peace, concord and mutual help.[68]

The explicitly theological ladder on which this structure of thought was built would ultimately be kicked away, giving rise to a revised eighteenth century self-understanding of Protestantism as having organically gestated a natural religion of reason that now stood on its own as the necessary maturation of Reformation's rejection of superstition and ritual. Troeltsch comments that on this view, looking backwards from the middle of the nineteenth century, 'the theology of the Enlightenment was [perceived as] indistinguishable from Socinianism and Arminianism. Kant, Fichte, and Hegel could hold that they were only reformulating philosophically the fundamental idea of the Reformation. Goethe at the Reformation Festival [of 1817] could suppose that he was at one with Luther in protesting against all obscurantism and clericalism.'

This is 'the heartland and origin' of the modern transvaluation of freedom of conscience from a religious ideal bound to a theological subjectivity ascending to Grace and Redemption, to a secularizing and subjectivistic ideal of self-legislating reason: 'a more general freedom of the individual to act and be permitted to conduct himself in accordance with his own law as laid down for his own conscience... In this sense, freedom of conscience was chiefly actualized by ideological liberalism and particular tendencies of political liberalism and the democratic left.'[69] The nineteenth century was one of intensifying polarization and conflict over the diverse institutionalized religious settlements that had persisted in Europe since 1648, and the nascent forces of liberal nationalism and socialism. At stake in these conflicts was the legacy of the French Revolution and Napoleonic Empire's radical attempt to secularize state and society, and the reaction against it by restorationist alliances of throne and altar. When the papal encyclical *Mirari Vos* of 1832 declared liberty of conscience an 'absurd and erroneous proposition' stemming from the 'shameful font of indifferentism' that led only to 'ruin in sacred and civil affairs',[70] it was drawing a battle line that would be joined across European states in the nineteenth century. The restoration only temporarily suspended the conflicts over the deconfessionalization of the state inaugurated by the Revolution and its aftermath. The instability, and latent and patent religious political conflict:

[68] Taylor (n. 33) 290, 293. Taylor's argument here accords with Weber's short remarks on deism, which he describes as a 'charismatic glorification of Reason' founded in the 'belief of the Enlightenment in the workings of individual reason which, if unimpeded, would result in the at least relatively best of all worlds, by virtue of Divine providence and because the individual is best qualified to know his own interests'. Weber (n. 14) 1209.

[69] Böckenförde (n. 44) footnote 18.

[70] Gregory XVI, 'Mirari Vos—On Liberalism and Religious Indifferentism' (1832).

> ... involved processes of mass mobilization and societal polarization. [The conflicts] embraced virtually every sphere of social life—schools, universities, press, marriage, gender relations, burial rites, associational culture, control of public space, folk memory, and symbols of nationhood... [T]he mobilization of clerical (and liberal anti-clerical) allegiances became interwoven with... the expansion of political participation that occurred within the European states in the middle and later decades of the century.[71]

On the one side, Catholic discourse projected a 'Manichean vision of the forces of Christ versus Satan', while on the other, ideas of 'nation, science and rationality' coalesced to form the common-sense of a 'self-confident European bourgeoisie that regarded itself... as the embodiment of modernity'.[72]

'Freedom of conscience' achieved a special polemical quality which refracted these conflicts, castigated on the one hand as a 'font of indifferentism' and civilizational collapse because of its dissolution of the objective unity of moral and political authority; and, on the other, as the very source of the unity of reason and freedom itself, unencumbering state and society from irrational ritual and superstition and establishing a foundation for religious belief within the limits of reason alone. Nineteenth century freedom of conscience was in this sense 'a modern combat concept', tied to its deployment in various philosophical histories that 'prophesied that Protestant [and Catholic] confessional religion was... about to be superseded or secularized, supposedly by a rational religion or moral philosophy in which man's capacity for rational self-consciousness and self-governance would be fully realized'.[73] In the real political conflicts over the German constitutional reform of 1848, Hunter notes:

> ... rival philosophical-political factions proposed to transcend the [Westphalian] constitutional meaning of the secular as the political and juridical maintenance of a plurality of revealed confessional religions, in favor of an all-embracing secularity grounded in the nature of human reason and its historical realization... This was the context that permitted the factions to first use the term 'secularization' to refer to the epochal transformation of a Christian into a rational society.[74]

The inner voice of conscience, deeply indebted to the sectarian Protestant metaphysic and ethic, became the load-bearing keystone of the rationalist critique of a certain kind of religious subjectivity; the latter entails not only internal beliefs and ideas *about* transcendent realities, but rituals, practices, and bodily habitus that perform lived relationships *with* and connectedness *to* a nomos not of human origin: the sharp line between *foro interno* and *foro externo* rested itself on an archetype of religion and religious belief.[75] In this ideal of rationalizable religious belief, both Catholicism and Judaism were suspect not only because of the former's apparent divided loyalties between nation and Church,[76] but also because (in the case of the

[71] Clark, 'From 1848 to Christian Democracy' in I. Katznelson and G.S. Jones (eds), *Religion and the Political Imagination* (2010) 190, 190–213, 196.

[72] Ibid. 200. [73] Hunter (n. 12) 15. [74] Ibid. 29–30.

[75] Asad, 'Thinking about Religion, Belief and Politics' in R.A. Orsi (ed.), *The Cambridge Companion to Religious Studies* (2012) 36.

[76] For the actual intellectual struggle of Catholic intellectuals to reconcile with 19th-century nationalism, see Perreau-Saussine, 'French Catholic Political Thought from the Deconfessionalization of the

latter) of the refusal of religious Jews to accept their assimilation to a more rational ideal of religious belief. Thus Bruno Bauer's *Jewish Question*—written in the throes of the turmoil over the demand for German constitutional change leading up to the failed revolution of 1848—epitomizes the stigmatization of alien religion as not only backward but incapable of assimilation to national democratic citizenship. In his famous critique of Bauer, Marx radicalizes the Hegelian logic by insisting that what is necessary is not the repudiation by Jews of *their* religion, but of the overcoming of the alienation that gives rise to the irrational need for *all* religion.[77]

The Catholic Church's rapprochement with freedom of conscience, and with subjective constitutional rights more generally, would await the end of Catholic doctrine's Manichean self-understanding of its role as a restrainer against the forces of nihilism and civilizational decay—and the tragic consequences of its flirtation with corporatism, authoritarianism, and fascism. This rapprochement would be an important source for another, distinct, moment in the history of freedom of religion and freedom of conscience. Recent historical work on the drafting of the guarantees of freedom of conscience in the Universal Declaration of Human Rights (Article 18) and the European Convention on Human Rights (Article 9) highlights two important contextual influences on how the concept was shaped in its drafting: Catholic Christian personalism,[78] and ecumenical missionary movements.[79] The latter emphasized the right to change religion in light of longstanding efforts to proselytize in the former lands of the Ottoman empire, and under the shadow of inter- and post-war attempts to protect Christian interests ('shrines and souls') in the looming national territorial conflict developing in Mandatory Palestine.[80] The former transformed European Catholic Christian social thought from a rejection of bourgeois individualism to an embrace of the 'absolute value of the human person'.[81] Early twentieth-century Christian political thought largely dismissed rights as indi-

State to the Recognition of Religious Freedom' in I. Katznelson and G.S. Jones (eds), *Religion and the Political Imagination* (2010) 150.

[77] Farris, 'From the Jewish Question to the Muslim Question: Republican Rigorism, Culturalist Differentialism and Antinomies of Enforced Emancipation', 21, *Constellations* (2014) 296.

[78] S. Moyn, *Christian Human Rights* (2015); M. Duranti, *The Conservative Human Rights Revolution: European Identity, Transnational Politics, and the Origins of the European Convention* (2017). See also the potted history in Invernizzi-Accetti, 'Is the European Union Secular? Christian Democracy in the European treaties and jurisprudence', *Comparative European Politics* (2017), available at: https://link.springer.com/article/10.1057/s41295-017-0091-0 (last visited 13 June 2018).

[79] For further argument, see Bhuta, 'Two Concepts of Religious Freedom in the European Court of Human Rights', 113, *South Atlantic Quarterly* (2014) 9.

[80] L. Lindkvist, *Religious Freedom and the Universal Declaration of Human Rights* (2017) Ch. 2. Lindkvist sets out the attenuated Christian theological underpinning of this position as articulated by O. Frederick Nolde, Director of the New York office of the influential ecumenical body, the Commission of the Churches on International Affairs (Nolde, through his links with Charles Malik and also Eleanor Roosevelt, had some influence during the drafting of the Universal Declaration):

> 'The ecumenical movement's efforts, Nolde argued, were not only rooted in the responsibility of Christians to contribute to the making of a just and peaceful political order. They also rested on the conviction that human rights would benefit what remained the primary mission of the Church and of every individual Christian, namely the promotion of the Gospel of Christ ... 'Because we believe that all men should have the opportunity to hear and accept the Gospel, we seek to promote religious liberty.' Ibid. 84.

[81] Moyn (n. 78) Ch. 2.

vidualist and materialist, accoutrements of an enfeebled liberal parliamentarism that was unable to stem the moral pathologies of modern politics. But the Catholic Church's anti-totalitarian turn after 1937, and the exile of prominent inter-war Catholic activists such as Luigi Sturzo and Jacques Maritain, led to a pivotal change in orientation: 'Catholic political refugees came back from Britain and the United States with a changed normative hierarchy in which individual liberty was . . . more important before, thus pointing the way towards the more liberal Christian democracy of postwar western Europe.'[82] Moyn shows how Maritain's embrace of rights was part of an attempt to provide a 'plausible alternative to secularism east and west'.[83] The concept of the person meant not the liberal solipsism of the rational subject but emphasized the primacy of the spiritual essence of human life, implied and protected by natural right: 'In either the stroke of a master, or a sleight of hand, or both, Maritain—as if the Thomistic movement had not long and unanimously rejected modern [subjective] right—claimed . . . [above all that] only the Christian vision placing the personal entitlements in the framework of the common good could afford a persuasive theory of rights.'[84] Freedom of (religious) conscience was understood to play a critical role in this limitation of secularizing modern politics, protecting the innermost spiritual core of the person against the excessive claims of the state and of materialist ideologies such as Communism. What distinguished the 'human person' from the (liberal) 'individual' was 'the capacity to transcend the finitude of this world by the right use of mind and conscience . . . [T]his liberty originated in the intrinsic purpose of human existence . . . the freedom realized in the act of responding to God's call to partnership.'[85]

3.

This chapter has presented two distinct but interrelated thought-formations—secularity and freedom of conscience—and I have tried in broad strokes to paint a picture of their intertwining histories. Secularity and freedom of conscience emerge neither as necessary implications of each other, nor as inherently complementary concepts, but as constituent threads of a seam-line that runs along the unity presupposed by the modern state. The secular is a stance or posture towards the religious, from a vantage point of a political unity (however constructed or imagined); freedom of conscience is a carrier for historically and sociologically specific kinds of religious subjectivity (or, in the case of the ideal-type of individualist rationalism, a seat of 'ultimate, independently formulated, individual convictions about life,

[82] W. Kaiser, *Christian Hegemony and the Origins of the European Union* (2007) 150.

[83] Moyn, *Jacques Maritain, Christian New Order and the Birth of Human Rights* (2008), available at https://dx.doi.org/10.2139/ssrn.1134345, at 5 (last visited 13 June 2018).

[84] Moyn (n. 78) 83. Lindkvist adds: 'Maritain's main contribution to these [Christian personalist movements] was probably to provide an exemplary revision reading of the history of human rights where the Enlightenment and the Atlantic revolutions were pushed aside by stoicism, scholasticism, and ultimately, the Gospel. With roots stretching back to the birth of Western civilization, human rights arose as a potential rallying cry for a united religious front against the ills of secular modernity.' Lindkvist (n. 80) 42.

[85] Lindkvist (n. 80) 43.

released from its religious role').[86] In the case of the subjectivities of conscience, I have suggested that they have also rested on a kind of inner unity of the subject with, inter alia, God's Being, His Law, the Holy Spirit, or even self-legislating reason. It is in the casuistic negotiation of the boundaries of these out-worldly and in-worldly unities, that we might locate the problematics, tensions, and dilemmas of freedom of religion in the modern state. These problematics are always particular to the political and constitutional histories of any given state, but nonetheless evince common logics that in my argument correspond to a deeper structural relationship revolving around the constant problem of the foundation of the unity of the political order—that 'operative concept of the substance' to which I refer in section 1, on which the intelligibility of any claim of the unity of the state rests. On my account, both the political unity presupposed by the secular, and the theological subjectivity presupposed by various iterations of freedom of conscience, make claims to be a final bearer of the authority to decide the extent of the application of a theological Truth in this-worldly affairs. Thus, in both inheres a possibility of profound intolerance, and one way of understanding the tangled history of the interrelationship between secularity and freedom of conscience is a continuous (and sometimes violent) struggle over the *organization and management of intolerance*:[87] of what, by whom, for what ends, and under what conditions or limits.

From this point of view, one gains a new appreciation of Böckenförde's observation in the context of German constitutional jurisprudence that so long as the German state 'still saw itself in Christian terms and because of the consensus among the Christian denominations with regard to social morality... the possibilities of conflict between law and conscience remained slight'.[88] But where the religious substance presupposed by the state and within society itself had irreversibly dissipated, freedom of conscience was a right 'whose substance was hardly understood at all'.[89] One way of giving content to the right would be through the pure self-legislating subjectivity posited by nineteenth-century rationalism,[90] but Böckenförde's rejection of this possibility tellingly dramatizes it as threatening the unity of the legal and political order of the state itself:

> Surely absolute, unconditional freedom of conscience will logically entail surrendering the validity of the entire legal system to private judgment—in conscience—of citizens and thus in practice nullifying it. It will take the *quis judicabit* so indispensable to the peaceful organization of the state away from the state and from the nation as a whole represented therein and give it back to individuals, thus incapacitating and undermining the authority of the organs of the state and eventually dissolving the state itself.[91]

Böckenförde proposes a resolution to this dilemma which is specific to the liberal democratic constitution of post-war Germany.[92] But the theoretical premises of the

[86] Böckenförde (n. 44) (forthcoming).

[87] I'm indebted to my colleague Peter Drahos for this marvellous formulation.

[88] Böckenförde (n. 44) (forthcoming).

[89] Ibid. (forthcoming).

[90] Although as Troeltsch noted, 'this rationalistic Individualism passed more and more into a Relativism' and led to a crisis of subjectivism. Troeltsch (n. 15) 25.

[91] Böckenförde (n. 44) (forthcoming).

[92] Ibid. (forthcoming).

particular solution may yield a more generalizable logic for working through, somewhat casuistically, the relationship between the secular and freedom of religious conscience. Böckenförde declines to define conscience by recourse to 'theological or philosophical notions or interpretations of conscience'[93] on the grounds that these are already partisan in their posture towards the state order. Rather, he reaches for Luhmann's sociological description of conscience as essentially a mediator of a subject's relationship with its environment, 'ensuring... that what starts out as an infinite number of possible ways of behaving is reduced... to an internally coherent representation of self and style of conduct'.[94] The implication of this account of conscience is to grasp it as an active and passive producer of subjectivity, inevitably produced pre-reflexively by state, society, family, religious authority, and other objective social relationships, but also self-producing during certain junctures of possibility, crisis, or in reaction to the social environment. 'Conscience' in this sense is an essential site for the reproduction of social integration and political unity, as well as necessarily a critical source of challenges to them. What becomes a question of conscience cannot be delimited as a matter of substance, because under contemporary conditions 'any kind of behavior critically affecting the integrity and identity of the personality may become a matter of conscience... [C]onscientious convictions may express themselves not only in general principles but equally in concrete imperatives tied to given situations.'[95] Thus, questions of conscience (including religious conscience) tend to be defensive and reactive: not arising on a daily basis but in response to an environmental pressure that challenges the integration of the personality in some basic way—'I cannot be the sort of person who does that.' This need not be limited to reflexively articulated beliefs and ideas, but can extend to a variety of collective and individual practices and behaviours that evince a fundamental relationship with a religious *nomos*.

Viewed from the standpoint of the management and organization of intolerance within any given state and society, the function of religious conscience is always somewhat paradoxical: it both holds out the promise of integration and threatens it; in any given context it might serve to reinforce historical domination and homogenization of belief and culture, or it might act as an irritant against the thick background of a dominant religious *or secular* belief and release new possibilities for practical freedom and reduced intolerance.[96] In an example from Indian political history, Bilgrami remarks:

> In the aftermath of Indian independence, Muslims in India, after much fascinating discussion during the Constituent Assembly debates, were allowed by constitutional provision to live by their own personal and family laws [and Hindus were not granted a similar concession].

[93] Ibid. (forthcoming). [94] Ibid. (forthcoming). [95] Ibid. (forthcoming).

[96] See, for example, Urbinati's observation that religious reasons can be public political reasons where there is a long history of religious uniformity (itself, the product of historical repression of alternative beliefs). Under these circumstances, the pre-reflexive integrative force of religious uniformity sets boundary conditions for the articulation and expression of political argument, without explicitly being theological argument. Urbinati (n. 35).

[The motivation for this was] not that the Muslim community is being granted its demand for living by its own personal and family laws on the grounds that their standpoint... has the truth on their side. Rather the thinking was this: in the aftermath of independence, the Muslims who remained in India and did not migrate to Pakistan lost a great deal—they lost their count in numbers [due to migration and pogroms], they lost jobs, they lost land,... they even lost their language Urdu [in the sense of its wide availability for instruction in schools and colleges]. In the face of these losses and the demoralization it generated, depriving them of the cultural aspects of their lives that are centered in their family and personal laws would be an inhumane blow for a state to deliver to a minority community.[97]

By contrast, the personal laws and rituals of the Hindu majority (among them dowry, and untouchability) were not granted a legal status and were instead reformed by the state in the name of the constitutional commitment to equality. The underlying presumption seems to have been that the constitutional state's promise of equality between religious communities, and within them, is to be approached differently—one could say, *casuistically*—in light of their relative social, cultural and economic power, and in order to minimize the much greater risk of the stigmatization and demoralization faced by the minority in the name of equality of citizenship. From a categorical point of view, the results are unsatisfactory; but Bilgrami points out that another, dialectical kind of thinking was involved in this strategy:

Since citizens are historical subjects, history and the incoming states of information that it provides to those subjects in its course may well introduce... tensions and dissonance in the relations between their value commitments... The point then, is that even if at a given time, a value economy seems relatively unreachable by internal reasons because it is relatively coherent and unconflicted, so long as we think of moral-psychological economies as necessarily being *in history*, internal conflicts may be injected by historical developments into moral-psychological economies ...

... [What the Indian Constituent Assembly did was] to wait for history to bring into Muslim thinking the sorts of internal conflict that might give them reasons to... put aside their family and personal laws.[98]

There can be no simple guarantees that attempting to manage this potential tension between religious conscience and political unity in the furtherance of a general reduction of intolerance—intolerance towards religious belief, and intolerance towards non-belief—is, on balance, the most likely way to engender civil peace and civil equality. But in the end, these foundational goods that form the 'basic legitimation demand'[99] for the modern state form cannot be understood as categorical and abstract achievements of principle, to be dogmatically and inflexibly asserted in the name of an ideal of practical freedom. Such an understanding seems to me unnecessarily beholden to a Kantian vision of the state (and of freedom). Rather, what freedom of religion should become is a self-consciously casuistic concept, along with its counterpart, secularity. The possibility of dialectical progress towards greater tolerance, and with a reduction in intolerance, requires a forbearance from

[97] Bilgrami (n. 36) 120. [98] Ibid. 112, 120.

[99] Bernard Williams, 'Realism and Moralism in Political Theory' in B. Williams, *In the Beginning was the Deed: Realism and Moralism in Political Argument* (2009) 18.

categorical perspectives that all too readily become routes towards a friend-enemy perception of irreducible antagonism between rival Truths or values. This forbearance of course presupposes self-confidence, both on the part of the legal-political order, and on the part of a group invoking a claim of conscience but in respect of whom some limitation of the demands of Truth is being required by the political order.[100] Where conditions of polarization and latent enmity are advanced, such self-assurance and forbearance may well be the first things to vanish. Nonetheless, for all its uncertainties, contingencies, and possible pathologies, I would maintain that this mode of becoming of religious freedom and of the secular might hold out some hope of realizing the possibilities of practical freedom for concrete human personalities *in* history.

[100] Bilgrami (n. 36) 121: 'That Muslims could be reasonably expected to reform their personal laws by internal reasoning in the face of such harassment would be to utterly fail to understand the psychological preconditions for how internal reasons usually work in a historical context. A group's capacity to change via internal reasoning requires a great deal of psychological security and self-confidence, precisely what is undermined by the demoralization caused by such harassment.'

2

Reimagining Secularism

Respect, Domination, and Principled Distance

Rajeev Bhargava

1. Political and Ethical Secularism

In a previous article, 'Giving Secularism Its Due',[1] I introduced a distinction between ethical and political secularism. Ethical secularism means something like a comprehensive normative perspective by which to lead an individual or collective life, or both. Here secularism is a well-reasoned but partly speculative perspective on how best to lead one's life, here and now, in this world on the assumption that all ends pursued by humans pertain only to this world and this time.

Politico-moral secularism or political secularism for short, outlined a perspective on what earthly restraint, coercive or non-coercive, can be placed on the pursuit of the good life, regardless of whether one is an ethical secularist or not. Both secularists and the religious might agree that such restraints exist, indeed this might be an object of consensus among different kinds of secular and religious believers.

One of the objectives of the aforementioned article was to show that contrary to what many had hitherto believed, political secularism neither entails nor presupposes ethical secularism.

2. Secularism and Secularization

The paper also clarified the distinction between the process of secularization, studied widely by sociological theorists, and political secularism, then largely neglected by political theorists. I argued that political secularism is frequently needed precisely in those societies where either people belong to multiple religions, or religious believers and philosophical secularists, or all of them coexist or are engaged in prolonged conflicts. A society that is already fully secularized would not *need* a secular state because it would, in some form, already have it. Political secularism, I argued, is needed precisely in those conditions where complete secularization is impossible, unavailable as an option, or undesirable.

[1] See Bhargava, 'Giving Secularism Its Due', 29 *Economic and Political Weekly* (1994) 1784.

Reimagining Secularism: Respect, Domination and Principled Distance. First Edition.
Rajeev Bhargava © Rajeev Bhargava 2019. Published 2019 by Oxford University Press.

My focus then was not on secularization. Therefore, I did not specify its meaning. But I implied that it refers to a social process that gets under way and remains in motion largely but not wholly independently of intentional human action. Secularization was not launched as a programme of collective action. It has occurred, if, where, and when it has, because of the unintended consequences of human action. Indeed, in Europe, it appears to have happened as a result of changes within religion, induced by religious people out of very religious motives. Secularism, on the other hand, is a collective normative project. It sets out a plan of desirable collective action. It is probable that the more successful its realization, the more secularization there is, but to some extent secularization can occur even without secularism, perhaps despite its failure. I also implied that secularization had to some extent a negative relationship with religions—the more one is present the less available the other will be, and vice versa.

3. Secularization and Secularism in Crisis

Perhaps, mistakenly, I also took it for granted that, though not for societies such as India, for at least much of the West, the theory of secularization holds true. That assumption has turned out to be deeply questionable. In 1994, José Casanova published his *Public Religions in the Modern World* in which he claimed that the theory of secularization consists not of one but three distinct hypotheses, the validity of each of which has to be separately established.[2] It may not be very useful to think of it in general terms such as the decline of the social significance or public authority of religion, but rather as involving three quite distinct claims. First, the differentiation thesis: modernization brought about a differentiation of the spheres of economy, politics, law, science, the arts, and religion. Religion exists, perhaps even remains strong, but in a separate sphere of its own. Second, the privatization thesis: secularization has meant the gradual removal of religion from public life and its relegation into the private sphere. Finally, the thesis of the decline of religious beliefs: the number of religious believers has declined and the intensity with which such beliefs are held has weakened. Citing the cases of the United States, Latin America, and Poland, Casanova then argued that while the differentiation and decline theses might be true, the privatization thesis was quite definitely false. There has been an explosion of public religions in the modern world. Indeed, he argued that a causal relationship exists between differentiation and de-privatization, that differentiation, i.e. one dimension or form of secularization, has led to the emergence of public religions. Once their function as grand legitimators and regulators of society is reduced, religions begin to take a new form as movements and pressure groups competing with other similar secular groups in the public sphere. Today, along with social theorists such as Talal Asad, Casanova has grave doubts about the validity of even the other two hypotheses. The theory of secularization is in crisis.

[2] J. Casanova, *Public Religions in the Modern World* (1994).

The crisis of secular states and secularism is graver. The 1994 article spoke of the challenge faced by secularism in India. But well before its crisis there, secular states and the doctrine underpinning them had begun to come under strain elsewhere. Secularism was severely jolted with the establishment in Iran of the first modern theocracy, rejected partly because of the perception that it was a Western idea. By the late 1980s similar Islamic political movements had emerged in Egypt, Sudan, Algeria, Tunisia, Ethiopia, Nigeria, Chad, Senegal, Turkey, Afghanistan, Pakistan, and even Bangladesh.[3] Movements challenging secular states were hardly restricted to Muslim societies. Protestant movements decrying secularism emerged in Kenya, Guatemala, and the Philippines. Protestant fundamentalism became a force in American politics. Singhalese Buddhist nationalists in Sri Lanka, practitioners of religious ultra-orthodoxy in Israel, and diasporic communities in Canada and Great Britain all began to question the separation of state and religion.[4]

In short, Western conceptions of political secularism do not appear to have travelled all that well in other societies. More importantly such conceptions and the secular states they underpin are coming under strain even in Europe, where, until recently, they were believed to be firmly entrenched and secure. Why is this so? It is true that the substantive secularization of European societies has brought about the extensive secularization of European states; regardless of their religious affiliation, citizens have a large basket of civil and political rights unheard of in religion-centred states, past or present. Nevertheless, two problems remain.

First, migration from former colonies and intensified globalization have thrown together in Western public spaces Christian, Islamic, and pre-Christian faiths such as Hinduism.[5] The cumulative result is unprecedented religious diversity, the weakening of the public monopoly of single religions, and the generation of mutual suspicion, distrust, hostility, and conflict. This is evident in Germany and Great Britain but was dramatically highlighted by the headscarf issue in France, the cartoon affair in Denmark, and the murder of filmmaker Theo Van Gogh in the Netherlands shortly after the release of his controversial film about Islamic culture.[6]

Second, despite substantial secularization, in some European states inequities resulting from the formal establishment of the dominant religion have done little to bolster better intercommunity relations or to reduce religious discrimination. With the deepening of religious diversity, the religious biases of European states have become increasingly visible. European states have continued to privilege Christianity

[3] D. Westerlund, *Questioning the Secular State* (1996); G. Kepel, *The Revenge of God: The Resurgence of Islam, Christianity, and Judaism in the Modern World* (1994); I. Ahmed, *The Concept of an Islamic State: An Analysis of the Ideological Controversy in Pakistan* (1987); Mohsin, 'National Security and the Minorities: The Bangladesh Case', in D.L. Sheth and G. Mahajan (eds), *Minority Identities and the Nation-State* (1999).

[4] M. Juergensmeyer, *The New Cold War? Religious Nationalism Confronts the Secular State* (1994).

[5] Turner, 'Cosmopolitan Virtue: On Religion in a Global Age', 4 *European Journal of Social Theory* (2001) 131.

[6] See J. Bowen, *Why the French Don't Like Headscarves: Islam, the State and Public Spaces* (2007); Freedman, 'Secularism as a Barrier to Integration? The French Dilemma', 42 *International Migration* (2004) 5; Barker, 'Church and State: Lessons from Germany?', 75 *The Political Quarterly* (2004) 168; T. Modood, A. Triandafyllidou, and R. Zapata-Barrero (eds), *Multiculturalism, Muslims and Citizenship: A European Approach* (2006).

in one form or another. They have publicly funded religious schools, maintained clerical salaries and real estate holdings of Christian churches, facilitated the control by churches of cemeteries, and trained the clergy. In short, there has been virtually no impartiality within the domain of religion, and despite formal 'equality' this privileging of Christianity continues to have a far-reaching impact on the rest of society.[7] Even the widespread belief regarding the existence of a secular European public sphere is based largely on a myth. As a result, the formal or informal establishment of a single religion, even the weaker variety of establishment, continues to be part of the problem.

This challenge to secularism has come not only from politicians, civil society groups, and clerics but also from academics. Critics have argued that the conceptual and normative structure of secularism is itself terribly defective. There is something wrong with the ideal itself. Secularism has been linked to a flawed modernization, the repressive structures of the nation state, to an indefensible conception of science and rationality, and to an excessive individualism. It has been charged with trivializing faith and being insensitive to religious believers. Its failure to be impartial and universal is linked to its Christian biases.

4. Can Political Secularism Be Rescued?

I agree that secular states are in crisis, that the problems of secularism are real and run deep. However, it is the contention of this chapter that secularism is not irredeemable, and that while many of its conceptions are flawed one can still reimagine, redefine, and rescue it.[8] This is crucial because there is still no alternative to secularism on the horizon. Under present conditions it continues to be badly needed.

The criticism of secularism, I argue, looks indefeasible only because it has focused on a few doctrinal versions of Western secularism. I argue that it is time we shifted focus away from doctrines and towards the constitutional provisions and normative practices of a wide variety of states, including the best practices of non-Western states such as India. Once we do so, we will begin to see secularism differently and might realize that we do not need an alternative to, but an alternative conception of, secularism. Identifying a defensible alternative conception is not always easy. It can be done only if we make two crucial moves. First, we must leave the standard church-state models and focus instead on secularism as a response to religious diversity. Second, as already mentioned, we must pay more attention to normative practices rather than to existing doctrinal formulations. Allow me to elaborate on these points.

Most societies today are characterized by religious diversity. The pressing question before us, then, is how is this diversity, and the problems that accompany it, to be handled? What does religious diversity mean? It means both diversity *of* religion and diversity *within* religion. Diversity of religion exists in a society when it has a popu-

[7] J. Klausen, *The Islamic Challenge* (2005).

[8] For a detailed discussion, see Bhargava, 'Rehabilitating Secularism' in C. Calhoun, M. Juergensmeyer, and J. VanAntwerpen (eds), *Rethinking Secularism* (2011) 92.

lace professing faith in, say, Christian, Jewish, or Islamic ideals. Diversity within religion may be of two kinds. The first might be called horizontal diversity, which exists when a religion is internally differentiated. For example, different confessions, denominations, and sects within Christianity and Islam. Religions are characterized, however, by another kind of diversity, which may be called vertical diversity. Here, people of the same religion may engage in diverse practices that are hierarchically arranged and might include certain kinds of practices that other members of the religion are excluded from. For example, caste-ridden Hinduism makes a distinction between pure and impure practices, and women or *dalits* may not be allowed entry into the inner sanctum of temples and in many cases even into the precincts of an upper-caste temple. This example already brings home a point that I ought to have made at the very outset of this discussion. Every form of diversity, including religious diversity, is enmeshed in power relations. It further follows that inherent in religiously diverse societies is the possibility of both inter-religious and intra-religious domination—a broad term that encompasses discrimination, marginalization, oppression, exclusions, and the reproduction of hierarchy. (Two other forms of domination are also possible: the domination by the religious of the non-religious and the domination of the religious by the non-religious.)

This shift allows me to conceive secularism as a response to a deeply distorted form of sociability within the domain of religion, as a normative stance that seeks to facilitate better social relations within and across religious groups. Secularism in this view is not against religiosity per se but is opposed to institutionalized religious domination. Allow me to draw an analogy with one of Karl Marx's better known ideas. Marx claimed that in order for production of material goods to take place, humans must enter into a production relationship with one another. He further claimed that such production frequently takes place within structures of exploitation and dominance. His entire project might be viewed as an attempt to emancipate the production process from distorted human relations. Likewise, one might view the production of symbolic goods as requiring a certain relationship of production. However, the production of most symbolic goods, including religious goods, almost always takes place under the conditions of domination within and between religions. Secularism might then be viewed as an attempt to emancipate the production of symbolic goods, values, and services from inter- and intra-religious domination. That is what I mean when I say that secularism is not against religiosity but fiercely opposes institutionalized religious domination. To rescue secularism requires a profound reconceptualization of what secularism means.

A second equally crucial move to reimagine secularism is this: a set of distinctions must be drawn and kept in mind to retrieve a defensible secularism. First, we need to distinguish between the entire complex of practices and institutional arrangements that either connect religion to, or disconnect religion from, the state and a subset of these practices and arrangements that embody norms—that is, an implicit sense of how states and religions *should* relate to one another. Whereas the former include the normative and the non-normative and operate entirely at the *practical* level, the latter operate only at the *normative* level. Second, these norms are then articulated in representations and ad hoc, unstable reflections found in statements of politicians, laws enacted by legislators, executive decisions, judicial pronouncements, and constitutional articles. These articulations operate at the *discursive* level. Finally, the normative conceptions implicit in these practices and either subtly or explicitly articulated in the legal and political discourse are then posited as a normative ideal that is sometimes expressed as ideology and doctrine and that occasionally becomes an object of theoretical inquiry, thus operating at both the *doctrinal* and the *theoretical* levels. The distinction between a comprehensive practical and the exclusively normative level is important because identifying secularism with any particular practice or institutional arrangement that relates religion and the state will not do. True, secularism needs to be institutionally grounded, but to distinguish secular from religion-centred states and, even more important, to articulate a critical, normative secularism, the distinction between the normative and the non-normative is crucial.

More to the point, I argue that secular norms conceived at the doctrinal and the theoretical levels are by now highly restricted and inadequate. This has happened because these levels are colonized by mainstream Western doctrines and theories of secularism. Reimagining secularism is virtually impossible unless we reduce our reliance on these formulations. These doctrines and theories have become part of the problem, they are hurdles to properly examining the issues at stake. Wittgenstein's warning that the hold of a particular picture is so strong that it prevents, even occludes, awareness of other conceptions of reality is apt here. We are so seized by one or two conceptions that we simply cannot see other conceptions that have been pushed into the background. Once we shift away from currently dominant models and focus on the normative practices of a broader range of Western states beyond the more familiar ones, and indeed also on non-Western states, we shall see that better forms of secular states and much more defensible versions of secularisms are available. And although in some contexts, minimally decent religion-centred states may be adequate, by and large they will not do because they, too, are as much a part of the problem as are some secular states.

So we need to move away from these doctrinal formulations of political secularism and unearth different versions found in the best practices of many states and in their judicial pronouncements and constitutional articles. Focusing on normative practices and constitutional articles and refashioning secularism will help us to displace a worn-out ideal and shift the norm, bringing it closer to how people wish to lead their lives, rather than how they should lead their lives in accordance with a more or less redundant ideal.

5. Models of Political Secularism

Which existing models am I referring to? There are two main ones: the French and the American. In addition, a third model is found in the rest of Western Europe. Let me critically examine each of these models.[9]

[9] See also Bhargava, 'Multiple Secularisms and Multiple Secular States' in A. Berg-Sørensen (ed.), *Contesting Secularism* (2013) 17.

A. The Idealized French Model

The idealized French conception holds that the state must be separate from religion while retaining the power to interfere in it. However, religion is divested of any power to intervene in matters of the .state. In short, separation means *one-sided exclusion*. For example, in March 2004, the French Assembly and the Senate introduced a law signed by the President, Jacques Chirac. The first article of the new law says 'In public primary, secondary, and high schools, the wearing of signs or dress with which the students manifest ostentatiously a religious affiliation is prohibited.'[10] As a result, 47 Muslim and three Sikh students who did not follow the new rules were expelled from their schools.[11] Clearly, the French state is less sensitive to the autonomy of religious associations and can brand them as dangerous and monitor them. But religions have no such influence on the state. This one-sided, exclusionary attitude continues a long-standing trend in France, after Catholic dominance in French public schools was replaced with a philosophically secular outlook. Since then, religious instruction has been abandoned. Organized prayer is forbidden and students cannot make a pledge that refers to God. The French exclude religious symbols and discourse from the public sphere. French public institutions have no prayer or reference to God. Over time, states that follow this conception also develop a hierarchy between the secular and the religious and may perpetuate the non-religious domination of the religious. This happens even more so when, to promote more rigorous non-religious conceptions of positive freedoms and substantive equalities, states cross minimal thresholds of morality, formal equality, and decency.

States governed by this conception typically have a single, robust conception of the good life that translates into deep scepticism about the truth claims and value of religion and about its public role and capacity to prevent forms of oppression and domination. Typically, this secularism does not understand the believer's life as it is lived from the inside. It misses out on perhaps the most significant feature of most religions: that they encourage their members to choose to live a disciplined, restricted, rule-bound, and desire-abnegating life. To be sure, even such an anti-religious stance may help states to deal with cases of intra-religious domination where some members of a religious community dominate members of their own religion, as occurs with anti-clericalism in France. But often their relative blindness to religion makes states driven by such conceptions insensitive to religious freedoms, particularly to the religious freedoms of minorities. As a result, states may even, wittingly or unwittingly, perpetuate inter-religious domination.

Many segments in virtually every society, on the right but particularly on the left, are tempted to follow the anti-pluralist French model, largely because they view religion—in Europe, more specifically Islam—as a 'problem' and believe that its solution requires the coercive power of the state. Such an approach would be detrimental to interfaith relations particularly because while strongly interfering with

[10] *Loi no. 2004–228 du 15 mars 2004* [Law 2004–228 of 15 March 2004].

[11] A. Kuru, *Secularism and State Policies Towards Religion: The United States, France, and Turkey* (2009) 108.

non-Christian faiths, it leaves the formal or informal establishment of a single Christian religion untouched. A striking example is the accommodation of majority Catholics in public schools. School cafeterias serve fish for those Catholics who abstain from meat, but no such provision exists for those students who eat only halal meat. Catholic chaplains in France operate in approximately half of French public secondary schools. French prisons and hospitals also have chaplains. Other exceptions to the secular laws exist in the region of Alsace-Moselle and overseas colonies. The French state and local government have owned and funded the maintenance of the grand majority of the 45,000 Catholic churches, half of the Protestant churches, and about 10 per cent of synagogues.

The French state also pays about 80 per cent of the budget including the salary of teachers in Catholic schools that follow the national curriculum and are open to students of all faiths.[12] Jocelyne Cesari stresses that 'the collective dimension of Islam was confined to the intimate space of the residences, the hearths, the provided places at hotels, or the backs of the shops'.[13]

It is evident that attempts to further intervene in religions is likely to meet with resistance not only from Muslims but from non-Muslims as well. Moreover, any reliance on the heavy-handed and one-sided French model is likely to exacerbate problems. In addition, a remedy normatively unsuitable for European states will be rejected outright elsewhere. Indeed, states that have drawn inspiration from this model—for example, communist states such as China and the Kemalist state in Turkey—have a very poor record of protecting religious freedoms or sustaining intra- and inter-religious equality.

B. The Idealized American Model

The idealized American self-understanding interprets separation to mean *mutual exclusion*. Neither the state nor religion is meant to interfere in the domain of the other. This mutual exclusion is held to be necessary to resolve conflicts between different Christian denominations, to grant some measure of equality between them, and—most crucially—to provide individuals the freedom to set up and maintain their own religious associations. The protection of religious liberties more generally is viewed as the raison d'être of this model. This strict or 'perfect separation', as James Madison has termed it,[14] must take place at each of the three distinct levels of ends, institutions and personnel, and law and public policy. The first two levels make the state non-theocratic and disestablish religion. The third level ensures that the state has neither a positive nor a negative relationship with religion. On the positive side, for example, there should be no policy of granting aid, even non-preferentially, to religious institutions. On the negative side, it is not within the scope of state activity to interfere in religious matters even when some of the values professed by the state, such as equality, are violated within the religious domain. Consider President

[12] Ibid. 109.

[13] Cesari, 'Demande de l'Islam en banlieue: un défi à la citoyenneté', 19 *Cahiers d'Etudes sur la Méditerranée Orientale et le monde Turco-Iranien* (1995), cited in Kuru (n. 11) 120–1.

[14] L.W. Levy, *The Establishment Clause: Religion and the First Amendment* (1994).

Barack Obama's helplessness in the face of the recent threat in America to publicly burn the Quran. As Leonard W. Levy puts it: 'Congress simply has no power to legislate on any matter pertaining to religion.'[15]

This non-interference is justified on the grounds that religion is a privileged, private (i.e. non-state) matter, and if something is amiss within this private domain, it can be mended only by those who have a right to do so within this sphere. This view, according to its proponents, is what religious freedom means. Thus the freedom that justifies mutual exclusion is negative liberty and is closely enmeshed with the privatization of religion. However, privatization here means non-officialization. American political secularism does not promote secularization in two of the three senses mentioned earlier in this section. It encourages a vibrant presence of religion in the non-state, public domain and does little to discourage religious beliefs or practices.

This model of secularism encourages the state to passively respect religion. Since any intervention is tantamount to control, the only way to respect religion is to leave it alone. Idealized American secularism, then, has some resources to fight inter-religious domination (for instance, it necessitates the disestablishment of the dominant religion) but few resources to wage a struggle against deeper, more structural aspects of this domination. The state's hands-off approach binds it to not facilitate freedoms or equality *within* religions. The American state may have worked out other strategies to minimize such domination. However, states that lack its more conciliatory history or that possess religions that do not easily allow the option to exit would perpetuate religion-related domination in following the American model. Moreover, by interpreting separation as exclusion, this model of secularism betrays its own sectarianism; it can live comfortably with liberal, protestantized, individualized, and privatized religions, but it has fewer resources to cope with religions that mandate greater public or political presence or that have a strong communal orientation. This group insensitivity makes it difficult to accommodate community-specific rights, such as the right of religious communities to set up and maintain their own educational institutions, and therefore virtually impossible to protect more robustly the rights of religious minorities.

Furthermore, as a product of the Protestant ethic, American secularism's greatest drawback is its universal pretension. It presupposes a Christian civilization, something easily forgotten because over time this civilization has silently slid into the background. Christianity allows this self-limitation, and much of the world innocently mistakes this somewhat cunning self-denial for Christianity's disappearance.[16] But if this is so, this 'inherently dogmatic' secularism cannot coexist innocently with other religions.[17] Given the enormous power of the state, it must try to shape and transform other religions—a clear instance of illegitimate influence. Thus, despite all its claims of leaving religions alone and granting religious liberty, this secularism has in the past been inhospitable to non-liberal, non-Protestant

[15] Ibid. See also P. Hamburger, *Separation of Church and State* (2002).

[16] W.E. Connolly, *Why I Am Not a Secularist* (1999) 24.

[17] Keane, 'Secularism', 71 *The Political Quarterly* (2000) 5, 14; Madan, 'Secularism in Its Place' in R. Bhargava (ed.), *Secularism and Its Critics* (1998) 297, 298.

believers,[18] and it can be inhospitable to non-believers as well. In March 2000 Michael Newdow, an atheist, filed a lawsuit pleading that the daily recitation of the pledge of allegiance that included the phrase 'one nation under God' harmed his daughter and violated the Establishment Clause of the First Amendment. Though he lost in the district court, he won the case in the court of appeals. But both houses of legislature reaffirmed the words 'under God' with a heavy majority endorsing strong religious expression in American public life.[19] This is widely seen as a virtual affirmation of the establishment of Christianity. If so, and whenever it happens, prospects of inter-religious discrimination loom large. Indeed, an excessive focus on religious freedom from the state may enhance inter-religious domination. As I say this I am conscious that this is not an empirical claim about American society or politics. Instead I am suggesting that if such a model is followed elsewhere it may neither protect people from some forms of inter-religious domination nor from intra-religious domination.

The current theoretical formulations of this model—represented, for example, by philosophical liberalism—only exacerbate these problems. Thus liberal secularist theories enjoin the citizen to support only those coercive state laws for which there is public justification. If others are expected to follow a law based on terms that they do not understand and for reasons they cannot endorse, the principle of equal respect is violated—so the reasoning goes.[20] Coercive principles must be as justifiable to others as they are to us and therefore must be based on terms that all citizens can accept on the grounds of their common reason.[21]

Because a religious rationale is a paradigmatic case of a basis for conduct that other citizens have good reasons to reject, it does not count as public justification; thus a law grounded solely in a religious rationale must never be enacted. In short, purely religious convictions or commitments have no role to play in democratic and pluralist polities. This requirement that religious reasons be excluded from liberal-democratic politics is offensive to religious persons who, like others, wish to support their favoured political commitments according to their conscience.[22] If people believe that their politics must be consistent with their morality as derived from religion, why should they be discouraged or stigmatized for grounding their politics in religious convictions? By asking the religious to exercise restraint and exclude theological reasons from their justification for a coercive law, liberal secularism forces them to act against their conscience and, in so doing, violates its own principle of equal respect. Indeed, the demand that restraint be exercised is counterproductive because exclusion from the larger public sphere forces the religious to form their

[18] Hamburger (n. 15) 193–251. [19] Ibid. 42–5.

[20] Audi, 'The Place of Religious Argument in a Free and Democratic Society', 30 *San Diego Law Review* (1993) 677; Solum, 'Faith and Justice', 39 *DePaul Law Review* (1990) 1083; S. Macedo, *Liberal Virtues: Citizenship, Virtue and Community in Liberal Constitutionalism* (1990) 249; J. Rawls, *A Theory of Justice* (1991) 337–8; Weithman, 'Religion and the Liberalism of Reasoned Respect' in P. Weithman (ed.), *Religion and Contemporary Liberalism* (1997) 1, 6.

[21] C. Larmore, *The Morals of Modernity* (1996) 137.

[22] Sandel, 'Freedom of Conscience or Freedom of Choice' in T. Eastland (ed.), *Religious Liberty in the Supreme Court* (1993) 483.

own narrow public one where resentment and prejudice will flourish.[23] This response would lead not only to the freezing of identities but also to the building of unbreachable walls between religious and non-religious citizens. Therefore, 'engagement with religious people is typically better than shunning them'.[24]

Furthermore, these theories of secularism rely excessively on a rationalist conception of reason that imposes unfair limits on the manner in which issues are to be brought into the public domain. Some issues are constitutively emotive; others become emotive because they are articulated by people who are not always trained to be rational in the way that secularists mandate.[25] Overall, the model of moral reasoning typical of such secularism is context-insensitive, theoreticist, and absolutist (or non-comparative), enjoining us to think in terms of this or that since it is too heavily reliant on monolithic ideas or values considered to be true, superior, or wholly non-negotiable. In sum, both French and American versions developed in the context of a single-religion society and as a way to solve the problems of one religion, namely Christianity. They were not designed to deal with deep religious diversity. Both the idealized French and American versions of secularism understand separation as exclusion and make individualistically conceived values—individual liberty, or equality between individuals, or both—the grounds for separation. Overall, it would not be wrong to say that they force upon followers of secularism a choice between active hostility and benign indifference to religion. Because of their diversity-resistant and individualistic character, these two models have become part of the problem.

C. Political Secularism in European Societies

Neither of these two models adequately captures the models of secularism actually in play in most European societies. These states follow neither the French nor the American model. Virtually all European states have a stable regime of individual rights that includes the right to religious liberty. None could have managed to install this regime without having attacked the power and privilege of their churches in the past, a stridency that would not have been possible without some degree of state-church separation. Yet, unlike in France, there is no lingering hostility towards religion in other European state structures. In Europe initial hostility was followed by active support.[26] Virtually all European states have developed an institutional arrangement that grants some privilege or public recognition to their church. Indeed, some still have an established church, a privileged arrangement that goes well beyond recognition. Tariq Modood finds the combination of separation of church and state and support for religion compatible with secularism; he calls it 'moderate secularism'.[27]

[23] J. Spinner-Halev, *Surviving Diversity: Religion and Democratic Citizenship* (2000) 150–6.

[24] Ibid. 155. [25] Connolly (n. 16) 1999.

[26] A. Stepan, 'The Multiple Secularisms of Modern Democratic and Non-Democratic Regimes' in C. Calhoun, M. Juergensmeyer, and J. VanAntwerpen (eds), *Rethinking Secularism* (2011) 114.

[27] Modood, 'State-Religion Connections and Multicultural Citizenship' in J. Cohen and C. Leborde (eds), *Religion, Secularism and Constitutional Democracy* (2015) 182. See also Bhargava, 'Beyond Moderate Secularism' in P. Losconczi and W. Van Herck (eds), *Secularism, Religion and Politics* (2014) 57.

Such is the context in which non-Christian migrants to Europe, the majority of whom are Muslims, have been arriving, settling, and making claims that relate to the place of religious identity in the public sphere. But it is precisely here that a sense of a crisis of secularism can be found. Since the advent of large-scale, non-Christian migration, moderate secularism has had a precarious life in Europe.

Europe's political secularism is currently destabilized. Europe cannot just go on with the same moderate secularism and properly face this destabilization. Modood hopes that the historical compromises between church and state will be extended to other religions, particularly to Islam.[28] However, the multiculturalization of this secularism is neither easy nor sufficient. It is not easy because it presupposes massive change in the cultural background. Institutional adjustment is bound to be difficult because an internal link exists between the collective secular self-understanding of European societies and deeply problematic institutional arrangements. Quite plainly, current European institutions are deeply biased. They have accommodated Christians but will not be able to accommodate Muslims. They are not sufficient because simple accommodation without some accompanying 'hostility' or critical questioning may not work for all Muslim citizens. For instance, many Muslim women might welcome hostility to some customs that have come to be associated with their religion.

Why are institutional adjustments difficult to achieve? Using a broad brush, we might say that European secularisms arose in predominantly single-religion societies. Issues of radical individual freedom and citizenship equality arose in European societies *after* religious homogenization. The birth of confessional states was accompanied by the massive expulsion of subject communities whose faith differed from the religion of the ruler. Such states eventually found some place for toleration in their moral space, but as is well known, toleration was consistent with deep inequalities and with a humiliating, marginalized, and virtually invisible existence. The liberal democratization and the consequent secularization of many European states has helped citizens with non-Christian faiths to acquire most formal rights. But such a scheme of rights neither embodies a regime of inter-religious equality nor effectively prevents religion-based discrimination and exclusion. Indeed, it masks majoritarian, ethno-religious biases.

The new reality of deepening religious diversity has brought the religious biases of European states into increasingly sharper relief.[29] Despite all changes, European states have continued to privilege Christianity in one form or another, as noted earlier. In short, there has been no impartiality within the domain of religion, and despite formal equality, this lack of impartiality continues to have a far-reaching impact on the rest of society.

Thus these biases are evident in different kinds of difficulties faced by Muslims. For example, in Great Britain one-third of all primary school students are educated by religious communities, yet applications for state funding by Muslims are frequently turned down. Veit Bader informs us that in 2007 there were only five

[28] Modood (n. 27).

[29] J. Klausen, *The Islamic Challenge, Politics and Religion in Western Europe* (2005).

Muslim schools, compared to 2,000 run by the Roman Catholic Church, and 4,700 run by the Church of England.[30] Similar problems persist in other European countries. In both France and Germany not a single school run by Muslims is subsidized by the state. This bias is also manifest in the failure of many Western European states to deal with the issue of headscarves (most notably France), in unheeded demands by Muslims to build mosques and therefore to properly practise their own faith (Germany and Italy), in discrimination against ritual slaughter (Germany), and in unheeded demands by Muslims for proper burial grounds of their own (Denmark, among others). Given that in recent times Islamophobia has gripped the imagination of several Western societies—as exemplified by the cartoon controversy in Denmark and by the minarets issue in Switzerland—it is very likely that their Muslim citizens will continue to face disadvantages due only to membership in their religious community.

Removing the biases of European states will not be easy because of resistance from the right, institutional resilience, and differences between Christianity and Islam, not to mention between Christianity and non-Semitic religions such as Hinduism. Moderate secularism will be severely tested. Indeed, the test has already begun, which is why talk of strain or even crisis is justified.

So far I have been talking as though the initiative lies squarely with only one agent, the European state (and its supporters), and as though Muslims will respond enthusiastically to any initiative from this reformed (i.e. multiculturalized) state. But this view is too sanguine about the self-understanding of Muslims and about their current condition in Europe. It underestimates their alienation and ghettoization. Only with a better and deeper understanding of Muslims in different parts of Europe can we learn about what should and should not be accommodated and about what currently can and cannot be accommodated. Indeed, only in a more relaxed atmosphere can a plurality of voices—the more vulnerable voices—emerge and be better heard, a change that will have a huge bearing on our collective judgment of what should and should not be accommodated. (As of now, we hear two dominant voices: that of the ultra-orthodox Muslim and that of the lapsed Muslim, a convert to radical secularism.) These voices may necessitate not just accommodation but also more active state intervention either to foster or to suppress some hitherto unnoticed beliefs and practices of Muslims. It is entirely possible that the state may not only have to support some religious practices but also have to inhibit others. European states may be only too happy to abort some Muslim practices, but such intervention would entail a massive shift in their conception of secularism—from first separating religion from the state and then moving from a position of only supporting religion to sometimes supporting it and at other times inhibiting it—what I call *principled distance*. In short, they may have to set aside their moderate stance of accommodating, rather than being hostile to, religion. Currently, the practice of most European states is to offer little official support, to provide no accommodation, and with few exceptions, to stay indifferent to massive societal intolerance. What might be required is more support of some religions, less support

[30] V. Bader, *Secularism or Democracy? Associational Governance of Religious Diversity* (2007) 161.

of others, and active interference in societal intolerance—that is, an attempt by the state to tackle both inter- and intra-religious domination.

In sum, extending moderate (i.e. accommodative) secularism to Muslims, under existing conditions, will be very difficult, for it presupposes massive shifts in background cultural conditions for which Europe may not yet be prepared. It would not be too far off the mark to say that not appreciating deep religious and cultural diversity is one of the central failures of modern Europe. To my knowledge, overcoming this issue is a bigger challenge than any other. Even the conceptual resources for such change appear to be missing. In any case, moderate secularism's accommodation will not be sufficient because the modern (i.e. democratic) state must have the legitimacy to also negatively intervene in some socio-religious practices, if only to protect the interests of vulnerable internal minorities. This in part entails abandoning moderate secularism. To respond to the challenge of deep diversity, Europe might be better off with an altogether different conception of secularism.

What I have said above needs some qualification, for it ignores two facts. First, it neglects the informal politics of state and non-state actors, where interesting changes might be occurring. Second, it does not take into account the existence of European constitutional values, which are very different from the constitutions of individual European states. I acknowledge the importance of both. These factors could make a substantial difference. But difficulties block progress here too. First, nothing prevents individual states from ignoring the European constitutional values. Would France, Belgium, or Italy listen to the European Union if it declared the banning of the burqa to be unconstitutional? Second, moderate secularism stands in the way of nurturing norms of principled distance embedded in the informal politics of state and non-state actors.

I believe then that the doctrinal, ideological, and theoretical formulations of Western secularism have become highly restricted and inadequate, as too have the formal politics and laws inspired by these doctrines and ideologies. A reimagination of secularism is virtually impossible unless we reduce our reliance on these formal practices and formulations, including the French and the American models of exclusionary separation of church and state as well as the formal, institutional political practices of most European states. If we remain in the grip of these formulations and practices, we will simply not notice other conceptions that have probably been pushed into the background. Once we shift away from these alternate perspectives and start to focus on the normative informal practices of a broader range of Western and non-Western states, we shall see that better forms of secular state and much more defensible versions of secularism are available.

D. The Indian Model of Secularism

Can a version of secularism be found that is sensitive simultaneously to the moral integrity of both liberal and non-liberal religious ways of living, as well as able to address religious or religion-based oppression and exclusions—one that goes beyond liberal, libertarian, and republican theories? Although theoretically less developed, another model of secularism exists—one not generated exclusively in the

West—that meets the needs of societies with deep religious diversity and also complies with the principles of freedom and equality. This model meets the secularist objection to non-secular states and the religious objection to some forms of secular state. To identify it, we must consider the *normative* and *discursive* levels and look at some of the developing normative practices of the French, British, and even American states. Take the example of the public funding of faith-based schools. Officially, American secularism does not sanction public financing of religion. Yet public funding of religion exists—albeit without proper assessment of the dilemmas of recognition and cooperation. Likewise, in practice, the French state not only directly and indirectly funds Roman Catholic schools but also tries to accommodate even Muslim minorities. In the Netherlands, at least until recently, 46 Muslim schools were directly funded by the state. However, the best place to find this version of secularism is within the best inter-communal practice in the subcontinent of India and in the country's Constitution appropriately interpreted. In India the existence of deep religious diversity has ensured a conceptual response to problems not only within religions but also between them. Without taking it as a blueprint, the West must examine the Indian conception in the hope of learning from it.

Several features of Indian secularism can be identified that distinguish it from other variants.[31] First, multiple religions are not extras added on as an afterthought but were present at Indian secularism's starting point as part of its foundation. Indian secularism is inextricably tied to deep religious diversity. Second, this form of secularism has a commitment to multiple values, namely liberty, equality, and fraternity—not conceived narrowly as pertaining to individuals but interpreted broadly to cover the relative autonomy of religious communities and their equality of status in society—as well as other more basic values such as peace, toleration, and mutual respect between communities. It has a place not only for the right of individuals to profess their religious beliefs but also for the right of religious communities to establish and maintain educational institutions crucial for the survival and sustenance of their distinctive religious traditions.

The acceptance of community-specific rights brings me to the third feature of Indian secularism. Because it was born in a deeply multi-religious society, it is concerned as much with inter-religious domination as it is with intra-religious domination. Whereas the two Western conceptions of secularism have provided benefits to minorities only incidentally (Jews benefited in some European countries such as France not because their special needs and demands were met but because of a change in the general climate of the society), under the Indian conception even community-specific political rights (through political reservations for religious minorities) were almost granted during the drafting of the Constitution but were withheld at the last moment only for contextual reasons. In fact, it is arguable that a conceptual space is still available for these rights within the Indian Constitution.

[31] For a detailed discussion, see R. Bhargava, *The Distinctiveness of Indian Secularism in the Future of Secularism* (2005); Bhargava, 'How Should States Deal with Deep Religious Diversity: Can Anything Be Learnt from the Indian Model of Secularism?' in T.S. Shah, A. Stepan, and M. Duffy Toft (eds), *Rethinking Religion and World Affairs* (2012) 73.

Fourth, Indian secularism does not erect a wall of separation between religion and state. There are boundaries, of course, but they are porous. This situation allows the state to intervene in religions in order to help or hinder them without the impulse to control or destroy them. This intervention can include granting aid to educational institutions of religious communities on a non-preferential basis and interfering in socio-religious institutions that deny equal dignity and status to members of their own religion or to those of others—for example, the ban on untouchability and the obligation to allow everyone, irrespective of their caste, to enter Hindu temples, as well as, potentially, other actions to correct gender inequalities. In short, Indian secularism interprets separation to mean not strict exclusion or strict neutrality but what I call *principled distance*, which is poles apart from one-sided exclusion, mutual exclusion, strict neutrality, and equidistance.

Fifth, Indian secularism is not entirely averse to the public character of religions. Although the state does not identify with a particular religion or with religion more generally, official and therefore public recognition is granted to religious communities. The model admits a distinction between de-publicization and de-politicization, as well as between different kinds of de-politicization. Because it is not hostile to the public presence of religion, it does not aim to de-publicize it. It accepts the importance of one form of de-politicization of religion. Sixth, this model shows that in responding to religion, we do not have to choose between active hostility and passive indifference or between disrespectful hostility and respectful indifference. We can combine the two, permitting necessary hostility as long as there is also active respect. The state may intervene to inhibit some practices as long as it shows respect for other practices of the religious community and does so by publicly lending support to them. Seventh, by not fixing its commitment from the start exclusively to individual or community values and by not marking rigid boundaries between the public and the private, India's constitutional secularism allows decisions on these matters to be made either within the open dynamics of democratic politics or by contextual reasoning in the courts. Eighth, one might say that Indian political secularism shows a marked preference for morally grounded secularization in each of the senses mentioned earlier, in section 3. No process exists which cannot be brought partially under human (democratic) control. Nor must an attempt be made for a blanket, morally insensitive restriction, privatization, or decline of religion. Ninth, it opens up the possibility of different societies working out their own secularisms. In short, it opens out the possibility of multiple secularisms. Tenth, it breaks out of the rigid interpretative grid that divides our social world into the Western modern and the traditional, indigenous, non-Western. Indian secularism is modern but departs significantly from mainstream conceptions of Western secularism. Finally, the commitment to multiple values and principled distance means that the state tries to balance different, ambiguous, but equally important values. This makes its secular ideal more like a contextual, ethically sensitive, politically negotiated arrangement—which it really is—rather than a scientific doctrine conjured by ideologues and merely implemented by political agents.

A somewhat forced, formulaic articulation of Indian secularism goes something like this. The state must keep a principled distance from all public or private and individual-oriented or community-oriented religious institutions for the sake of the equally significant—and sometimes conflicting—values of peace, worldly goods, dignity, liberty, equality, and fraternity in all of its complicated individualistic and non-individualistic versions. Indian secularism, then, is an ethically sensitive, negotiated settlement between diverse groups and divergent values. This model thus embodies what I call *contextual secularism*.

Allow me to elaborate on two features of the Indian model: principled distance and contextual secularism.

1. *Principled distance*

The idea of principled distance unpacks the metaphor of separation differently. It accepts a disconnection between state and religion at the level of ends and institutions but does not make a fetish of it at the level of policy and law; this distinguishes it from all other models of secularism, moral and amoral, that disconnect state and religion at this level. It accepts that humans have an interest in relating to something beyond themselves, including gods, goddesses or God, and that this manifests itself as individual belief and feeling as well as social practice in the public domain. It also accepts that religion is a cumulative tradition[32] as well as a source of people's identities. But it insists that even if it turns out that God exists and that one religion is true and others false, this will not give the 'true' doctrine or religion the right to force itself down the throats of others who do not believe it. The moral obligation to ensure the equal distribution of liberties and other valuable resources would prevent discrimination.

At the same time, a secularism based on principled distance accepts that although religion may not have special public significance antecedently written into and defining the very character of the state or the nation, it does not follow that religion has no public significance at all. A second idea distinguishes it from strict neutrality, which dictates that the state must help or hinder all religions to an equal degree and in the same manner; if it intervenes in one religion, it must also do so in others. This makes principled distance rest upon a distinction explicitly drawn by the American philosopher Ronald Dworkin between equal treatment and treating everyone as equals.[33] The principle of equal treatment in the relevant political sense requires that the state treat all citizens equally in the relevant respect—for example, in the distribution of a resource of opportunity. In contrast, the principle of treating people as equals entails that every person or group is treated with equal concern and respect. This second principle may sometimes require equal treatment—say, equal distribution of resources—but it may also occasionally dictate unequal preferential treatment. Treating people or groups as equals is entirely consistent with differential treatment. This idea is the second ingredient in what I have called principled distance.

[32] W. Cantwell-Smith, *The Meaning and End of Religion* (1991) 154–69.
[33] Dworkin, 'Liberalism' in S. Hampshire (ed.), *Public and Private Morality* (1978) 113, 125.

When I say that principled distance allows both for engagement with or disengagement from, and does so by allowing differential treatment, what kind of treatment do I have in mind? First, religious groups have sought exemptions when states have intervened in religious practices by promulgating laws designed to apply neutrally across society. This demand for non-interference is made on the grounds either that the law requires them to do things not permitted by their religion or that it prevents them from doing things mandated by their religion. For example, Sikhs demand exemptions from mandatory helmet laws and from police dress codes to accommodate religiously required turbans. Muslim women and girls demand that the state not interfere in the religious requirement that they wear the chador. Rightly or wrongly, religiously grounded personal laws may be exempted. Elsewhere, Jews and Muslims seek exemptions from Sunday closing laws on the grounds that such closing is not required by their religion. Principled distance allows a practice that is banned or regulated in the majority culture to be permitted in the minority culture because of the distinctive status and meaning it has for the minority culture's members. For the mainstream conception of secularism, this variability is a problem because of a simple and somewhat absolutist morality that attributes overwhelming importance to one value—particularly to equal treatment, equal liberty, or equality of individual citizenship. Religious groups may demand that the state refrain from interference in their practices, but they may equally demand that the state interfere in such a way as to give them special assistance so that they are able to secure what other groups are routinely able to acquire by virtue of their social dominance in the political community. The state may grant authority to religious officials to perform legally binding marriages or to have their own rules for or methods of obtaining a divorce. Principled distance allows the possibility of such policies on the grounds that holding people accountable to a law to which they have not consented might be unfair. Furthermore, it does not discourage public justification—that is, justification based on reasons endorsable by all. Indeed, it encourages people to pursue public justification. However, if the attempt to arrive at public justification fails, it enjoins religiously minded citizens to support coercive laws that, although based purely on religious reasons, are consistent with freedom and equality.[34]

However, principled distance is not just a recipe for differential treatment in the form of special exemptions. It may even require state intervention and, moreover, in some religions more than in others, consideration of the historical and social condition of all relevant religions. To take first examples of positive engagement, some holidays of all majority and minority religions are granted national status. Subsidies are provided to schools run by all religious communities. Minority religions are granted a constitutional right to establish and maintain their educational institutions. Limited funding is available to Muslims for *Hajj*. But state engagement can also take a negative interventionist form. For the promotion of a particular value constitutive of secularism, some religions, relative to other religions, may require more interference from the state. For example, suppose that the value to be advanced is social equality. This requires in part undermining caste and gender hierarchies.

[34] C.J. Eberle, *Religious Convictions in Liberal Politics* (2002).

Thus there is a constitutional ban on untouchability, Hindu temples were thrown open to all, particularly to former untouchables should they choose to enter them. Child marriage was banned among Hindus and a right to divorce was introduced.

Consider once again laws that interfere with Hinduism. The relevant consideration is not whether they immediately encompass all groups but whether or not they are just and consistent with values under-pinning secularism. Three reasons exist to explain why all social groups need not be covered by these laws. First, they may be relevant only to Hindus. Take the abolition of child marriage and *devadasi* dedication[35] or the introduction of the right to divorce. Here, before deciding whether it was necessary to enact a special provision for Hindus, the legislature took into account their social customs and beliefs. Similar laws for Muslims were simply redundant. Second, laws in liberal democracies require legitimacy; the consent of at least the representatives of communities is vital. If consent has indeed been obtained from the representatives of only one community, it is sometimes prudent to enact community-specific laws. It is wise to apply the general principle in stages, rather than not have it at all. Finally, 'it is perfectly within the competence of the legislature to take account of the degree of evil which is prevalent under various circumstances and the legislature is not bound to legislate for all evils at the same time. Therefore, an act passed by the legislature cannot be attacked merely because it tackles only some of the evils in society and does not tackle other evils of the same or worse kind which may be prevalent.'[36] Thus, if the legislature acting on these considerations wanted to enact a special provision in regard to, say, bigamous marriages among Hindus, it cannot be said that the legislature was discriminating against Hindus only on the ground of religion.[37] The Indian courts have frequently followed this line of reasoning. They have defended a policy if they found that its purpose is the eradication of a social evil traceable to religious practices, even if the policy was targeted at specific communities. It has argued that so long as the state has taken gradual steps towards social welfare and reform and has not introduced distinctions or classifications that are unreasonable or oppressive, equality before law is not breached. A state interfering in one religion more than in others does not automatically depart from secularism. Indian secularism rejects the assumption that 'one size fits all'.

To sum up, in responding to a variety of values, the state can neither strictly exclude considerations emanating from religion nor keep strict neutrality with respect to religion. It cannot antecedently decide that it will always refrain from interfering in religions or that it will interfere in each equally; it may not relate to every religion in exactly the same way or intervene in each to the same degree or in the same manner. Wanting to do so would plainly be absurd. All the state must ensure is that its relationship with all religions is guided by non-sectarian motives consistent with some secular values and principles.

[35] *Devadasi* refers to low-caste girls dedicated to worship and service of a deity or a temple for their entire lives.

[36] *The State of Bombay v. Narasu Appa* AIR (1952), Bom. 84.

[37] Ibid.

2. Contextual secularism

A context-sensitive secularism, one based on the idea of principled distance, is what I term contextual secularism. It is contextual not only because the precise form and content of secularism will vary from one context to another and from place to place but also because it embodies a certain model of contextual moral reasoning. It is a multi-value doctrine. To accept its multi-value nature is to acknowledge that its constitutive values do not always sit easily with one another. On the contrary, they are frequently in conflict.

Some degree of internal discord, and therefore a fair amount of instability, is an integral part of contextual secularism. For this reason, it forever requires fresh interpretations, contextual judgments, and attempts at reconciliation and compromise. No general *a priori* rule of resolving these conflicts exists, no easy lexical order, no pre-existing hierarchy among values or laws that enables us to decide that, no matter what the context, a particular value must override everything else. Almost everything, then, is a matter of situational thinking and contextual reasoning. Whether one value will override or be reconcilable with another cannot be decided beforehand. Each time the matter will present itself differently and will be differently resolved. If this is true, the practice of secularism requires a different model of moral reasoning than the one that straitjackets our moral understanding in the form of well-delineated and explicitly stated rules.[38] This contextual secularism recognizes that conflicts between individual rights and group rights, or between equality and liberty, or between liberty and the satisfaction of basic needs cannot always be adjudicated by recourse to some general and abstract principle. Rather, they can be settled only case by case and may require a fine balancing of competing claims. The eventual outcome may not be wholly satisfactory to either claimant but may still be reasonably satisfactory to both. Multi-value doctrines such as secularism encourage accommodation—not the giving up of one value for the sake of another, but their reconciliation and possible harmonization so that apparently incompatible concepts and values may operate without changes to their basic content.

This endeavour to make concepts, viewpoints, and values work simultaneously does not amount to a morally objectionable compromise. This is so because nothing of importance is being given up for the sake of something less significant, something without value, or even with negative value. Rather, what is pursued is a mutually agreed-upon middle way that combines elements from two or more equally valuable entities. The roots of such attempts at reconciliation and accommodation lie in a lack of dogmatism, in a willingness to experiment—to think at different levels and in separate spheres—and in a readiness to make and accept decisions on a provisional basis. The pursuit of this middle way captures a way of thinking characterized by the following dictum: 'Why look at things in terms of this or that, why not try to have both this and that?'[39] This way of thinking recognizes that, although we may currently be unable to secure the best of both values and may therefore be forced to

[38] Taylor, 'Justice After Virtue' in J. Horton and S. Mendus (eds), *After MacIntyre: A Critical Perspective on the Work of Alasdair MacIntyre* (1994) 16.

[39] G. Austin, *The Indian Constitution: Cornerstone of a Nation* (1972) 318.

settle for a watered-down version of each, we must continue to have an abiding commitment to searching for a transcendence of this second-best condition.

It is frequently argued that Indian secularism is contradictory because it tries to bring together individual and community rights and that those articles in the Indian Constitution that have a bearing on the secular nature of the Indian state are deeply conflictual and at best ambiguous.[40] This characterization, however, misrecognizes a virtue as a vice. In my view, the attempt to bring together seemingly incompatible values is a great strength of Indian secularism. Indian secularism is an ethically sensitive negotiated settlement between diverse groups and divergent values. When it is not treated as such it turns either into a dead formula or into a facade for political manoeuvres.

Two other serious objections are frequently raised against this model. First, it assumes that the state has the capacity to impartially arbitrate among conflicting religious groups. But is any state ever impartial towards all religious groups or between the religious and the secular? Are not structural biases present in every state? Second, the notion of principled distance is found to be problematic. It is claimed that it is far too pragmatic in the crude opportunistic sense, the assumption here being that any negotiation or compromise is morally wrong. In what follows I shall try to counter these objections.

It is not my claim that the state has no biases. Indeed a commitment to certain goals makes the state bend in the direction of those objectives. Only those who have a God's-eye view of impartiality or neutrality expect the state not to have any biases. Since I believe that all humans and human-made entities are laden with some interest or values, I reject a God's-eye view of impartiality, an absolutist impartiality from nowhere.[41] Yet, the state can embody a set of minimal values that all citizens, if they were to use their powers of reason and empathy, can agree on and without which a decent, egalitarian social life is impossible. For instance, they can all agree not to subordinate themselves to each other and to live their lives in accordance with conceptions of the good they have worked out with each other's help, though without undue influence. More importantly, a state not only embodies a set of professed values but reflects the overall cultural ethos within which it is located.

This ethos may or may not be made of multicultural strands of equal weight or strength. For example, if a state is situated within a lively Christian tradition, it is, if it is examined closely enough, likely to reflect the character of that tradition. The more important issue then is what the state does once it begins to recognize its own cultural and religious leanings—those which are not stated and have even been disavowed but are nonetheless present in its institutions and practices. An example would help. In India a very large and significant number of people either call themselves Hindu or are assumed to be so. Though not entirely, the ethos of many of India's social and political institutions is saturated, it might be reasonably claimed, by one or the other strand of 'Hinduism'. So, regardless of our evaluative judgment,

[40] Tambiah, 'The Crisis of Secularism in India' in R. Bhargava (ed.), *Secularism and Its Critics* (1998) 417, 445–53.

[41] See Bhargava (n. 1).

it would not be entirely incorrect to say that these institutions are somewhat Hinduized or wear a Hindu look. Yet, India also has Muslims, Christians, Parsees, Buddhists, Jains, Sikhs, atheists, and people with many other not so easily definable outlooks. Sections of Hindus may find the practices of such communities disagreeable, morally discomforting, or just downright strange but they tolerate them. They may collectively have the power to interfere in them, even banish them, but they refrain from doing so. Of course, legally they have no other option. These religious communities have rights not to be interfered with in their religious and cultural practices. But the minorities will not be able to effectively exercise their rights if Hindus do not possess the capacity for other-related self-restraint. Most Hindus do as a matter of fact exercise such restraint. But is this sufficient for a morally justified co-existence between Hindus and minority communities? Suppose, then, that community-specific rights of minorities are respected but Hindu self-assertion becomes more pronounced. Let us say they build new temples around every corner, ensure that these are mightier in size than mosques and churches, fund new radio and television channels that stream Hindu teachings and no other, introduce text books that speak largely of and glorify Hindu gods and goddesses, change national and state symbols in order to make them explicitly and exclusively Hindu, and so on. What would the impact of such actions be on the psyche of the minorities? Most likely, it would increase their sense of social and cultural alienation. It would force them to feel left out of many public domains. It might even lower their self-esteem. Alternatively, Hindus can show some self-related self-restraint, so as not to show off, to not always wear their own religion and culture on their sleeve, to not always advertise their wares, as it were. Indeed, to persistently announce in public that you are the boss in your own country might be a definitive sign of deep-rooted insecurities and anxieties, one that is both potentially damaging to others and to oneself. Abandoning this self-related self-restraint might then adversely affect everyone, and destroy the very fabric of contemporary Indian society.

A second, related objection can be answered by spelling out what kind of state I have in mind when I speak of 'the state'. I am certainly not talking here about an authoritarian, centralized state. I take it for granted that the state is democratic not only in the sense that its own institutions are so but also in the other sense that it is continually nourished by a democratic ethos. A state with democratic institutions can be impartial to some degree, if at least some politicians behave as statespersons, some judges scrupulously make decisions that are legally sound and wise, and so on. But for its biases to be revealed and rectified, in short for a state to act in a properly secular and democratic manner, it is imperative that there be a free and vibrant press, committed social activists, and an alert citizenry. An impartial and secular state is dependent on multiple agents both within its structure and outside it. There is no way to ensure that the first act of the state on a relevant issue be properly and unmistakably secular. However, if the state is understood as multiple agent-dependent, then over time it can shed most of its significant biases for one religion and emerge instead as secular and impartial. A frequently asked question is who decides what is right and properly secular and my answer is always: a relatively correct and endorsable decision cannot be taken without the involvement of all relevant agents including those who are directly and adversely affected by the decision. All decisions in a democratic state are taken over time and invariably involve a large number and different kinds of agents. So must the case be with decisions of the state that are expected to be appropriately secular. They take time and must involve a number of agents if they are to arrive at a sound and endorsable decision. Indeed, such decisions involving multiple agents do take a long time even if it turns out that they are mistaken, as is attested by the French hijab issue which was sparked off in 1989 and resolved by law 15 years later, in 2004.

On principled distance, all I have to say is this: I have used the term 'distance' to distinguish my account from a separationist reading of political secularism. On the latter view, separation of state and religion means a somewhat strict and wholly unambiguous exclusion of religion from the state at each of the three levels mentioned previously. As indicated earlier, I find this interpretation of separation neither desirable nor possible. Distance is a less extreme mode of relation. Keeping a distance from something does not prevent one from relating to it in multiple ways. It implies only that there is neither identity nor closeness. The rest is left unspecified, opening a terrain of multiple possibilities. It allows for flexibility when it is desperately needed and, therefore, for change in perspective and practice when the situation demands. But it is precisely this openness and flexibility that has led some critics to the mistaken conclusion that virtually any mode of relation between state and religion is permissible. Does this not allow anything and everything to barge in? Does it not introduce an ad hocism or opportunism that is conceptually defeating and morally outrageous? Thus, it is alleged that this model of secularism allows for state involvement in or detachment from religion grounded purely in reasons of say, vote-bank politics or appeasing the tantrums of particular religious groups. But then it is precisely to block such interpretation that the term 'principled', so crucial in the phrase 'principled distance', is used. Every action of the state in relation to all religious communities must be grounded in, supported by, and justified in terms of principles or values. Given this, it would be preposterous to think of principled distance as a purely tactical and opportunistic policy adopted for self-aggrandisement, for purely political and financial consideration. Principled distance is *not* opportunistic distance. Furthermore, the not so visible plurality of principles can hardly be overemphasized. Multiple values always come into play in the process of any decision-making. I am committed to value pluralism and therefore to a potential conflict of values. There are very few instances where a single value applies unambiguously. Most human situations are saturated with multiple and competing values and therefore any decision requires a sensitive interpretation, negotiation, and balancing of all relevant values. I consider it wrong if any one value unreflectively and unambiguously overrides other values relevant to the situation, almost as wrong as taking a decision grounded in pure considerations of wealth or power despite the need to take into account human values.

All compromises are not wrong or despicable. If something of value is sacrificed for the sake of pure consideration of self-interest, say in the pursuit of power, wealth, or fame, then clearly the compromise is morally dubious, but if one begins with the recognition that multiple values are at stake, then provided issues of self-interest are set aside, any negotiation or balancing among values is entirely appropriate from a moral point of view. Indeed such negotiations are morally required. My entire contextualist, morally sensitive approach to secularism as principled distance will lose its distinctiveness and individuality if it is viewed in any way that is Machiavellian.

Thus, the decision arrived at by a defensible secular state must be viewed as a practical judgment, a result of an elaborate public reasoning with citizens over a long period of time. By its very nature it is not final but provisional and revisable. It just happens to be the best possible answer to a problem, under the circumstances, at that point of time, which retrospectively may even be understood as part of a long, continuing series of similar morally sensitive practical judgments.

I hope to have convinced readers that this alternative model of reasoning is more nuanced. It simply has to be, if every value is not to be ordered beforehand. Let me take a concrete example to show that the best practice of the Indian state has frequently vindicated the principled distance model of secularism. Under scrutiny, for this purpose, is the important 1995 Supreme Court judgment, *Prabhoo v. Kunte*.[42] By looking at this judgment, I hope to show that the judiciary has understood the principles of secularism in much the same way as I have interpreted them in this chapter. Put differently, the best practice of the Indian state conforms to my interpretation of constitutional secularism.

The judgment I examine pertains to the inflammatory speeches by Shiv Sena supremo Bal Thackeray during the election campaign of Ramesh Prabhoo, a candidate for the Maharashtra State Legislative Assembly. Examples of speech cited by the judgment are:

> We are fighting this election for the protection of Hinduism. Therefore, we do not care for the votes of the Muslims. This country belongs to Hindus and will remain so.

And:

> You will find Hindu temples underneath if all the Mosques are dug out. Anybody who stands against the Hindus should be showed or worshipped with shoes. Prabhoo should be lead to victory in the name of Hindu. Though this country belongs to Hindus, Ram and Krishna are insulted. We do not want Muslim votes. A snake like Shahabuddin is sitting in the Janata Party. So, the voters should bury this party.[43]

The election of Prabhoo, an independent candidate supported by Shiv Sena, was declared void by the Bombay High Court on the ground that he and his agent Bal Thackeray had appealed for votes on the basis of the returned candidate's religion and that Thackeray's election speeches promoted feelings of enmity and hatred among citizens of India on grounds of religion and community. Both Thackeray and Prabhoo contested this judgment and appealed to the Supreme Court, claiming that their acts did not constitute a violation of the Representation of the Peoples Act, 1951, which prohibits *only* a *direct* appeal for votes on the ground of the religion of the candidate. (They also argued that their public speeches did not amount to an

[42] Supreme Court of India, *Dr Ramesh Yeshwant Prabhoo v. Shri Prabhakar Kashinath Kunt and Others*, Judgment of 11 December 1995, 1996 AIR 1113, 1996 SCC (1) 130.

[43] Ibid. 31.

appeal for votes on the ground of their religion because Hindutva means the Indian culture and not merely the Hindu religion. Shockingly, the Court accepted this view. Thus we have a judgment which exemplifies a combination of the best and worst practice of the Indian judiciary.) Their counsel argued that, because they violate the fundamental right to free speech given by Article 19(I)(a) of the Constitution, sub-sections 3 and 3A of section 123 of the Act are unconstitutional.

The Supreme Court rejected the arguments of the appellants, particularly their contention that sub-section 3 of section 123 is violated only when an election speech makes a direct appeal for votes on the ground of the candidate's religion. In the view of the Court, the nature of the speech is determined by its substance as well as by the manner in which it is meant to be understood by the audience within a particular social setting, and if a reasonable interpretation of the speech leads to the same conclusion as a direct appeal, then the speech violates the relevant sub-section of the Act. The purpose of enacting the provision, the Court argued, was to ensure that no candidate at an election gets or is denied votes only because of his or her religion.

Is this judgment of the Court consistent with secularism? More specifically, which version of secularism does it endorse? According to the judgment, it is part of the meaning of secularism that the state has no religion. The judgment claims that a secular state guarantees all its citizens the right to follow their religion according to their own convictions. It further clarifies that secularism is one facet of the right to equality, for it means equality in matters of religion to all individuals and groups. In several passages, the Court also endorses equality of citizenship. However, in the opinion of the Court, secularism cannot allow the mixing of religion and politics. Its professed goal is violated when a candidate appeals for votes on the ground of his religion. Does it mean that the Court understands separation to mean the exclusion of religion from politics? If so, its understanding of secularism is very different indeed from the principled distance version outlined earlier.

Fortunately, the Court clarifies that this secular principle must not be understood simplistically. The mere mention of religion in an election speech is not forbidden by the Act. Religion may figure in an election speech as long as its introduction does not amount to an appeal to vote on the ground of the candidate's religion or an appeal not to vote for the opponent on the ground of his religion. For example, an election speech made in conformity with the fundamental right to freedom of religion guaranteed under Articles 25–30 of the Constitution cannot be treated as anti-secular. Similarly, if a speech refers to discriminatory acts against any particular religion and promises removal of this imbalance, then, because its objective is the promotion rather than the denial of equality and justice, the speech is entirely consistent with secularism. This means that the Court endorses Articles 25–30 where every group is protected from discrimination on grounds of religion and is granted the right to obtain funds from the state for educational purposes on a non-preferential basis. Only when an electoral or political speech promotes enmity between religious communities, thereby trying to alienate the electorate from a candidate on the ground of his religion or when the candidate wants to gain political mileage for himself simply on the ground of his own religion, does mixing religion with politics become inappropriate and anti-secular. Thus when the use of religion in political or electoral speeches creates alienation among citizens instead of encouraging solidarity, when it violates the principle of equal citizenship, only then is secularism violated. It was to uphold the principle of equal citizenship or political fraternity and to prevent political alienation among citizens that, according to the Court, the makers of the Constitution rejected separate electorates. Forbidding the use of religion for gaining votes is in line with the rejection of separate electorates. Both mix religion and politics in an inappropriate manner. This distinction between appropriate and inappropriate mixing of religion and politics is at the heart of the idea of principled distance. Since this distinction is accepted or presupposed by the judgment, it follows unambiguously that separation is understood not as exclusion of religion but in terms of the idea of principled distance.

Notice also the subtle and deft contextual reasoning of the judgment. Contextual secularism is contextual not only because it captures the idea that the precise form and content of secularism will vary from one context to another and from place to place, but also because it embodies this second model of contextual moral reasoning. This it does because of its character as a multi-value doctrine. To accept that secularism is a multi-value doctrine is to acknowledge that its constitutive values do not always sit easily with one another. On the contrary, they are frequently in conflict. Some degree of internal discord and therefore a fair amount of instability is an integral part of contextual secularism. For this reason, it forever requires fresh interpretations, contextual judgments, and attempts at reconciliation and compromise. No general *a priori* rule of resolving these conflicts exists; no easy lexical order, no pre-existing hierarchy among values or laws that enables us to decide that, no matter what the context, a particular value must override everything else. Almost everything, then, is a matter of situational thinking and contextual reasoning. Whether one value overrides or is reconciled with another cannot be decided beforehand. Each time the matter presents itself differently and will be differently resolved. If this is true, then the practice of secularism requires a different model of moral reasoning than the one that straitjackets our moral understanding in the form of well-delineated, explicitly stated rules.[44] This contextual secularism recognizes that the conflict between individual rights and group rights, or between claims of equality and liberty, or between claims of liberty and the satisfaction of basic needs, cannot always be adjudicated by a recourse to some general and abstract principle. Rather they can only be settled case by case and may require a fine balancing of competing claims. The eventual outcome may not be wholly satisfactory to either but still be reasonably satisfactory to both. Multi-value doctrines such as secularism encourage accommodation—not the giving up of one value for the sake of another but rather their reconciliation and possible harmonization, that is, to make each work without changing the basic content of apparently incompatible concepts and values.

This endeavour to make concepts, viewpoints, and values work simultaneously does not amount to a morally objectionable compromise. This is so because nothing of importance is being given up for the sake of a less significant thing, one without

[44] Taylor (n. 38) 16–43.

value or even with negative value. Rather, what is pursued is a mutually agreed middle way that combines elements from two or more equally valuable entities. The roots of such attempts at reconciliation and accommodation lie in a lack of dogmatism, in a willingness to experiment and think at different levels and in separate spheres, and in a readiness to make decisions on a provisional basis. It is frequently argued against Indian secularism that it is contradictory because it tries to bring together individual and community rights and that articles in the Indian Constitution that have a bearing on the secular nature of the Indian state are deeply conflictual and at best ambiguous. This is to misrecognize a virtue as a vice. In my view, this attempt to bring together seemingly incompatible values is a great strength of Indian secularism.

Two further objections might still be raised. First, it might be said: look at the state of the subcontinent! Look at India! How deeply divided it remains! What about the violence against Muslims and Christians? How can success be claimed for the Indian version of secularism? I do not wish to underestimate the force of this objection. The secular ideal in India is in periodic crisis and is deeply contested. Besides, at the best of times, it generates as many problems as it solves.

But it should not be forgotten that a secular state was set up in India *despite* the massacre and displacement of millions of people on ethno-religious grounds, and it has survived in a continuing context in which ethnic nationalism remains dominant throughout the world. As different religious cultures claim their place in societies across the world, it may be India's development of secularism that offers the most pro-diversity, freedom-sensitive, and democratic way forward. In any case, this account must not be read as an apologia for the Indian state but as a reasonable and sympathetic articulation of a conception that the Indian state frequently fails to realize. My discussion is meant to focus on the comparative value of this conception and its potential for the future and not on how in fact it has fared in India. And why should the fate of ideal conceptions with transcultural potential be decided purely on the basis of what happens to them in their place of origin?

Second, it might be objected that I do not focus on the best practices of Western states and emphasize the more vocal articulations of Western secular conceptions. But this criticism would be unfair. Part of my point throughout has been that a gap has opened up everywhere between the dominant doctrinal formulations and practice even in the West. Consider France. The practice of the French state has often deviated from the principles of French *laïcité*. Much of this adjustment began in order to sustain French colonial projects in Africa. For example, to win over Arab nationalists, the French encouraged Muslims to undertake the pilgrimage to Mecca. A Muslim institute was created in Paris almost as a cover for a public mosque that would have been disallowed by the 1905 law on the state's abstention from supporting religion. In order to be consistent with that law the French government created an Islamic Cultural Centre with a conference room, library, and residences, as well as a mosque. As the interior minister of France, Nicolas Sarkozy made several attempts to co-opt Muslims into what was virtually a state-run body. In the same spirit there have been demands that the state should grant long-term leases of land to mosques and finance the trainings of Imams. Thus, several attempts are afloat in

France which combine state control with religious autonomy—something akin to the idea of principled distance.

Similar chasms between doctrine/theory and practice appear in the United States. For example, in *Goldman v. Weinberger* in 1986 the US Supreme Court decided by 5–4 that the Air Force had the right to ban an officer from wearing religious headgear (a yarmulke, in the case).[45] The Court stressed that the armed forces were different from civil institutions, and that the 'purpose of the military and its need to foster cohesiveness were regarded as appropriate justifications to restrict the religious rights of individuals'. Nevertheless, the following year Congress passed legislation that reversed this decision by allowing the members of the armed forces to wear religious apparel.[46] Likewise, in 2004, a school in Oklahoma banned a sixth-grade Muslim girl, Nashala Hearn, from wearing a headscarf.[47] In April 2004, the US Justice Department intervened on the side of the student and said: 'No student should be forced to choose between following her faith and enjoying the benefits of public education.'[48] Islamic organizations applauded this action as a 'message to... [France that] banned hijabs in schools'.[49] There is a certain whiff of the policy of principled distance exhibited in this stance.

The voucher system provides an alternative to the financial separation of state and religion. It reimburses the tuition expenses of the parents who send their children to private schools.[50] This funding can be used by parents to pay the tuition of either religious or secular private schools. Strict separationists have opposed the system on the ground that this indirectly funds religious schools whose central mission is religious training. Conservatives, on the other hand, support the system precisely for that reason. When the matter went up to the US Supreme Court, it affirmed that a decision to use federal funds to supply computer hardware, software, and library materials to religiously affiliated schools did not violate any constitutional principle because the aid was made in a non-discriminatory manner to both religious and secular schools. Although the doctrinal interpretation of church–state separation or mutual exclusion is violated by the voucher system, secularism itself is not abandoned so long as it is interpreted as principled distance. Non-preferential aid to religious groups is as consistent with the principles of secularism as is a policy of forbidding aid to all religious schools. I am not suggesting that the implementation of the voucher system is morally endorsable, but merely pointing out that in itself it does not violate secularism understood as principled distance.

Many of these examples show that the dominant conception of Western secularism is derived from an idealized self-understanding of two of its versions rather than from the best practices of Western states, including the practices of the United States and France. The normativity embedded in these practices contests these formal conceptions, and rightly so. My point, it might be recalled, is not that principled distance is absent from French or American practice but rather that it exists informally and when it enters the formal sphere it remains unacknowledged, making no

[45] A. Kuru, *Secularism and State Policies Towards Religion: The United States, France, and Turkey* (2009) (n.11) 46
[46] Ibid. 46–7. [47] Ibid. [48] Ibid. [49] Ibid. 46. [50] Ibid. 68–70.

difference to existing doctrinal formulations. These doctrinal conceptions, on the other hand, (a) obstruct an understanding of alternative conceptions worked out on the ground by morally sensitive political agents; (b) frequently distort the practice of many Western and non-Western states by influencing politicians and citizens alike; and (c) mask the many ways in which inter-religious or intra-religious domination persists in many Western societies. Moreover, it is this conception that has travelled to all parts of the world and is a continuing source of misunderstanding of the value of secular states. My objective is to displace these conceptions or at least put them in their place.

I hope to have demonstrated that the principled distance model is the best among available versions. I do not wish to suggest that this alternative model is found only in India. The Indian case is meant to show that such an alternative exists. It is not meant to resurrect a dichotomy between the West and the East. As I have mentioned, I am quite certain that this alternative version is embedded in the best practices of many states, including those Western states that are deeply enamoured of mainstream conceptions of political secularism. My objective in this chapter has been to draw attention to the point that political theorists do not see the normative potential in the secular practices of these different states because they are obsessed with the normativity of just one variant, the mainstream model of secularism. Western states need to improve their understanding of their own secular practices, just as Western secularism needs a better theoretical self-understanding. Rather than getting stuck on models they developed at a particular time in their history, they would do well to more carefully examine the normative potential in their own political practices or to learn from the original Indian variant.

This problem of misunderstanding secularism affects India, too. Both the self-proclaimed supporters of secularism and some of its misguided opponents in India could learn from examining the original Indian variant of constitutional secularism. Indeed, it is my conviction that many critics of Indian secularism will embrace it once they better understand its nature and point, something that can be done only when we loosen the grip of dominant models of secularism and recognize the existence of multiple secularisms, including the principled distance variant.

One last point: since it differs so extensively from other models, why use the term 'secular' at all for this model? Why use the terms secular and secularism which some people argue carry a negative connotation and should therefore be replaced by liberal democracy or a civic state? Such a view has been expressed by Veit Bader, especially in relation to my work.[51] Now both Bader and I agree that in an amorphous and diffused world, concepts bring order and clarity by directing our case and helping us to focus on specific matters. What does the concept of 'secular' help us to do? What does secularism achieve in our context? For Bader virtually nothing. Therefore he considers it should be dropped. For me it prevents the bland lumping together of all forms of discrimination and oppression under the same rubric and helps us to demarcate institutionalized religious domination from other kinds of domination such as those stemming from class, gender, race, and ethnicity, and reassures those

[51] Bader, 'Reply', 9 *Ethnicities* (2009) 566.

threatened by religious or religion-based exclusion, marginalization, discrimination, or oppression that the state is deeply committed to preventing these. If societies go the European way and continuously follow this trajectory of a general recession of Christianity into the background, they may not use the word 'secular' and may call themselves something else, perhaps liberal democratic. However, in societies with multiple religions with a very real possibility of inter- or intra-religious domination, religion is bound to be profoundly salient and the state would be equally bound to use a term that underscores its impartiality towards all religions, reaching out to religious minorities to assure them that they shall not be persecuted or treated as unequal. Not all freedom-loving and democratic states are automatically sensitive to issues of religious domination. They frequently need to underline that in addition to every other thing they value and want to be they are also against institutionalized religious domination. Such states would not choose between secularism and democracy but would opt for both. This is what happened in India. Therefore, I reject the general precept that the terms secular and secularism be dropped from public discourse. Whether these terms are to be used or not should be decided by contextual reasoning rather than by academic legislation.

6. Conclusion

Political secularism must be viewed as part of critical social secularism, indeed, as a self-critical social perspective, against neither religion nor faith but against institutionalized religious domination—as part of a family of perspectives against four types of domination: inter-religious, intra-religious, domination of religious by secular, and domination of secular by religious. We also need to give up the binary opposition between the secular and the religious. A new, refashioned conception of secularism must not see a necessary opposition between the secular and the religious. On the contrary, it must encourage a way of conceiving a world inhabited by both religious and non-religious people. Second, we should jettison seeing political secularism as a mere strategy, even as an institutional strategy. Third, secularism should sever its ties with amoral secular states. This means coming to realize that, somewhat paradoxically, secularism is against some secular states. Fourth, the state cannot avoid having or endorsing a policy towards religion or religious organizations. Religion plays an important part in the lives of many people, and religious institutions function in this world like purely secular institutions. So, separation cannot mean the exclusion of religion from the domain of the state. Separation of church and state should also not be interpreted as absolute or strict neutrality. No state can possibly help or hinder all religions in the same manner and to the same degree. The state may interfere with religion and refrain from such interference, depending entirely on which of these promotes the values of freedom and equality or undermines inter-religious and intra-religious dominations. Thus, we must rethink disconnection or separation and talk instead in terms of principled distance. Furthermore, values of freedom and equality must be interpreted both as rights of individuals and, wherever required, as rights of communities. Community rights are particularly important if religious groups are vulnerable or, because of their small number, have relatively little power to influence the process of decision-making.

To conclude, secularism must be neither servile nor hostile to religion. It must manifest an attitude of neither blind deference nor indifference but rather of critical respect toward all religions. Secularism that professes principled distance and is sensitive to multiple values cannot avoid making contextual judgments. Contextual judgments allow for ethically sensitive balancing and compromise.

If secularism is to survive as a transcultural normative perspective, it must be de-Christianized, de-Westernized, de-privatized, and de-individualized. In saying so, I do not mean that it must wholly sever its links with Christianity or the West, but its ties with them must be loosened. It should be able to accommodate other civilizations and community-based rights. Only with this form of secularism and a state nourished by it can deep religious diversity be managed.

3

Citizenship, Religious Rights, and State Identity in Arab Constitutions

Who is Free and What are They Free to Do?

Nathan J. Brown

Since the first constitutions governing the Arab world were written in the nineteenth century, they have contained provisions for religious freedom and the rights of religious communities that appeared to offer considerable concessions, even as the same constitutions took pains to proclaim Islam as the official religion and protect it from perceived insults and assaults. Arab constitutions seem to be promising freedom, protection, and support to individuals, communities, entire religions, and Islam. How can they make promises to entities that sometimes conflict with each other? What does it mean to protect individuals and religions at the same time? The mix is confusing but there is some consistency to the blend.

In this chapter, I will show how apparently contradictory constitutional clauses can be best understood as products of a set of historical circumstances and political realities that render their overall effect very coherent, if not always liberal. Religious freedom is guaranteed but also circumscribed by the interests of community, official religion, and state—each of which are seen as having their own claims and rights. Understanding the outcome as resulting from the pressures exerted by the various actors with rights—and seeing the constitutional text as the place where those rights are specified—helps us to understand how the definition of religious rights does the precise opposite of separating religion and state. Instead, guaranteeing the rights of various actors thoroughly enmeshes religion and state, to the extent they can become difficult to separate even for analytical, much less normative, purposes.

This chapter will be based primarily on a textual analysis of Arab constitutions, but one that places them within a political and historical context. We will begin by examining the apparent paradoxes in Arab constitutions in more detail. We will then consider how these patterns were set in early constitutional texts that governed the Arab world—in Tunisia, the Ottoman Empire (not an Arab entity but one that governed much of the Arab world and was the starting point for many Arab efforts of the twentieth century), and Egypt. We will then follow the evolution of one particular case, the Constitution of Egypt, to see how the basic patterns continued despite the vicissitudes of specific constitutional provisions.

Citizenship, Religious Rights and State Identity in Arab Constitutions: Who is Free and What Are They Free to Do? First Edition. Nathan J. Brown
Published 2019 by Oxford University Press.

1. Introduction: Paradoxical Particularities

In 1955, Egyptian Christian religious leaders from a variety of denominations cancelled Christmas Eve ceremonies in an act of stark political protest against an action taken by Egypt's new army-led regime.[1] What was the offence to the freedom of religion for Christians in Egypt that occasioned such a drastic move? The regime was abolishing separate personal status courts for each religious community in the country in order to create a single set of courts for all Egyptians. Why was this seen as such an objectionable step? There was to be no change in the law applied. *Shari'a* court judges, also covered by the move, had taken similar symbolic steps in the past but this time offered no resistance. But for Christian religious leaders, the overall impact was to subordinate matters of religiously inspired practice in the most intimate sphere to state oversight, enforcement, regulation, and control. And the officials given such authority—judges in a personal status branch of the civil court system—were largely Muslim. An authoritarian state, with its passion for uniformity and control, was clearly infringing on freedoms that Egyptian Christians had the right to enjoy.

Or, at least, so thought the leaders of various Egyptian churches. They may have been right, but the matter is far more complex than just religious rights and transgressing states.

Indeed, there were several levels to this issue, all revolving around the matter of religious freedom. First, there is the matter of the state and political authority—is it a source of protection or of threat for religion? But there is also a question of the closeness of the link between belief and practice—the action appeared to govern only the second but of course the practices involved matters of faith. And finally, there is the tie between individual and the community—was the state's action problematic for each Christian as an individual, or for the churches and their communal leaderships?

Arab constitutions almost always include provisions for religious freedom that will be familiar to anyone well versed in various European constitutional traditions.[2] And, indeed, there has been a strong textual influence from Europe (sometimes directly and sometimes through the Ottoman and Egyptian traditions, themselves deeply informed by various strains of European constitutional thought and language). But the political and religious context has been very different and the clauses often contain differences in wording that appear subtle but have substantial implications. And those clauses are placed alongside other ones that might be termed strongly establishmentarian and communal in nature. The result is a particular conception of—and protection of—religious freedom.

Taken together, the mix of provisions tends to protect communal practice far more than individual freedom of conscience (though they often acknowledge some

[1] Chase, 'Abolition of the Shari'a and Melli Courts Announced', 4 January 1956, *United States National Archives* 774.31/1–456.

[2] A survey of provisions regarding religion in Muslim states (not restricted to the Arab world) can be found in T. Stahnke and R. Blitt, *The Right to Freedom of Religion or Belief: An Analysis of Muslim Countries* (2005).

version of the latter principle); they seek to protect religion and religious practice more than the rights of individuals (though again, the latter are acknowledged); they require the state to recognize and license religious communities even as they allow the communities some authority to determine their own practices and rites; they deny such protections to any faiths or practices that are not recognized; they view Islam specifically and religion in general as requiring state protection and, in a sense, entities with their own rights (though no explicit provision is made to that effect); and they are predicated on a state that is friendly to all recognized faiths but especially friendly to Islam. Non-Muslims may struggle against some aspects of this formula, but may actually work to protect other aspects.

A tradition of constitutional interpretation that views a constitutional text as the will of a single legislator predisposes constitutional interpreters in the Arab world against the view that the constitutional provisions on individual freedoms could be in tension or contradict each other, further entrenching a tendency to read such individual freedoms through the prism of a state obligated to protect and promote religion and the practice of specific religious communities.

In legal and constitutional terms, there is a clear general approach in most states in the Arab world that might be summed up (a bit too schematically, perhaps) as follows:

> Believe whatever you wish. When it comes to practising religion, choose any one of a menu of state-recognized faiths—or rather have your parents (especially your father) select yours for you. Changing your mind about your faith can get a bit complicated and even dangerous (especially if it is away from Islam), but we would prefer not to specify the consequences in clear legal form. Changing within sects of the same religion is generally much easier; sometimes you may be allowed to switch sects simply to change the provisions of family law that govern you—though sometimes we will obstruct that path. The state is there to help you, your family and your community practise your religion within certain bounds; it is also there to help ensure that it is taught to your children. When you marry, divorce, or inherit, you will do so according to the way that state officials interpret and apply the teachings of your own religious community; they have generally consulted with scholars versed in your religion in coming up with their interpretations. The state favours the religion of Islam by sponsoring a significant role for the religion—as state-supported religious officials define it—in public life. And it takes it as a duty to protect Islam as a religion deserving rights and respect. But other recognized religions obtain protection as well.

In comparative terms, this appears at first to be a very state-centric conception of religion and a view of religious freedom that ranges from the odd and idiosyncratic to the Orwellian. But the devil in the details suggests a far more complicated and contentious reality.[3]

The contention is not necessarily over the formula itself. There are complications to this picture in some countries (especially where sectarian differences are strongly

[3] A very useful analysis is provided by H.A. Agrama, *Questioning Secularism: Islam, Sovereignty, and the Rule of Law in Modern Egypt* (2012).

marked among Muslims[4]) and a few countries (most notably Saudi Arabia[5]) give far less recognition to religions other than Islam. But in most places, contestation on religious matters largely takes place within the boundaries of this set of conceptions of religion, rights, and public life.

But note how capacious those boundaries are—and how much they enable contention within an apparently broad social consensus.[6] First, within each community there are struggles over authority, leadership, interpretation, and practice. What is the role of church versus lay leadership for Egyptian Christians? When does an Iraqi Shiʿi approach a marjaʿ for guidance? When a preacher on the payroll of the Palestinian Ministry of Religious Affairs denounces Yusuf al-Qaradawi on official instruction, do those assembled for Friday prayers learn from, ignore, or criticize their prayer leader? Who speaks for the community to those outside it? Allowing a community freedom to structure its own affairs raises as many questions as it answers.

Secondly, and perhaps most obviously, this formula writes political authority so thoroughly into religious affairs that it would be impossible to avoid tripping over the state even under the most benign regime—and there are few regimes that most citizens of the Arab world would view as benign.

But thirdly, and most profoundly if least obviously, the formula folds religion, with all its controversies, directly into the state apparatus.[7] When the state (through various of its officials) codifies personal status law based on religious sources, broadcasts prayers, teaches students, appoints religious officials, adjudicates disputes on the basis of religious teachings, issues fatwas, designates a particular scholar as authoritative, preaches on television, and participates in religious dialogues, it rarely does so in a coherent manner. Not only does it replicate the diversity of religious views within its own ranks, the state also offers privileged points of entry to specific groups, approaches, and even social movements and political parties.

And it is this third phenomenon that I think deserves far more of our attention. The overall effect on the relationship between religion and politics owes a bit less to Orwell's Big Brother than may often appear and far more to the pilot in Saint Exupéry's *The Little Prince*, who as a child drew a picture of a boa constrictor digesting an elephant.[8] By folding religion into itself, it is not clear whether the state is

[4] For an examination of some of the issues involved in working Islam into constitutional texts, with some comments on the special challenges for Iraq with its mixed population and Shiʿi majority, see Rabb, '"We the Jurists": Islamic Constitutionalism in Iraq', 10 *University of Pennsylvania Journal of Constitutional Law* (2008) 527.

[5] For an analysis of the distinctive Saudi basic law, see Al-Fahad, 'Ornamental Constitutionalism: The Saudi Basic Law of Governance', 30 *Yale Journal of International Law* (2005) 30.

[6] T. Asad, *Formations of the Secular: Christianity, Islam, Modernity* (2003).

[7] For a provocative argument that state law has become a form of Islamic law in some Muslim states, see C. Lombardi, *State Law as Islamic Law in Modern Egypt: The Incorporation of the Shariʿa into Egyptian Constitutional Law* (2006).

[8] I introduced this perhaps far-fetched metaphor in Brown, 'Egypt: Cacophony and Consensus in the Twenty-first Century' in R. Hefner (ed.), *Sharia Politics: Islamic Law and Society in the Modern World* (2011). George Orwell's *Nineteen Eighty-four* (1949) describes a dystopian future in which subjects are governed by a totalitarian state led by a figure known only as 'Big Brother', whereas in Antoine de Saint-Exupéry's *The Little Prince* (1943), the pilot's drawing consists simply of a brown shape that was thin on either end but very wide in the middle so that adults could only see it as a hat.

dominating religion, whether it is the other way around, or whether what has been produced is something else entirely that requires great imagination to understand.

2. The Constitutional Arrangement is Born

The constitutional formula for state–religion relations just described developed out of political practices and power relationships dating back to the nineteenth century: a time when the Arab world was largely governed by the Ottoman Empire, though pockets of it remained outside direct Ottoman control and some political entities (most notably Egypt and Tunisia) had considerable autonomy from Istanbul. There were large legal areas that were governed by edicts from rulers, but, at least in theory, Islamic law and courts that were based on Islamic law retained general jurisdiction. Disputes among members of recognized non-Muslim communities were generally governed by their own law and courts. And through various kinds of capitulatory agreements, citizens of European powers generally had extraterritorial status, governed by their own law not only in internal disputes, but also often in any civil or criminal dispute with a Muslim subject.

That situation began to change in most of the region—or was steadily remoulded—under pressure from two contrasting trends. First, European penetration of the region in all spheres (economic, political, and cultural) greatly raised the salience of treatment of non-Muslims and tilted the application of the capitulatory agreements heavily in favour of European citizens (including some long-time residents of the societies in question, who quickly learned how advantageous European citizenship could be under such circumstances and laid claim to it in order to escape local law and taxation). Secondly, most states (or autonomous systems) within the region attempted state-building programmes that involved bureaucratic strengthening, construction of military forces, ambitious economic development, and administrative centralization.[9]

The first trend gave many non-Muslim populations a protected status. The second trend led to reform programmes that greatly increased the role of the state but also fostered a sense of a need for uniformity and clarity and sometimes even citizenship. And the two trends combined in some odd ways: it was often, for instance, in the interests of Middle Eastern states to provide guarantees to non-Muslim subjects that played down the legal distinction between Muslims and non-Muslims: not only did this foster a sense of loyalty and citizenship, but it also robbed European powers of a justification for intervention (or reassured them that it was not necessary). Similarly, when European states asserted direct control, they often sought to pick their battles in internal matters by allowing large pockets of law to remain out of their hands. Indeed, it was precisely this strategy that led to the creation of the category of 'personal status law' and its position as the last domain in which Islamic jurisprudence directly shaped the law applied. 'Personal status law' itself was unknown as a category in Islamic jurisprudence prior to this time; it was an island

[9] I have examined this topic in more detail in N.J. Brown, *The Rule of Law in the Arab World* (1997).

carved out so that European states could assure colonized populations that they would not enter their most intimate sphere and so that non-colonized (or post-colonial) states could assure non-Muslims that they would respect their religious practice.[10]

We can follow the institutional arrangements that developed in four cases—Tunisia, the Ottoman Empire, Egypt, and Iraq—to see that, however much the particularities varied, there were strong commonalities with regard to result: religious freedom was associated both with ambitious states and European imperialism; practice and communal standing were both far more significant areas of attention than individual conscience or belief; communities themselves (majority and minority) were often very protective of their communal rights; religion understood in this way was given positive state protection; and none of these arrangements were deemed as antithetical to a strong official role for Islam. When religious provisions were written about such rights and freedoms, they took place in a context not of individual rights and certainly not of secularism in any of its guises, but of colonialism, state building, and emphasis on community practice.

A. Tunisia

The *qanun al-dawla al-tunisiyya* [law of the Tunisian state or dynasty] of 1861 was the first written constitution in the Arab world.[11] The document was issued in the midst of a period of political changes introduced by an ambitious, centralizing administration operating at a time of increased European influence.[12] At the time, Tunisia formed a virtually independent province within the Ottoman Empire; the reform programme followed by the country's rulers loosely followed the Ottoman *tanzimat* in content and vocabulary. It involved an assertion of central control over loosely administered outlying areas and the construction of a more powerful military. The programme was pursued unevenly at best, encountering difficulties because of the rudimentary administrative structure as well as fiscal constraints. Growing European (especially French and British) interest in Tunisia affected the course of political reform: an outbreak of Muslim-Jewish tension in Tunis led the European powers to demand that the Tunisian *bey* adopt some of the reforms recently promulgated in the Ottoman Empire.[13] Thus, in 1857, the *bey* issued the *'ahd al-iman* (Charter of Faith), which promised protection of persons and property, regulariza-

[10] On the invention of the category, see Cuno, 'Muhammad Qadri's Code of Personal Status Law in Egypt', paper presented at the annual meeting of the Middle East Studies Association, Washington DC, December 2011.

[11] Portions of this and the following two sections are based in part on N.J. Brown, *Constitutions in a Nonconstitutional World: Arab Basic Laws and the Prospects for Accountable Government* (2001).

[12] This account on the background to the Tunisian Constitution of 1861 is based on the following sources: L.C. Brown, *The Tunisia of Ahmad Bey 1837–1855* (1974); L. Anderson, *The State and Social Transformation in Tunisia and Libya 1830–1980* (1987); and Harber, 'Reforms in Tunisia 1855–1878' (1970) (Ph.D. dissertation on file with Ohio State University).

[13] The most noted incident involved the execution of a Jew accused of insulting Islam in a street dispute. For more details, see Harber (n. 12) Ch. II.

tion of taxation, military service and justice, and concessions to non-Muslims in the adjudication of disputes.[14]

Shortly after the issuance of the *'ahd al-iman*, the *bey* formed a commission of Tunisian officials to study the application of centralizing Ottoman legal reforms—ones that tended to move from legal categories based on religious communities to those based on state sovereignty and citizenship—and to draft a constitution. This document was drawn up in consultation with European officials and was formally issued on 26 April 1861.[15] While there was, therefore, much European interest and participation in the composition of the document, the Tunisian Constitution of 1861 actually reflects European structure and practice less than almost any other Middle Eastern constitutional document, in part because no standardized formats and vocabulary had developed in the Arab world and European constitutional traditions were only becoming established.

The Constitution consists of 13 sections. The 12th section covered the rights and duties of Tunisians, and affirmed the guarantees of the *'ahd al-iman* for legal equality regardless of residence, social position, and religion. Very few of the economic and civil rights customarily mentioned in twentieth-century constitutions appeared in the Tunisian Constitution: there was no mention of freedom of expression or association, for instance. Yet the right to security of person, honour, and fortune were guaranteed; residents of Tunisia who were subjects of friendly states did receive recognition, granting them many of the same rights and guarantees.

The Tunisian Constitution of 1861 was viable only for three years. It was clearly designed in part to obtain European support but also to serve the Tunisian political elite, essentially providing for a self-perpetuating political authority. A reading of the Tunisian Constitution reveals that it promises no democracy and seeks accountability only within the political elite; it supports the rule of law but the legislative process is thoroughly elitist. Such a reading can be measured against the writings of Khayr al-Din al-Tunisi, a leading Tunisian politician of the period. Khayr al-Din was a minister and the president of the Grand Council during the constitutional period until he had a falling out with his father-in-law, Mustafa Khaznadar, the *bey*'s chief minister. He later replaced Khaznadar and also briefly served as the grand *wazir* of the Ottoman Empire. Khayr al-Din was, therefore, involved in the writing and operation of the Constitution, but not in its abrogation. A few years after the end of the Tunisian constitutional experiment he wrote an extended treatise on government. While he did not mention the Tunisian Constitution, he provided a thorough ideological justification for its structure and content. The treatise advances a powerful argument for a constitutionalist polity, and locates constitutionalism not only in European practice but also in the Islamic tradition. While his vocabulary was Islamic, his argument was reminiscent of the *Federalist Papers*: human beings need government to restrain them, but those who exercise power are themselves human and need to be restrained.

[14] The text of the *'ahd al-iman* can be found in 'A. 'Umar and Q. Sa'id (eds), *Nusus wa-watha'iq siyasiyya tunisiyya* (1987).

[15] The text is in 'Umar and Sa'id (n. 14).

[S]ome form of restraint is essential for the maintenance of the human species, but if the person exercising this restraint were left to do as he pleases and rule as he sees fit the fruits to be expected from this need to have a restrainer would not appear to the *umma* [community of Muslims], and the original state of neglect would remain unheeded. It is essential that the restrainer should have *his* restrainer to check him either in the form of a heavenly *shari'a* or a policy based on reason, but neither of these can defend its rights if they be violated. For this reason it is incumbent upon the *'ulama* [Islamic scholars] and the notables of the *umma* to resist evil. The Europeans have established councils and have given freedom to the printing presses. In the Islamic *umma* the kings fear those who resist evil just as the kings of Europe fear the councils and the opinions of the masses that proceed from them and form the freedom of the press. The aim of the two [i.e. European and Muslim] is the same—to demand an accounting from the state in order that its conduct may be upright, even if the roads leading to this end may differ.[16]

Khayr al-Din therefore argued for a political system in which rulers would be required to account for their actions to the *ahl al-hall wa-l-'aqd*, the phrase used in the Tunisian Constitution for the members of the Grand Council. For Khayr al-Din, such people would include both notables and the *'ulama*. Viewed in light of Khayr al-Din's writings, the Tunisian Constitution appears to be an attempt to develop a constitutionalist system that is Islamic but not democratic. It promised a form of civic equality to non-Muslims out of a sense that such a move was consistent with both constitutional and *shari'a*-based governance.

B. Ottoman Empire

While the Ottoman Empire was a multinational entity ruled from Istanbul in what today is Turkey, it not only governed much of the Arab world but also bequeathed a set of institutional arrangements to successor states in the Arab regions. It therefore makes sense to consider it in any historical analysis of the Arab world.

The Ottoman Constitution of 1876 was issued in circumstances quite similar to those surrounding the Tunisian Constitution of 1861.[17] Its fate initially seemed quite similar because it was suspended after only a short period of operation. In the longer term, however, not only was it eventually revived for the Ottoman Empire in its final decade, but it also served as the basis for many Arab constitutions of the twentieth century. The Ottoman Empire faced a profound crisis in the mid-1870s. Like Tunisia, it had embarked on a programme of administrative centralization and

[16] L.C. Brown (ed.), Khayr al-Din al-Tunisi, *The Surest Path: The Political Treatise of a Nineteenth Century Muslim Statesman; A Translation of the Introduction to The Surest Path to Knowledge Concerning the Condition of Countries* (1967) 84.

[17] Scholarly writings on the Ottoman Constitution of 1876 are reasonably extensive, but because of the declining interest among scholars in legal and political history, the most comprehensive works tend to be older. The account here depends primarily on such older works, including R. Devereux, *The First Ottoman Constitutional Period: A Study of the Midhat Constitution and Parliament* (1963); Davison, 'The Advent of the Principle of Representation in the Government of the Ottoman Empire', in *Essays in Ottoman and Turkish History, 1774–1923: The Impact of the West* (1990); R.H. Davison, *Reform in the Ottoman Empire 1856–1876* (1963); and S.J. Shaw and E.K. Shaw, *History of the Ottoman Empire and Modern Turkey, Volume II: Reform, Revolution, and Republic: The Rise of Modern Turkey, 1808–1975* (1977).

rationalization coupled with an attempt to build a powerful standing military force. The Ottoman programme was far more extensive and sustained than its Tunisian counterpart (indeed, the Tunisian programme was partly modelled on the Ottoman), but by 1875 the Ottoman government faced a series of related problems. Internally, several provinces in the Balkans were in open revolt. The political and military programme had been expensive, leading the government to borrow so extensively that it could not avoid bankruptcy. Externally, the military position of the Empire had eroded to such an extent that it could not resist European encroachment without diplomatic manoeuvrings designed to solicit European support and play European powers off against each other.

In this environment, a group among the political elite of the Empire evinced increasing interest in constitutional government as the key to political and fiscal rationalization and reform. The idea was controversial, partly because a constitution had the potential to encroach on the prerogatives of powerful individuals and groups. Not only might it restrict the authority of the Sultan, it might also further the legal equality between Muslims and non-Muslims and diminish the role for *shari'a*-based law in the administration of justice.

A group of senior officials, military leaders, and *'ulama* was appointed to draft a constitution; they considered a number of drafts and proposals. The draft they finally submitted to the Sultan most closely resembled the Belgian Constitution of 1831; others noted parallels with the Prussian Constitution, itself a more royalist version of the Belgian model. The Sultan submitted the draft to the cabinet, which made some changes before promulgation.

As finally adopted, the Ottoman Constitution of 1876 had 12 sections. The first defined the nature of the state and of the Sultan, designating him as Caliph and protector of Islam and enumerating his prerogatives (without limiting his authority to those designated in the constitution). The second section granted Ottoman subjects rights and equality under the law. Article 11 of the Constitution stated directly: 'The constitution Islam is the state religion.' But, while maintaining this principle, the article hastened to add that 'the state will protect the free exercise of faiths professed in the Empire, and uphold the religious privileges granted to various bodies, on condition of public order and morality not being interfered with'. The same type of balance was reflected in Article 16: 'Proper means will be devised for harmonizing and regulating the instruction given to all the Ottomans, but without interfering with the religious education in the various districts.'

Given the crises faced by the Ottoman government—bankruptcy, military weakness, internal rebellion, and European diplomatic pressure—it was natural that the newly created parliament would take its responsibility for oversight fairly seriously. This soon led to a clash between the cabinet (and implicitly the Sultan) and the parliament.[18] Rather than accept the parliamentary effort to transform the Constitution into a basis for a constitutionalist system, the Sultan disbanded

[18] I have relied heavily on Devereux (n. 17) for this account of the parliamentary period. See especially at 238–44.

the parliament, ordering all deputies to leave the city. Parliament was not reconvened for three decades.

The Ottoman Constitution thus had a far more contentious history than its equally short-lived Tunisian predecessor. It was written to conform to conflicting visions of the proper political order. Religion was among the matters which proved especially divisive in the process of drafting. Some members of the *'ulama* so bitterly and publicly opposed the entrance of non-Muslims into the parliament that they were exiled. Yet while they lost the battle over the constitutional text, the victors were far from secularists. The final draft clearly established Islam as the state religion in various institutional and symbolic ways. The authors of the Constitution most likely sought to further legitimate positive legislation alongside the Islamic *shari'a*; they also probably wished to wean non-Muslims onto loyalty to the Empire and away from separatist hopes. (Indeed, an earlier proposal had been based on federalizing the government of the Empire.)

The nature of these debates—and the short history of the Constitution itself—suggest that the Ottoman political elite was badly divided in the 1870s. The Constitution served only to focus these divisions rather than resolve them. On the one hand stood constitutionalist politicians. While they were anxious to establish an assembly, the goal was less to provide for an element of democracy in Ottoman governance than it was to provide for a measure of accountability. The authority of state actors was not to be diminished, but it was to operate on a more legal and rationalized basis. Accountability, fiscal reform, and rationalization would serve as tools to strengthen the Empire and enable it to face its formidable domestic and international challenges. On the other hand stood those who did not see the Constitution as a valid instrument for an Islamic state and, more powerfully, those (including ultimately the Sultan) who did not see restraints on the head of the state as an appropriate tool.

Robert Devereux writes:

> As crisis followed crisis the liberals became convinced that the safety, if not the very existence, of the Empire lay in a radical reshaping of its faulty government structure. Above all they perceived a need to end the absolute rule of the Sultan and to substitute a constitutional form of government. Although they viewed non-Muslim co-operation and participation as an essential element of the new regime, they were by no means advocates of abandonment of Turkish-Muslim supremacy. They appear to have been constitutionalists not because they desired a constitution as an end in itself but because they saw in a constitution the best hope for the regeneration of the Empire. Comparing the strength and vigor of the Western European states and impressed by the form without fully understanding its basis, they appear to have become imbued with the idea that the creation in Turkey of a regime patterned on those of Europe would *ipso facto* restore to their country its vanished strength and vigor.[19]

Devereux's description of the motivations of the constitutionalists seems quite fair, though his comment that they lacked a full understanding of the basis of European constitutionalism is puzzling. More to the point, however, his description of this group as 'liberals' needs to be qualified: the Ottoman constitutionalists were very

[19] Ibid. 28.

much members of the political elite. By trying to regularize the authority of the sultan and introduce a measure of accountability they were, in a sense, attempting only to render their own positions more effective and efficient. The precarious international and domestic position of the government allowed them to negotiate an ambiguous document that secured some of their ends. The Constitution that resulted did not emanate from the population of the Empire, nor did it really empower any group other than elements of the existing political leadership. When the ambiguous structures and procedures established by the Constitution seemed to be leading to real constitutional government, its opponents were powerless to prevent its suspension.

While the effective life of the Ottoman Constitution was short (it was restored in the years before the Empire's demise after World War I), its provisions lived on in the constitutions of Arab states in following years.

C. Egypt

The history of the Egyptian Constitution of 1923 is much more complex than that of its Tunisian and Ottoman predecessors but its effective life was far longer (it survived until 1952 with two suspensions). The British occupied Egypt in 1882 but did not formally detach it from the Ottoman Empire until World War I, when they declared it a protectorate. While they prepared to incorporate Egypt into the British Empire after the war, a nationalist uprising in 1919 led the British to abandon those plans and negotiate limited independence with the Egyptian government, at that time headed by a Sultan who was regarded with some suspicion by the nationalist leadership. Unable to negotiate an arrangement, the British finally unilaterally declared Egypt independent in 1922, subject to four reservations (the Suez Canal, defence, Sudan, and protection of foreigners) over which the British claimed continued oversight until negotiation of an agreement (eventually reached in 1936).

Egyptians, though their independence remained limited, were confronted with the need to define a political structure. The king appointed a committee to draft a constitution, but the committee was forced to work in difficult circumstances. The British had reduced but not eliminated their role in matters of internal governance. The Wafd rejected the British reservations on independence and demanded that a constitution be written by a popularly-elected constituent assembly. Many leading politicians, legal figures, and jurists were willing to participate in the committee despite the Wafd's suspicions, but it was not clear how much constitutionalism the king would tolerate.

While the committee worked in a difficult political atmosphere, it was able to draw on European and Ottoman, as well as Egyptian, experience. The minutes of the drafting committee, later published, show its members to be very conversant in matters of constitutional law and design.[20] While they worked predominantly from

[20] The minutes were published by the Egyptian Senate under the title *Al-dustur: ta'liqat 'ala mawadihi bi-l-a'mal al-tahdiriyya wa-l-munaqashat al-barlamaniyya* [The Constitution: Commentaries on its Articles in the Preparatory Works and Parliamentary Discussions] (1940).

Ottoman and continental European constitutional design, they showed particular interest in drafting a document that would help the country to assert its independence and establish a measure of parliamentary rule.[21]

To secure independence, the drafting committee prepared a draft proclaiming the country's monarch 'King of Egypt and Sudan'. This step angered the British who had not fully accepted Egyptian sovereignty, much less inclusion of the Sudan. More subtly, the drafters included an article that implicitly recognized the capitulations—legal arrangements that effectively granted extraterritorial status to citizens of foreign states—as a way of undermining the British claim of responsibility for protecting foreign interests and communities in Egypt.[22] In that sense, guarantee of minority rights (and most but not all of those with capitulatory privileges were non-Muslims) was a nationalist gesture.

In addition, a list of political and civil rights and freedoms which were to be guaranteed or defined by law was given. Such phrasing made rights less than absolute, since they depended on implementing legislation to give them meaning (and potentially limits): a feature that was not lost on the constitutional drafters.[23]

The 1923 Constitution has been portrayed as British-inspired, but such a view is untenable.[24] The minutes of the drafting committee make clear that those who wrote the document were extremely anxious to avoid any recognition of the British role in the country; neither did they want to give the British any excuse for intervention in Egypt's internal affairs (therefore, treatment of foreigners was a particularly vexatious issue).[25]

The document acknowledged the Islamic nature of the polity, though only in very general ways. The committee drafting the Constitution discussed religious clauses with little acrimony. The final document granted Islam official status without making any mention of the Islamic *shari'a*. This formulation, however weak it appears in retrospect, was in fact proposed by Egypt's former mufti, Shaykh Muhammad Bakhit (often identified as a conservative).[26] Shaykh Bakhit did unsuccessfully object to an article granting state protection to all religions as risking offence to existing religions in the country. The final draft included strong language on religious free-

[21] For discussions of the work of the drafting committee, see M. Deeb, *Party Politics in Egypt: The Wafd and its Rivals, 1919–1939* (1979) 58–61; and Kedourie, 'The Genesis of the Egyptian Constitution of 1923' in P.M. Holt (ed.), *Political and Social Change in Modern Egypt* (1968).

[22] Article 154 pledged that agreements and customs involving foreigners would not be disturbed. In the discussion of the article, Husayn Rushdi, one of the most prominent and active members of the committee, explicitly cited the need to make the British understand that foreigners were to be protected by the Constitution. See the section on Art. 154 in *Al-dustur* (n. 20). For the politics surrounding the capitulations more generally, see Brown, 'The Precarious Life and Slow Death of the Mixed Courts of Egypt', 25 *International Journal of Middle East Studies* (1993) 33.

[23] See, for instance, the discussion of freedom of the press in M.H. Haykal, *Muzakkirat fi al-siyasa al-misriyya* (1978) 166–7.

[24] For a different view, emphasizing the British role, see E. Kedourie (n. 21).

[25] Article 154 recognized Egypt's 'agreements with foreign states' and asserted that 'the rights of foreigners in Egypt by virtue of laws, international treaties, and observed customs will not be disturbed'. The minutes of the drafting committee make clear that this wording was intended to communicate to the British that Egypt was capable of protecting foreigners and their interests without British oversight or intervention. See *Al-dustur* (n. 20) esp. Part III, 3459.

[26] See the discussions recorded in *Al-dustur* (n. 20).

dom, with Article 3 barring religious discrimination and Article 11 proclaiming the inviolability of freedom of belief.

The document's silence on difficult issues related to Islam (the source of sovereignty, the relationship of Islamic law to positive law, and even the religious identity of the ruler) attracted little public debate. After the Constitution became effective, debates about religion were rarely phrased in constitutional terms. Some cited the official status of Islam in objecting to the visit of an American missionary in 1928, but other references to constitutional provisions on religion were rare indeed.[27] Even Hasan al-Banna, the founder of the Muslim Brotherhood, described Egypt's constitutional system as close to Islam, criticizing it only for failing to ban some behaviour prohibited by the *shari'a*.[28]

3. Early and Later Patterns

The Tunisian, Ottoman, and Egyptian experience thus set the framework for later constitutional experimentation. Most subsequent documents mirrored these early models, even as they used different language. The constitutions promised an increasing list of freedoms (sometimes in an increasingly vague way), but when they came to religious issues they would often tread carefully. It was not individual belief that was at issue—sometimes promises of something resembling individual freedom of conscience were tossed off carelessly. But drawing far more attention were matters of personal status, the official role of Islam, and issues regarding non-Muslim minorities. In all these areas, constitutional drafters were generally anxious to protect religion and even religious freedom and they often borrowed some familiar language from the West but cast it in a context that furthered rather than limited these characteristics. The status of religious minorities was sometimes tightly bound up with nationalist concerns, especially in countries where the capitulations had been particularly prominent, or European powers especially active in asserting a duty to protect such minorities during the pre-colonial and colonial period.

An early example of the pattern came in Iraq, where the British set to work drawing up a constitution for Iraq after taking control of the country in the aftermath of World War I. The document was originally drawn up by British officials in Baghdad, who based their work primarily on the Ottoman Constitution, though other constitutions were consulted. The Egyptian Constitution, then being drafted, was

[27] On the dispute on the missionary's visit, see ibid. Pt III, 3381. It is true that there was potential for controversy, especially regarding individual liberties protected by the Constitution and attempts by some within the Islamic establishment to curtail the voices of those deemed threatening to Islam (the 'Ali 'Abd al-Raziq case was the most prominent but hardly the only such case). Yet such controversies were not cast in constitutional terms, perhaps because the Egyptian judiciary did not clearly assert a right to review the constitutionality of legislation and official actions until the end of the 1940s. Thus, controversial legal issues did not become constitutional issues—a situation that changed only in the 1980s with the emergence of the assertive Supreme Constitutional Court.

[28] See *Majmu'at Rasa'il al-Imam al-Shahid Hasan al-Banna* [Collection of Letters of the Martyred Imam Hasan al-Banna] (1993) 170–4 and 215–18.

influential, especially with regard to the rights provisions.[29] They submitted the draft to the Colonial Office in London and to Faysal, the incoming king of Iraq, shortly after he took the throne.[30] The original draft was a British product to such an extent that it was initially drafted in English.[31] But the rights provisions of the Constitution were expanded, generally along lines that rapidly became standard in most Arab constitutional texts. Personal liberty, resort to the courts, and freedom of expression, meeting, association, and religion (extending to the freedom of religious minorities to operate their own schools) were all guaranteed.

As time went on, these patterns only deepened. Official recognition of Islam was generally strengthened, in a process that I have described elsewhere as 'Islamic inflation'.[32] Non-Muslim communities were generally represented by religious leaders in the constitutional drafting efforts with the result that communal protections were often strong while language against discrimination was lofty but toothless. It was, in that sense, churchgoing and not everyday Christians who were receiving recognition and constitutional status, and the protection they received was one that pulled the state into regulating their internal affairs, implicitly by empowering specific kinds of leaders and even explicitly by ensuring that the law would regulate (in the guise of supporting) religious practice and the construction of houses of worship.

The evolution of this pattern could be seen most clearly in Egypt, which underwent a series of constitutional changes, beginning in 1971 with the promulgation of the country's 'permanent' Constitution (and indeed its longest-lasting one). The Constitution itself did claim (in Article 2) that 'Islam is the religion of the state and Arabic its official language. The principles of the Islamic shari'a are a main source of legislation', without explaining precisely how that source was to be used or by whom. Article 40 barred discrimination based on religion; since major parts of the Egyptian state apparatus (such as the military and the police) were largely (though not totally) devoid of Christians (who composed perhaps a tenth of the population) it was not clear what, if anything, the article meant in practice. More specific provisions included Article 46, providing for freedom of religious belief and practice (though the formula used—insisting that the state should guarantee these things—opened the door to state regulation of religion in both doctrine and in practice[33]). Article 19 mandated religious instruction as a subject in all schools, again a step taken with the support of religious leaders, but also one which suggested that it was the Ministry of

[29] Davidson, 'The Constitution of Iraq', 7 *Journal of Comparative Legislation and International Law* (1925) 44.

[30] A.H. Jamil, *Al-khalifiyya al-siyasiyya wa-l-ijtima'iyya li-l-awda' allati kan yutabbiq fi thulliha dustur 1925 fi al-'iraq* [The Politial and Social Background to the Conditions in which the Constitution of 1925 in Iraq Were Applied] (1986) 13–14.

[31] See the Foreword by E.M. Drower, adviser to the Ministry of Justice in Iraq, in C.A. Hooper, *The Constitutional Law of Iraq* (1928) vii.

[32] See Brown, 'Islam and Constitutionalism in the Arab World: The Puzzling Course of Islamic Inflation' in A. Bali and H. Lerner (eds), *Constitution Writing, Religion and Democracy* (2017).

[33] On how these clauses were interpreted and applied by Egypt's Supreme Constitutional Court, see Lombardi and Brown, 'Do Constitutions Requiring Adherence to Sharia Threaten Human Rights?: How Egypt's Constitutional Court Reconciles Islamic Law with the Liberal Rule of Law', 21 *American University International Law Review* (2006) 379.

Education that would be deciding how to instruct children in their religion. The minutes of the drafting committee survive, and reveal that religious matters came up in several debates that are slightly obscured by the final text.[34] For instance, provisions for women's rights provoked a debate between those advocating strong and definitive language and those who were concerned that this would lead to violations of the Islamic *shari'a*. The result was a careful compromise protecting both a paternalistic version of state guarantee for women's rights with a protection for the rulings of the Islamic *shari'a*. Another avenue for debate concerned freedom of religious practice: Coptic members of the committee unsuccessfully sought constitutional protection for building houses of worship.

Over the course of its life, the 1971 Constitution was amended in two ways directly related to religious issues. In 1980, the phrase in Article 2 referring to the principles of the Islamic *shari'a* as 'a' source of legislation was amended to make them 'the' source. And in 2007, parties with a religious reference were barred and ideological provisions proclaiming citizenship were inserted into the Constitution. The 1980 amendment was designed to burnish the regime's Islamic credentials but does not seem to have been intended to have operative meaning; the 2007 amendments were designed to bar any party connected with the Muslim Brotherhood but also to build an ideological basis for the state that was non-religious and non-sectarian—not to render the Egyptian state secular but to give it a way to repudiate an Islamist movement that was calling for a 'civil state with an Islamic reference', a formula that seemed to generate a feeling that an official retort was needed.

In 2012, Egypt received an entirely new constitution. While the new document copied very heavily from its 1971 predecessor, the largely Islamist assembly that drafted it both increased its commitment to Islamic principles and tried to placate critics by offering concessions, chiefly to recognized religious communities—but only as religious communities (churchgoing 'Sunday Christians')—with little offered to non-recognized faiths.[35] The 2012 Constitution allowed Christians and Jews the right to be governed by their own *shari'a* in matters of personal status, religious affairs, and selection of religious leaders (Article 3; something already recognized in law but now constitutionally entrenched). Article 43 proclaimed grandly that freedom of belief was inviolable but then went on to a more carefully hedged commitment that the state would guarantee the freedom to practise religious rites and build houses of worship in a manner organized by law—for 'heavenly religions' (i.e. Islam, Christianity, and Judaism).[36]

In 2014, in the wake of a military coup that ousted the Brotherhood-led regime and suspended the 2012 Constitution, a new document was issued (technically a

[34] I consulted the minutes in the library of the Egyptian parliament in 1999.

[35] I analysed the Islamic provisions in the document in an article with Clark Lombardi, Lombardi and Brown, 'Islam in Egypt's New Constitution', *Foreign Policy*, 13 December 2012, available at http://foreignpolicy.com/2012/12/13/islam-in-egypts-new-constitution (last visited 20 April 2015).

[36] The 2012 Constitution provoked an enormous amount of analysis and commentary. A good introduction to the issues is contained in al-Ali, 'The new Egyptian constitution: an initial assessment of its merits and flaws', International Institute for Democracy and Electoral Assistance (IDEA), 23 January 2013, available at http://www.idea.int/wana/the-new-egyptian-constitution-an-initial-assessment-of-its-merits-and-flaws.cfm (last visited 30 October 2015).

thorough revision of its 2012 predecessor). While the drafters tinkered with most of the provisions and removed some of the Islamic innovations, the provisions for religious freedom were strengthened only mildly. Once again, only Christians and Jews received recognition in Article 3. And Article 64 replaced the previous Article 43 making freedom of belief 'absolute' and tweaking (and thus strengthening) the references to religious practice and construction of houses of worship for 'heavenly religions' to be 'rights organized by law'. Since the state immediately clamped down on unauthorized mosques and preachers, it was clear that such a right was to be governed by the state as its top officials saw fit.

Egypt's four constitutions represented here—the 1923 establishment of a parliamentary monarchy; the 1971 presidential (and socialist) republic); the 2012 Islamist-led majoritarian democracy; and the ambiguously democratic and authoritarian blend of 2014—appear, when taken as a whole, to 'run in place' very enthusiastically on matters of religious rights and protections.

4. Conclusion

And indeed, the point for Egypt can be made more generally: the formulas designed a century and a half ago have gone through many permutations but the essentials remain unchanged. So long as religions are protected in this way—given recognition in specific realms (personal status, education), it will be necessary for the political order to decide what is a religion and what is not, who speaks for a religious community, and what religious issues will be given some kind of constitutional insulation. This very process involves the state in religious affairs and folds religion into the state.[37] Protection there is aplenty—for states, religious communities, religious leaders, Islam, specific religious rights and freedoms and, to some extent, individual freedom of conscience. The result is neither liberal nor secular but instead a complicated intertwining of religion and state that leaves the relationship between the two very difficult to unravel.

[37] On this point generally, see Agrama (n. 3).

4

Communal Religious Rights or Majoritarian Oppression

Conversion and Proselytism Laws in Malaysia and India

Carolyn Evans and Timnah Rachel Baker

1. Introduction

Religious freedom as it is framed in international law and in domestic constitutions is often held up as 'the ultimate freedom'[1] and even as the 'foundation'[2] of the human rights regime. As with all rights, there are cases in which clear violations of the right to religious freedom take place. However troubling these violations may be, they do not undermine the importance of the right or its legal status any more than the fact that people continue to kill one another undermines the criminalization of murder. Over time, however, a more complex set of questions has arisen with respect to religious freedom and its scope. On the one hand, there are those who simply deny the importance or relevance of the right at all—sometimes from the standpoint of belonging to the 'one true' religion which should yield no ground to 'false' religions and at other times from those hostile to religion who see it as inherently unworthy of protection. On the other hand, there are debates and tensions between those who claim to genuinely subscribe to the notion of religious freedom but have very different conceptions of what that might mean.

Nowhere are these tensions more pronounced than in the context of proselytization and conversion. The twin practices of conversion and proselytization often become the fault lines of religious freedom as it is conceptualized and applied in different jurisdictions. They take place in the liminal space between religious groups and therefore introduce uncertainty into many national and cultural landscapes. This is particularly true in Asian countries, where the open-textured nature of religious freedom is overlaid with complex legacies of colonialism and with the inherent tensions between liberal conceptions of religious freedom expressed in terms of individual rights, and Asian conceptions of communal rights.

[1] Hasson, 'Religious Liberty and Human Dignity: A Tale of Two Declarations', 27 *Harvard Journal of Law and Public Policy* (2003–4) 81, 88. Quoted in R. Ahdar and I. Leigh, *Religious Freedom in the Liberal State* (2nd edn, 2013) 1.

[2] Hasson (n. 1) 88.

Focusing on two Asian countries—India and Malaysia—as illustrations, this chapter will examine the ways in which the tensions around proselytization and conversion highlight some of the conceptual difficulties of liberal theory formulations of religious freedom[3] and the way in which different cultures and religious groups are reinterpreting the traditional conception of religious freedom to better fit their own cultural context. The indeterminate and open-ended language of international conventions on religious freedom can be both a strength (allowing for areas of cultural difference in a flexible way) and a weakness (with no strong determinate boundaries around acceptable behaviour). The language of 'public order' in particular, generally included in both international law and in domestic constitutions as a legitimate limitation to religious freedom, is often invoked to legitimize a religious/ethnic majoritarian agenda. Religious freedom in a number of Asian countries is therefore transformed from the liberal notion of an autonomous individual making choices about fundamental questions of belief and practice and changed into the right of religious communities to maintain traditional practices underpinned by appeals to public order to prevent individuals from challenging those arrangements. Rather than rejecting the notion of religious freedom, the countries discussed in this chapter challenge how the decades-old language of international religious freedom should be understood and applied.

The presence of this pattern in the context of two such disparate constitutional arrangements has implications for the way we view the limits of religious freedom. As Goldie Osuri asks in the context of India, if the *Hindutva* (or other majority groups) 'are able to articulate their "rights" through the discourse of religious freedom and human rights, are these discourses adequate to the task of addressing discrimination and violence toward religious others?'[4] This chapter will argue that despite its mandate of 'protecting... the freedoms of others',[5] the indeterminacy of 'religious freedom' often leaves religious minorities and dissenting individuals vulnerable to discriminatory or oppressive treatment at the hands of the state and dominant religious groups. Such a position is, of course, hardly unique to Asian countries but some of the political history and social structures of countries in this region make them a particularly compelling case study of the complexities of religious freedom.

2. Proselytism and Conversion in Asia

The 'correct' balance between the freedom to manifest religion and its valid limitation cannot be meaningfully addressed in abstract terms. The notion of religious freedom as a constitutionally protected human right has different resonance de-

[3] See generally Danchin, 'Of Prophets and Proselytes: Freedom of Religion and the Conflict of Rights in International Law', 49 *Harvard International Law Journal* (2008) 249; and Danchin, 'Suspect Symbols: Value Pluralism as a Theory of Religious Freedom in International Law', 33 *Yale Journal of International Law* (2008) 2.

[4] G. Osuri, *Religious Freedom in India: Sovereignty and (Anti) Conversion* (2013) 126.

[5] International Covenant on Civil and Political Rights 1966, 999 UNTS 171, Art. 18(2).

pending on where, when, and by whom it is being claimed. The shifting and highly contextualized meaning of 'public order' in the context of religious freedom has been observed by many scholars. Natan Lerner, for example, has made the following observation:

> Particularly complicated problems have arisen when rites, customs, and rules of behavior of specific religious groups clash with norms related to public order, health, or public morality as seen by the general society. Regulation of such problems depends, of course, on the constitutional and legal framework of each country.[6]

Public morality is a particularly open-textured concept and raises complex issues with respect to religious freedom, given how interconnected religion, morality, and culture are in many societies. Yet even public order, a seemingly more constrained and less contextual conception, plays out in different ways in different contexts. The extent to which given societies at given points in their history can genuinely tolerate disruptions to the public order differs—consider the differential impact of religious disputes in a country recovering from a civil war along religious lines compared to a stable liberal democracy. The extent to which challenges to the religious majoritarian beliefs and practices cause disruption to public order also differs. And the willingness of courts and governments to push back against religious majorities who disrupt public order when their dominance is challenged is strikingly different in different contexts.

Asia's political, historical, and religious landscapes make it a particularly fertile region for tensions around religious freedom to arise. The legacy of European colonialism, and the complex ways in which that experience has 'shaped particular conceptions of religious propagation and conversion',[7] inflect the application and interpretation of religious freedom standards. As Michael Feener writes: 'Asian countries have been on the receiving end of colonial projects and have formed a continuing deep suspicion of Christian missionaries and other religious outsiders. These histories form a crucial context in which debates about proselytism take place today.'[8] The colonial encounter in this region seems to have left in its wake a strong impulse for group self-preservation: it has shaped the way dominant groups view themselves (often in terms usually associated with minority groups) as under threat and vulnerable. The regulation of conversion and proselytism in these countries is often an extension of anxieties carried through a shared legacy of colonialism which is then projected onto existing demographic shifts in the religious landscape.

As the following case studies will illustrate, whatever its precise permutation, in both countries the formulation of religious freedom as a constitutionally protected right and its simultaneous subjection to prescribed limitations has resulted—to

[6] Lerner, 'Proselytism, Change of Religion, and International Human Rights', 12 *Emory International Law Review* (1998) 477, 514.

[7] See Feener, 'Official Religions, State Secularisms, and the Structures of Religious Pluralism' in J. Finucane and M. Feener (eds), *Proselytizing and the Limits of Religious Freedom in Contemporary Asia* (2014) 1, 5.

[8] Ibid. 3.

varying degrees—in the privileging of the approved or dominant religion, often at the expense of minority groups.

3. Malaysia

Malaysia's legal and constitutional arrangements are in many respects *sui generis* in the Muslim world. The Constitution enshrines Islam as the 'official religion' of the federation, but Malaysia prides itself on being a multi-religious, multicultural society.[9] Also unique is the fact that Malaysia has mostly managed to avoid the religious conflicts that have occurred in many parts of the Muslim world.[10] In terms of its modes of regulating religious freedom, however, Malaysia resembles other predominantly Muslim states. Restrictions on proselytism and conversion in Malaysia 'run in a single direction':[11] non-Islamic proselytism directed at Muslims is specifically prohibited by the Constitution, and conversion out of Islam is administratively difficult.[12]

The contours of religious freedom in Malaysia are in many ways a product of a perceived interdependence between the preservation of public order and harmony on the one hand, and the preservation of the Islamic faith on the other. This is so despite, or perhaps because of, Malaysia's status as a multi-religious society. As Andrew Harding stresses, in an important study of Malaysia's Constitution, Malaysia's pluralistic society 'is the crucial factor guiding all analysis of contemporary constitutional issues'.[13] The fact of pluralism has had a particularly distorting effect on the state's management of proselytism and conversion.

Cultural and legal pluralism[14] in Malaysia is a reality inherited from the former colonial rule, and may be viewed as a colonial imposition on a colonized society: both were the 'product of an alien culture and history, disseminated and introduced by the agency of imperial British rule'.[15] During British colonial power, Chinese and Indian labourers were encouraged to migrate to British Malaya, but little effort was made to assimilate them.[16] Upon independence, 'the Malaysian state inherited the segmented society left behind by the former colonial master'.[17] It also left behind economic disparities between the disparate religious groups, particularly between

[9] See generally A. Harding, *The Constitution of Malaysia* (2012) 224–47.

[10] Lemière, 'Conversion and Controversy: Reshaping the Boundaries of Malaysian Pluralism' in J. Finucane and M. Feener (eds), *Proselytizing and the Limits of Religious Freedom in Contemporary Asia* (2014) 41, 44.

[11] Stahnke, 'Proselytism and the Freedom to Change Religion in International Human Rights Law', 1 *Brigham Young University Law Review* (1999) 251, 306.

[12] Lemière (n. 10) 42.

[13] Harding (n. 9) 225.

[14] For a discussion on legal pluralism in Malaysia and the contested status of the common law, see generally Neoh, 'The Legitimacy of the Common Law in Post-Colonial Malaysia', 1 *Journal of the Law Association for Asia and the Pacific* (2010) 59.

[15] Harding, 'Editorial Preface' in A. Harding (ed.), *The Common Law in Singapore and Malaysia* (1985) iii, iii. Quoted in Neoh (n. 14) 59.

[16] Parmer, 'Constitutional Change in Malaysia's Plural Society', 26 *Far Eastern Survey* (1957) 145, 145.

[17] Neoh (n. 14) 70.

the wealthy Chinese minority and the Malay majority,[18] resulting in a powerful Us/Them mentality. As Diane K. Mauzy writes:

[T]he emphasis of nationalism in the country turned to the threat the 'other' posed to the essential survival of the nation. To the Malays, the 'others' were the 'non-Malays,' primarily the Chinese. A key feature of Malay nationalism was its highly developed sense of 'us versus them' and its keen sense of purpose in defending everything considered Malay.[19]

Despite the inter-group tensions, the British insisted on a degree of harmony and 'unity of purpose' before it would relinquish its control over Malaya.[20] The arc from colonialism to a post-independence recovery of precolonial unitary identity—whether real or imagined—is a hallmark of the postcolonial condition.[21] The flip-side of the postcolonial nation-building project is that the construction of national unity in Malaysia, as we shall see later, occasioned the oppression of religious minority groups who are/were an easy stand-in for the colonial 'Other'.

Demographically, Malaysia is a 'mosaic'[22] of religious and ethnic diversity. Broken up along religious lines, Muslims comprise about 60 per cent of the total population of Malaysia, Buddhists about 20 per cent; Christians about 9 per cent; Hindus about 6 per cent; and others about 6 per cent.[23] Looked at ethnically, the population of Malaysia can be broken down along three lines. Malays (or Bumiputera) constitute about 67 per cent of the population, the Chinese and Indians about 25 and 8 per cent of the population, respectively, and other non-Malay indigenous groups constitute 1 per cent of the population.[24] The Federal Constitution was the product of a 'tortuous' bargaining among the various ethnic and religious groups.[25] A.B. Shamsul offers a useful and concise account of the communal negotiations that took place during the complex drafting process of the Constitution:

In formulating a Constitution for the independent 'Federation of Malaya', the 'British', the 'Chinese' and the 'Indians' had to bargain hard with the 'Malays'. The 'Chinese' and the 'Indians' effectively became citizens of the independent state but they had to acknowledge ketuanan Melayu, or Malay dominance, which implied that they had to accept 'special Malay privi-

[18] Thio, 'Constitutional Accommodation of the Rights of Ethnic and Religious Minorities in Plural Democracies: Lessons and Cautionary Tales From South-East Asia', 22 *Pace International Law Review* (2010) 43, 62.

[19] Mauzy, 'From Malay Nationalism to a Malaysian Nation?' in L. Barrington (ed.), *After Independence: Making and Protecting the Nation in Postcolonial and Postcommunist States* (2006) 45, 50.

[20] Neo, 'Malay Nationalism, Islamic Supremacy and the Constitutional Bargain in the Multi-Ethnic Composition of Malaysia', 13 *International Journal on Minority and Group Rights* (2006) 95, 99.

[21] See, e.g., A. Smith, *Theories of Nationalism* (1971). Discussed in C. Jaffrelot, *The Hindu Nationalist Movement and Indian Politics, 1925 to the 1990s* (1999).

[22] J. Nagata, *Malaysian Mosaic: Perspectives from a Poly-Ethnic Society* (1979). Quoted in Lemière (n. 10) 41.

[23] Population Distribution and Basic Demographic Characteristics Report: Population and Housing Census, Malaysia (2010), available at https://www.dosm.gov.my/v1/index.php?r=column/ctheme&menu_id=L0pheU43NWJwRWVSZklWdzQ4TlhUUT09&bul_id=MDMxdHZjWTk1SjFzTzNkRXYzcVZjdz09 (last visited 23 August 2018).

[24] Ibid.

[25] Lee, 'Constitutional Amendments in Malaysia', 18 *Malaya Law Review* (1976) 59,59. Quoted in Neo (n. 20) 96.

leges' in education and government services, and 'Malay' royalty as their rulers, Islam as the official religion, and the 'Malay' language as the official language of the new nation-state.[26]

The final constitutional arrangement is marred with the kinds of tensions and competing forces one would expect of a postcolonial text. The Constitution[27] states in Article 3 that Islam is the religion of Malaysia. This is qualified by the second section of Article 3, 'but other religions may be practised in peace and harmony in any part of the Federation'. Article 3 sits alongside Article 11(1), which provides simply: 'every person has the right to profess and practice his religion and, subject to clause 4, to propagate it'. Clause 4, in turn, reads as follows: 'State law and in respect of the Federal Territories of Kuala Lumpur and Lubuan, federal law may control and restrict the propagation of any religious doctrine or belief among persons professing the religion of Islam.' Finally, Article 11(5) stipulates: 'This article does not authorize any act contrary to any law relating to public order, public health or morality.' Hashemi describes Article 11(4), the limitation clause, as 'additional or explanatory to' Article 11(5).[28] As we shall see, Article 11(4) is also invoked to justify a narrow reading of Article 11(1) as conditioned by, and subordinate to, the first section of Article 3.

Leaving aside for a moment the difficulties surrounding Article 3 and the inherent tensions between Article 3 and Article 11, the proselytism limitations contained in Article 11 have in and of themselves attracted much criticism. A 1988 United Nations (UN) report alleged that Article 11 has had a negative impact on 'the enjoyment of freedom of thought, conscience and religion'.[29] The Malaysian authority's response to the allegations is revealing of the government's official position on religious freedom, and bears quoting in full:

> [W]hen Malaysia achieved its independence in 1957, it inherited enormous national problems. Top of the list are the daunting problems of forging unity among the multiracial and multi-religious composition of the newly born country which are not easily appreciated by foreign observers... Malaysia, or Malaya then, was born from a land and State which had its own long established indigenous institutions characterized by Islamic teachings and belief... Malaysia was to be born as a multiracial and multi-religious nation.
>
> One important factor underlying the opportunity of forging ahead for the birth of a united nation then was the fact that this multi-religious and multiracial society had had little experience in religious and racial interaction... Yet, as civilized human beings, Malaysian leaders from the various ethnic communities worked out compromises between the ethnic groups... The compromises agreed to include the understanding that all institutions indigenous to the country must be preserved, the character of the country and all its attributes must not only be maintained but strengthened further, and the rights of the indigenous (Malays) must remain, while those of the other ethnic groups are guaranteed.

[26] Shamsul, 'A History of an Identity, an Identity of a History: The Idea and Practice of "Malayness" in Malaysia Reconsidered', 32 *Journal of Southeast Asian Studies* (2001) 355, 364.

[27] Laws of Malaysia: Federal Constitution, available at http://confinder.richmond.edu/admin/docs/malaysia.pdf (last visited 23 August 2018).

[28] K. Hashemi, *Religious Legal Traditions, International Human Rights Law and Muslim States* (2008) 58.

[29] Report of the Special Rapporteur on Religious Intolerance, E/CN.4/1989/44, 25, available at http://www.ohchr.org/EN/Issues/FreedomReligion/Pages/Annual.aspx (last visited 23 August 2018).

The spirit of the Constitution of Malaysia pertaining particularly to interracial and inter-religious relations between the various ethnic communities was derived from the above compromises. Indeed Article 11 and the various legislations passed in consonance with that article are reflective of the compromise that the character of the country and all its attributes should not only be maintained but strengthened. This is the wish of the indigenous people (Malays) who are Muslims and indeed if there should be a change in the characteristics mentioned above, it should only take place in accordance with the wishes of the Muslims. However, in keeping with the spirit of compromise, the Constitution at the same time guarantees freedom of worship to others.[30]

Malaysia sees itself as a fragile society precariously straddling two competing ideologies:[31] on the one hand, it is (or at least presents itself as) a proud pluralist, multi-religious society. On the other, its identity is bound up in an 'ethno-religious ideology where the interest of the [Islamic] dominant religious group is prioritized over other groups'.[32] The passages make clear, however, that the second aspect of Malaysia's identity is elevated above the first. The preservation of its pluralist identity is viewed as a concession: its ethnic identity is paramount, but its leaders are 'civilized human beings' who are willing to 'compromise' by ceding a portion of the country's integrity (its condition of being undivided and whole) to safeguard the rights of 'other ethnic groups'.

While many government officials pay lip service to multi-ethnicity and social harmony, pluralism is often viewed with suspicion, and as an impediment to national unity and the nation-building enterprise.[33] We can perhaps begin to make sense of this dissonance, and of the problematic religious freedom interpretations it has yielded, by attending to the drafting history of the Constitution.

In a previous article, one of us has mapped out two competing narratives inherited by Malaysia upon independence. On the one side is a narrative of 'continuity and connectedness to the community of British former colonies, with some indigenous elements to recognize the particularities of Malaysian culture and history'.[34] According to the terms of this narrative, the intention of making Islam the official religion of the Federation 'was primarily for ceremonial purposes'.[35] On the other side is a narrative of 'discontinuity—the constitutional moment was one of breaking away from the British colonial power and the establishment of a new state based on pre-colonial, Islamic traditions'.[36] The language used by the Malaysian government

[30] Ibid. 25–6. Cited and discussed in Stahnke (n. 11) 307.

[31] See generally Neo, 'What's in a Name? Malaysia's "Allah" Controversy and the Judicial Intertwining of Islam with Ethnic Identity', 12 *International Journal of Constitutional Law* (2014) 751.

[32] Ibid. 754.

[33] Z. Bagir and S. Cholil, *The State of Religious Pluralism in Indonesia* (2008) 12. Discussed in Feener (n. 7) 4. This refers to the situation in Indonesia, but their observation applies with equal force to Malaysia.

[34] Evans, 'Constitutional Narratives: Constitutional Adjudication on the Religion Clauses in Australia and Malaysia', 23 *Emory International Law Review* (2009) 437, 449.

[35] Fernando, 'The Position of Islam in the Constitution of Malaysia', 37 *Journal of Southeast Asia Studies* (2006) 249, 251. Citing Faruqi, 'Secularism and Theocracy: A Study of the Malaysian Constitution', paper delivered at the Malaysian Strategic Research Centre—Konrad Adenauer Foundation Intercultural Discourse Series (2002).

[36] Faruqi (n. 35) 450.

in its response to the UN Special Rapporteur absorbs the discourse from both narratives, even if it aligns itself with the latter.

The ambiguities surrounding certain points of friction—the role of the common law as against Islamic law,[37] the secularization as against Islamization of the state—generate problematic interpretations of the Constitution, which can shift depending on the lens or historical narrative through which it is refracted. Consider, for example, the following claim, authored by three academics from the Universiti Kebangsaan Malaysia: 'Although Article 11 of the Federal Constitution recognizes freedom of religion, other matters in the Constitution clearly show that freedom of religion does not amount to equal rights.'[38] This reasoning, almost unintelligible within a liberal rights framework, begins with a different set of assumptions from Western liberalism. It emerges from a framework and a social structure in which it is 'not contradictory for a government to be "democratic" while simultaneously favouring a specific religious tradition'.[39] Shad Saleem Faruqui, in attempting to argue against assertions that Malaysian laws prohibiting proselytism impact upon the right to religious freedom of non-Muslims, places the restrictions on religious propagation in historical and cultural context. His analysis, which has since been quoted by at least one Malaysian high court to justify such restrictions,[40] provides a telling insight into what Juliana Finucane calls the 'new regulatory frameworks' that have emerged from postcolonial Asia:[41]

> [M]any non-Muslims complain that [Article 11(4)] amounts to unequal treatment under the law because Muslims are allowed to propagate their religion to non-Muslims. It is respectfully submitted that Article 11(4) is part of the pre-Merdeka 'social contract.' Its aim is to insulate Muslims against a clearly unequal and disadvantageous situation. During the colonial era, many non-indigenous religions were vigorously promoted by the merchants, the military and the missionaries of the colonial countries... Malays see an inseparable connection between their race and their religion. Any attempt to weaken a Malay's religious faith may be perceived as an indirect attempt to erode Malay power. Conversion out of Islam would automatically mean deserting the Malay community due to the legal fact that the definition of a Malay in Article 160(2) contains four ingredients. Professing the religion of Islam is one of them. A Pre-Merdeka compromise between the Malays and the non-Malays was, therefore, sought and obtained that any preaching to Muslims will be conducted only by authorised Syariah authorities.[42]

[37] See Neoh (n. 14).

[38] Kusrin *et al.*, 'Legal Provisions and Restrictions on the Propagation of Non-Islamic Religions among Muslims in Malaysia', 31 *Kajian Malaysia* (2013) 2, 2.

[39] Finucane, 'Preface and Acknowledgment' in J. Finucane and M. Feener (eds), *Proselytizing and the Limits of Religious Freedom in Contemporary Asia* (2014) v, vii. The maintenance of established churches in many European countries even after the protection of religious freedom was established in the European Convention of Human Rights demonstrates that this position is far from unique to Malaysia or Asia. However, the degree of state support for Islam and overlapping national and religious identity exceeds that which Western countries give even to established churches.

[40] *Menteri Dalam Negeri and Others v. Titular Roman Catholic Archbishop of Kuala Lumpur* [2013] 6 MLJ 468, 491. See later discussion.

[41] Finucane (n. 39) vii.

[42] S. Faruqui, *Document of Destiny: the Constitution of the Federation of Malaysia* (2008) 138–9. The Court of Appeal in *Menteri Dalam Negeri and Others v. Titular Roman Catholic Archbishop of Kuala Lumpur* cites this passage to buttress its claim that 'the purpose and intention of the insertion of the words "in peace and harmony" in art 3(1) is to protect the sanctity of Islam as the religion of the country

In a similar way to India, as will be discussed later, the legacy of colonialism, and the threat posed by the missionary activity that attended it, has meant that Muslim Malaysians assume the posture of victimhood, or minority status, entitled to a level of protection and preservation, even as they hold a dominant or 'special' position within the social structures of Malaysia. Interestingly, Malaysia is 'one of the rare examples' of a state in which affirmative action policies are set up to favour a majority rather than a minority group.[43] The language of national unity and harmony, which was part of the British colonial project, has since been assimilated into official governmental discourse[44] and is used to preserve (and is increasingly being used to expand) the political and religious dominance of the Muslim community.[45]

Many of these issues came to a head in the highly controversial case of *Lina Joy v. Federal Territory Islamic Council*.[46] The case involved a young woman's application to change her name to Lina Joy and to have this reflected in an official identity card. While the High Court judgment did not deal at length with public order considerations, its implications for the regulation of religious freedom are far-reaching.

Lina Joy was raised a Muslim but later converted to Christianity as she was engaged to be married to a Christian.[47] Her name change was eventually approved, but the National Registration Department refused her application to remove Islam from her identity card unless she presented them with a formal certificate of apostasy from the Syariah court or religious authority. In her arguments, Lina Joy claimed a violation of her religious freedom based on Article 11. The Federal Court of Malaysia split 2–1 and rejected her appeal, holding that the authority was correct to refuse to change her registration without Syariah court grant.[48]

The Federal Court majority decision did not fully address some of the pressing constitutional issues surrounding the *Lina Joy* case, but the reasoning can be more easily unpacked[49] when it is read together with the majority decisions of the High Court[50] and the Court of Appeal.[51] Put simply, the High Court majority decision read Article 11 as conditioned by Article 3.[52] Dismissing the application, the High Court held that Article 11(1) 'should not be read in isolation',[53] and is qualified, among other sections, by Article 3(1).[54] More telling, however, was the fact that the primacy and precedence of Article 3 is justified with reference to Article 11(4). As the Court states: 'One of the natural consequences from the fact that Islam is the

and also to insulate against any threat faced or any possible and probable threat to the religion of Islam'. [2013] 6 MLJ 468, 490.

[43] Lemière (n. 10) 47.

[44] See, e.g., the 'One Malaysia Campaign' of Prime Minister Najib Tun Razak. See generally Hashim and Mahpuz, 'Tackling Multiculturalism via Human Communication', 2 *International Journal of Business and Social Science* (2001) 4, 16.

[45] As Juliana Finucane writes (referring to Sophie Lemière's analysis), 'the state has an interest not just in preserving social harmony, but also in maintaining the religious and political dominance of the Muslim majority'. Finucane (n. 39) viii.

[46] *Lina Joy v. Federal Territory Islamic Council* [2007] 4 MLJ 585.

[47] Evans (n. 34) 461.

[48] Ibid. 460–1.

[49] Ibid. 463.

[50] *Lina Joy v. Majlis Agama Islam Wilayah and Another* [2004] 2 MLJ 119.

[51] *Lina Joy v. Majlis Agama Islam Wilayah Persekutuan and Others* [2005] 6 MLJ 193.

[52] See Neoh (n. 14) 77.

[53] [2004] 2 MLJ 119, 127.

[54] Ibid. 128.

religion of the Federation is the limitation imposed on the propagation among persons professing the religion of Islam in art 11(4).'[55]

Interestingly, and perhaps unsurprisingly, 'public order' is used interchangeably with 'public harmony'. In paragraph 11, Faiza J makes the following claim: 'It is clear that cll (4) and (5) above preserve and protect the harmony and preserve the affairs and interests of Muslims and non-Muslims in this country whereby the rights of the various races and religions are also protected.' In a later passage Faiza J refers again to the 'harmony and well-being of the multi-racial and multi-religious communities of this country'.[56] The judge reasons that if the plaintiff were allowed to renounce her religion (a right which Faiza J concedes is covered by the first part of Article 11(1)) without first taking leave from the religious authorities:

> ... this will create chaos and confusion with the administrative authority which manages the affairs of Islam and the Muslim community and consequently the non-Muslim community as a whole. I am of the opinion that this threaten[s] public order and this cannot have been the intention of the legislature when drafting the [Federal Constitution].[57]

The 'public' in the public order arguments is framed narrowly, 'in terms of the harm that would be done to the Muslim community if conversion was permissible without the formal process of apostasy'.[58]

As Thio Li-ann points out, the majority holding stands in conflict with the holding in *Minister for Home Affairs Malaysia v. Jamaluddin bin Othman*[59] that proselytism activities do not pose a threat to public order.[60] In that case, a Christian was detained by the Minister of Home Affairs in order to prevent him from 'acting in a manner prejudicial to the security of Malaysia'.[61] The grounds for the detention stated that the petitioner 'was involved in a plan or programme for the dissemination of Christianity amongst Malays',[62] which allegedly resulted in the conversion of six Malays to Christianity.[63] The trial judge ruled that the detention was unconstitutional, and the Supreme Court dismissed the Appeal. While emphasizing that the freedom to profess and practise one's religion is subject to Article 11(5) (that is, to general laws relating to public order, public health, or morality), the Supreme Court ultimately held that the mere participation in meetings and seminars, even if they resulted in a number of conversions to Christianity, cannot by itself be regarded as a threat to the security of the country. The Supreme Court concluded with the following statement: 'The guarantee provided by art 11 of the Constitution, i.e., the freedom to profess and practise one's religion, must be given effect unless the actions of a person go well beyond what can normally be regarded as professing and practising one's religion.'[64]

It is difficult to see how a personal decision to change religious affiliation can constitute a threat to public order while activities explicitly aimed at the conversion of Muslims to the Christian faith do not. Moreover, while it is possible to accept that

[55] Ibid. 127. [56] Ibid. 132. [57] Ibid. 125. [58] Evans (n. 34) 465.

[59] *Minister for Home Affairs Malaysia v. Jamaluddin bin Othman* [1989] 1 MLJ 418.

[60] Thio, 'Apostasy and Religious Freedom: Constitutional Issues arising from the Lina Joy Litigation', 2 *Malayan Law Journal* (2006) i, para. 2.

[61] *Minister for Home Affairs Malaysia v. Jamaluddin bin Othman* (n. 59) 418. [62] Ibid.

[63] Ibid. [64] Ibid. 419.

public order arguments carry some water with respect to proselytism given its 'incendiary' nature,[65] those arguments do not have the same salience for laws that prohibit personal acts of conversion. The restrictions placed on Lina Joy's conversion expose the motivating force behind public order justifications, which are less about 'contemplating the trade-off between rights and social responsibilities'[66] than 'the imperative to protect Islam as the "main and dominant religion" of the federation and to recognize its superior status'.[67]

This iteration of the public order argument can only take place in the 'points of friction and rupture'[68] between two conflicting discursive spaces: between Islam as a dominant religion and Islam as a religion under threat. The brief for the Council of Islamic Religion in the *Lina Joy* case (unwittingly) expresses the crux of the tension: 'Malaysia would have become fully Islamic and with full Islamic law' (i.e. Islam is dominant) *but for* 'the intrusion of the colonial power' (i.e. Islam is under threat).[69] As Danchin points out with reference to the proselytism laws, but his observation applies with equal force to the public interest argument, 'the rationale derives from a certain perceived conception of the collective good of the state'.[70] Put differently, the argument treats conversion and proselytism as a collective group matter that has the potential to destabilize Malaysia's religious landscape, or its religious 'order', which itself relies on the privileged position of Islam. The protection of collective rights is not problematic in and of itself; it becomes so when the state has an interest in maintaining the religious and political dominance of a majority group, and frames that interest in terms of public order. Viewed in this way, it becomes clear that the language of public order in the context of Malaysia does not refer only, or even predominantly, to maintaining horizontal social orderliness or tranquillity. It refers to the preservation of a vertical or hierarchical arrangement. Izza Hussin's characterization of Malaysia's legal system as a 'hierarchy within [a] plurality'[71] brings into sharp focus the underlying impossibility of Malaysia's formulation of the public order argument. A pluralist democracy is by definition built upon 'communities living together and participating as equal partners in the national political life'.[72] Indeed, the principal of equality is enshrined in the Constitution, which provides in Article 8 that '[a]ll persons are equal before the law and entitled to the equal protection of the law'. The state uses the language of equality and public harmony, but it is often a politics of dominance disguised as public order.

65 Harding, 'Malaysia: Religious Pluralism and the Constitution in a Contested Polity', 4 *Middle East Law and Governance* (2012) 356, 373.

66 Neoh, 'Islamic State and the Common Law in Malaysia: A Case Study of *Lina Joy*', 8 *Global Jurist* (2008) 1, 12.

67 Thio (n. 60) para. 2.

68 Feener (n. 7) 5.

69 Brief for the Council of Islamic Religion, *Lina Joy v. Federal Territory Islamic Council* [2007] 3 MLJ 586, quoted in Evans (n. 34) 463.

70 Danchin, *Of Prophets* (n. 3) 275.

71 Hussin, 'Islam, Ethnicity and the Problem of Mixed Legality: Two Malaysian Cases', 1 *Yearbook of Islamic and Middle Eastern Law* (2010) 1, 2.

72 Mahajan, 'Indian Exceptionalism or Indian Model: Negotiating Cultural Diversity and Minority Rights in a Democratic Nation-State' in W. Kymlicka and B. He (eds), *Multiculturalism in Asia* (2005) 288, 313. Quoted in Neoh (n. 14) 72.

In 2014 the Federal Court[73] upheld a unanimous judgment of a Court of Appeal decision that took the public order justification to new extremes. The central issue in *Minister for Home Affairs and others v. Titular Roman Catholic Archbishop of Kuala Lumpur*[74]—commonly known as the '*Allah*' case—was whether the prohibition on the usage of the word 'Allah' in the Malay version of the publication of *The Herald* (a Catholic weekly newspaper) was lawful, and, specifically for the purposes of this study, whether it was in the interest of public safety and public order.[75] In three individual, and highly contested judgments, the Court upheld the government's prohibition, overturning the 2010 High Court decision[76] which came out in favour of the Church, and made explicit some of the underlying assumptions informing earlier decisions. In keeping with earlier decisions, the Court read Article 11(1) as conditioned by Article 3. But it took this already problematic construction a step further by asserting that the second portion of Article 3 ('but other religions may be practised in peace and harmony in any part of the Federation') must be read in light of the first portion ('Islam is the religion of the Federation'). This interpretive move allowed the Court to reason that 'the purpose and intention of the insertion of the words: "in peace and harmony" ... is to protect the sanctity of Islam as the religion of the country and also to insulate against any threat faced or any possible and probable threat to the religion of Islam'.[77] 'Peace and harmony', now understood as serving to protect the dominancy and sanctity of Islam, is almost explicitly viewed as synonymous with public order, such that all three provisions support each other to form a constellation of coordinates that point in a singular direction: the will and the interest of the dominant religion.

Drawing on a line of cases from India, where public order was defined as 'the even tempo of the life of the community',[78] Apandi Ali JCA concludes that the inclusion of the word 'Allah' in the weekly newsletter is 'not conducive to the peaceful and harmonious tempo of life in the country'.[79] The double manoeuvre is strikingly self-referential: a religious freedom clause which is meant precisely to protect the liberty of minority religions ('*but* other religions may be practised in peace and harmony') is viewed as identical with 'public order', which, according to the judgment, was inserted into the Constitution together with Article 11(4) to 'fortify the position of Islam in the Federation'. Every aspect of the legal framework—from the provisions under scrutiny, to the very arrangement of the constitutional text[80]—is filtered through the ethno-nationalist narrative.[81] Two of the judgments go so far as to quote a passage from Professor Andrew Harding's book, *The Constitution of Malaysia*, where he comments that 'the restriction of proselytism has more to do with the preservation of public order than with religious priority', to bolster their

[73] *Titular Roman Catholic Archbishop of Kuala Lumpur v. Menteri Dalam Negeri and Others* [2014] 4 MLJ 765 (Federal Court).

[74] *Menteri Dalam Negeri and Others v. Titular Roman Catholic Archbishop of Kuala Lumpur* [2013] 6 MLJ 468 (Court of Appeal) (hereinafter the *Allah* case).

[75] Ibid. 486.

[76] *Titular Roman Catholic Archbishop of Kuala Lumpar v. Menteri Dalam, Negeri and Another* [2010] 2 MLJ 78 (High Court).

[77] *Allah* case (n. 74) 490. [78] Ibid. 493. [79] Ibid. 496. [80] Ibid.

[81] Neo (n. 31) 5.

interpretation of 'peace and harmony'—a blatant misreading of his text that Harding himself disclaims.[82]

The *Lina Joy* case also makes reference to religious freedom in India. In the originating summons, the judge dismisses as erroneous the plaintiff's assertion that Article 11(1) can be equated with Article 25 of the Indian Constitution.[83] While it is right that the two constitutional arrangements are backlit with very different historical and cultural contexts, and while the judge may be correct in asserting that '[e]ach country frames its constitution according to its genius and for the good of its own society',[84] the public order clause is invoked in both systems to similar ends.

4. India

The regulation of conversion and proselytism has long been a site of controversy and friction in India.[85] Laws imposing restrictions on conversion were first enacted by a number of princely states during British rule,[86] motivated largely by 'concerns about public order or about foreign influences…in the context of encroaching colonialism'.[87] The postcolonial wave of anti-conversion discourse in many ways modelled itself on these early laws, and has continued to underpin its claims with reference to public order arguments.

The first wave of so-called 'Freedom of Religion' Acts were enacted in the late 1960s.[88] Since the rise to power of the Hindu nationalist party in the 1990s,[89] similar Acts have been enacted in several Indian states, including Gujarat, Chhattisgarh, Rajasthan, and Himachal Pradesh.[90] Despite the fact there have been very few actual convictions under the laws,[91] there appears to be a strong correlation between the passage of anti-conversion laws and increased persecution and violence

[82] Harding, 'Language, Religion and the Law' (27 February 2014), available online at http://www.loyarburok.com/2014/02/27/language-religion-law/ (last visited 23 August 2018).

[83] *Lina Joy v. Majlis Agama Islam Wilayah and Another* [2004] 2 MLJ 128.

[84] Ibid. 129.

[85] See Dhavan, 'Religious Freedom in India', 35 *The American Journal of Comparative Law* (1987) 209; see also Osuri (n. 4).

[86] See generally Jenkins, 'Legal Limits on Religious Conversion in India', 71 *Law and Contemporary Problems* (2008) 109.

[87] Ibid. 114.

[88] Orissa Local Act, No. 2 of 1968; Madhya Pradesh Freedom of Religion Act, No. 27 of 1968; Arunachal Pradesh Local Act, No. 40 of 1978. See Mahmood, 'Religion, Law, and Judiciary in Modern India', *Brigham Young University Law Review* (2006) 755, 761; Suleman, 'Freedom of Religion and Anti Conversion Laws in India: An Overview', 1 *ILI Law Review* (2010) 106, 107.

[89] See generally C. Jaffrelot, *Hindu Nationalism: A Reader* (2007) 1–25.

[90] Gujarat Freedom of Religion Act, 2003; The Chhattisgarh Dharma Swatantraya Adhiniyam, 1968 (now amended by the Chhattisgarh Dharma Swatantraya (Sanshodhan) Adhiniyam, 2006); Himachal Pradesh Freedom of Religion Act, 2006; Rajasthan Freedom of Religion Act, 2006. See Suleman (n. 88) 106–7; Osuri (n. 4) 2. See generally Arora, 'India's Defiance of Religious Freedom: A Briefing on "Anti-Conversion" Laws', 1 *International Institute for Religious Freedom* (2012) 59, 60; UN Human Rights Council, Report of the Special Rapporteur on Freedom of Religion or Belief, Asma Jahangir : addendum: mission to India, 26 January 2009, A/HRC/10/8/Add.3, available at http://www.refworld.org/docid/498ae8032.html (last visited 23 August 2018); AG Noorani and South Asia Human Rights Documentation Centre (SAHRDC), *Challenges to Civil Rights Guarantees in India* (2012) 207–38.

[91] Arora (n. 90) 61.

against religious minorities in the enacting states. The episodes of violence have sometimes taken extreme forms.[92] In March of 2002, for example, a campaign of extreme violence against Muslims took place in the state of Gujarat, killing between 800 and 2,000 people.[93] In its 2011 report, the United States Commission on International Religious Freedom noted that 'the harassment and violence against religious minorities appears to be more pronounced in states that have adopted "Freedom of Religion" Acts or are considering such laws'.[94] The Special Rapporteur on Freedom of Religion or Belief also noted that 'even in the Indian states which have adopted laws on religious conversion there seem to be only few—if any—convictions for conversion by the use of force, inducement or fraudulent means... [h]owever, such laws or even draft legislation have had adverse consequences for religious minorities and have reportedly fostered mob violence against them'.[95] In order to understand how these Acts have been issued against the backdrop of a secular Constitution which expressly guarantees equal freedom of religion, we need to consider closely the contours of India's constitutional organization as it relates to religious freedom.[96]

In 1976 an amendment added the words 'secular' and 'socialist' to the preamble to India's Constitution, and changed the words 'unity of the Nation' to 'unity and integrity of the Nation'.[97] The Preamble now reads as follows:

> WE, THE PEOPLE OF INDIA, having solemnly resolved to constitute India into a SOVERIGN SOCIALIST SECULAR DEMOCRATIC REPUBLIC and to secure to all its citizens:
> JUSTICE, social, economic and political;
> LIBERTY of thought, expression, belief, faith and worship;
> EQUALITY of status and of opportunity;
> and to promote among them all
> FRATERNITY assuring the dignity of the individual and the unity and integrity of the Nation.

Article 25 of the Indian Constitution proclaims: 'all persons are equally entitled to freedom of conscience and the right to freely profess, practise and propagate

92 See, e.g., Narula, 'Overlooked Danger: The Security and Rights Implications of Hindu Nationalism in India', 16 *Harvard Human Rights Journal* (2003) 41.

93 Kamat and Mathew, 'Mapping Political Violence in a Globalized World: The Case of Hindu Nationalism', 30 *Social Justice* (2003) 14, 93.

94 'USCIRF Annual Report 2011—The Commission's Watch List: India', available at http://www.refworld.org/docid/4dbe90bac.html (last visited 23 August 2018). Quoted in Arora (n. 90) 61.

95 UN Human Rights Council, Report of the Special Rapporteur on Freedom of Religion or Belief (n. 90). Quoted in Arora (n. 90) 61. More recently, the UN Special Rapporteur on religious freedom stated that India's 'anti-conversion' laws are a threat to religious freedom, available at http://blogs.wsj.com/indiarealtime/2014/03/10/un-official-indias-conversion-laws-threaten-religious-freedom/ (last visited 23 August 2018).

96 For a discussion on the debate over conversion during the drafting of the Indian Constitution, see S. Kim, *In Search of Identity: Debates on Religious Conversion in India* (2003) 37–58.

97 The Constitution of India, Preamble: amended by the Constitution (Forty-Second Amendment) Act, 1976. See Jenkins, 'Diversity and the Constitution in India; What is Religious Freedom', 57 *Drake Law Review* (2008–2009) 913, 918–19.

religion'.[98] The right to practise and propagate religion, however, is subject to constitutional limitations enshrined in Article 25 which further provides that 'public order, morality and health' may form the basis for valid limitations on religious freedom. Article 25 in its entirety reads as follows:

25. Right to Freedom of Religion
1) Subject to public order, morality and health and to the other provisions of this Part, all persons are equally entitled to freedom of conscience and the right freely to profess, practice and propagate religion.
2) Nothing in this article shall affect the operation of any existing law or prevent the State from making any law—
  (a) regulating or restricting any economic, financial, political or other secular activity which may be associated with religious practice;
  (b) providing for social welfare and reform or the throwing open of Hindu religious institutions of a public character to all classes and sections of Hindus.

Article 26, also contained in the Fundamental Rights category, guarantees to 'every religious denomination' the '[f]reedom to manage religious affairs', including the right to 'establish and maintain institutions for religious and charitable purposes', to 'manage its own affairs in matters of religion', and to own, acquire, and administer property. This Article too is '[s]ubject to public order, morality and health'.[99]

The anti-conversion Acts do not strictly ban all forms of conversion; rather they render illegal conversions made by force, fraud, or allurement. State-enacted anti-conversion laws are all framed in effectively the following terms: 'No person shall convert or attempt to convert, either directly or otherwise, any person from one religion to another by the use of force or by inducement or by any other fraudulent means.'[100] At a textual level, such laws are largely in keeping with human rights standards and with the Indian Constitution. In practice, however, and in application, the laws are profoundly problematic.

A problem that is immediately clear from the text is the imprecise language contained in the Acts. The South Asian Human Rights Documentation Centre (SAHRDC) has noted that the vague nature of such terms as 'fraud', 'force', and 'inducement' presents a 'danger of discriminatory abuse in their application'.[101] It concludes that the 'terminology used by these legislations transforms them from their purported role as protectors of constitutional rights into violators of these very guarantees'.[102] While a term such as 'force' likely does line up with the international prohibition on the use of coercion with respect to religious matters, the notion of inducement, in particular, is much more fluid and open to abuse. Possibly more troubling, however, which we shall return to later, is the discriminatory interpretation and application of the anti-conversion laws.

[98] The Constitution of India, Art. 25. For a discussion of India's Constitutional Framework, especially as it relates to religious freedom, see generally Noorani and SAHRDC (n. 90); R. Sen, *Articles of Faith: Religion, Secularism, and the Indian Supreme Court* (2012) 108–27; Jenkins (n. 97); Mahmood (n. 88) 756–70.

[99] The Constitution of India, Art. 26.

[100] See Noorani and SAHRDC (n. 90) 210.

[101] Ibid. Cited in Osuri (n. 4) 3.

[102] Osuri (n. 4) 3.

The cultural and historical forces that have given rise to the current wave of anti-conversion laws are difficult to trace. As Goldie Osuri notes in her book on religious freedom in India, the laws—commonly referred to as 'anti-conversion laws'—have been spearheaded by a body of Hindu nationalists.[103] A comprehensive analysis of the interplay between colonialism, anti-conversion sentiment, and Hindu nationalism is well beyond the scope of this chapter, but we can perhaps begin to unpack the tangled narratives by attending briefly to the genealogies of Hindu nationalism. Although Hindu nationalism did not begin fully to take hold of the public imagination until the early 1990s, as an ideology it crystallized between the 1870s and the 1920s.[104] From its inception, Hindu nationalism was largely constructed in reaction against British colonialism, Christian missionary activity, and the threat of Muslim mobilization.[105] The colonial project interfaced in complex ways with Christian missionary operations. While it is often observed that the two operations differed in significant ways, the differences took place 'within a shared colonizing project'.[106] In his historical appraisal of the anti-conversion phenomenon in India, Chad Bauman explains that the missionary activities that accompanied colonialism 'placed certain Hindus in a defensive posture, causing them to seek, as a bulwark against national disintegration, a primordial, unalterable and unifying cultural essence... Many identified "Hinduness" (*hindutva*) as that unifying essence'.[107] Whatever its reflection of historical realities, the perception of Christian complicity with British colonialism, and the 'militancy of the Muslim minority',[108] served to animate and embolden the nationalist project.

To those who subscribed to the *Hindutva* construction of national unity, converts (in both the transitive and intransitive sense) were viewed as a threat to Indian solidarity, and were thus treated as abject outsiders. The politics of 'other'-izing fed back into the nationalist project. The ideological basis of *Hindutva* maps directly onto the nation-building paradigm: it was 'premised on the creation of two groups... those who belong to the Hindu family, and those outside the fold of "Hinduness"'.[109] While the hostility toward Christianity and Islam, and perhaps toward religious 'others' altogether, was in many ways the 'manifestation of understandable postcolonial anxieties about the very survival and coherence of the Indian nation',[110] the abjection of Muslim and Christian minority groups facilitated their function as the 'outside' against which Hindu nationalism defined itself. As it has grown in political power, the 'other'-ing has extended beyond religions associated with colonialization and includes indigenous religions such as Buddhism.

The framing of conversion as a disturbance to public order was an essential component of the Hindu nationalist project. The development of this script can partly

[103] The Hindu nationalist organizations include the Vishwa Hindu Parishad (VHP), the Rashtriya Swayamsevak Sangh (RSS), and the Bajrang Dal (BD), as well as the Bharatiya Janata Party (BJP). See Osuri (n. 4) 2.

[104] Jaffrelot (n. 89) 3; Jaffrelot (n. 21) 11.

[105] Jaffrelot (n. 21) 11.

[106] P. van der Veer, *Imperial Encounters* (2001) 43.

[107] Bauman, 'Postcolonial Anxiety and Anti-Conversion Sentiment in the Report of the Christian Missionary Activities Enquiry Committee', 12 *International Journal of Hindu Studies* (2008) 181, 183.

[108] Jaffrelot (n. 21) 6.

[109] Kamat and Mathew (n. 93) 8.

[110] Bauman (n. 107) 182.

be attributed to the highly controversial 1956 *Niyogi Committee Report on Christian Missionary Activities*.[111] The Report was an official inquiry into the work of missionaries in the state of Madhya Pradesh. In a bid to underscore the centrality of 'public order' and 'morality' as valid limitations to religious freedom, the Report cites discussions that took place in the Constituent Assembly during the drafting of Article 25 of the Constitution (Article 19 of the Draft Constitution):

> Article 19 is really not so much an article on religious freedom but an article on what I may call religious toleration. It is not so much the words 'all persons are equally entitled to freedom of conscience and the right freely to profess, practise and propagate religion' that are important; what are important are the governing words with which the article begins, viz., 'Subject to public order, morality and health'... this article has been very carefully drafted and the exceptions and qualifications are as important as the right it confers.[112]

The reference in this passage to 'religious toleration' is likely an allusion to Mahatma Gandhi's *Tolerance* ideal, deployed in the 1920s against the backdrop of 'escalating Hindu-Muslim conflict amidst active competition for converts pursued in the name of religious freedom'.[113] Indeed, the Niyogi Report's invocation of Gandhi's *Tolerance* ideal is characteristic of the 'strange marriage between Gandhi and the Hindu nationalists',[114] who drew on Gandhi's critique of proselytism, often to majoritarian ends.[115] In a later passage, the Report cites directly Gandhi's call for 'unity in diversity',[116] and continues as follows:

> Following this dictum of the Father of the Nation, the framers of the Constitution, in their anxiety to preserve the secular nature of our State, have guaranteed equality to all religions. But if the followers of any one religion deny it not only in their mental attitude but in their outward conduct and behaviour, then it becomes the duty of the State to keep an eye on the religions [*sic*] activities of the votaries of different religions and to step in wherever there is any misuse of their rights threatening public order or solidarity of country. This is an obligation imposed by the Constitution.[117]

In the introductory letter to the Chief Secretary to Government, M.B. Niyogi stresses that members of the committee were:

> Guided solely by the necessity to maintain intact the solidarity and security of the country, to prevent disruption of society and culture, and to emphasize the essential secular character of the Constitution. If they have drawn attention to certain disruptive tendencies inherent in,

[111] Report of the Christian Missionaries Enquiry Committee Madhya Pradesh, Nagpur, 1956, available at http://voiceofdharma.org/books/ncr/ (last visited 23 August 2018). Reprinted in Christian Activities Enquiry Committee, *Vindicated by Time: The Niyogi Committee Report on Christian Missionary Activities* (1998) (hereinafter 'Niyogi Report').

[112] Niyogi Report (n. 111) Vol. 1, Pt III, Ch. II, para. 11.

[113] Adcock, 'Debating Conversion, Silencing Caste: The Limited Scope of Religious Freedom', 29 *Journal of Law and Religion* (2014) 363, 365. See generally C.S. Adcock, *The Limits of Tolerance: Indian Secularism and the Politics of Religious Freedom* (2014). Adcock provides a critical analysis of Tolerance as an Indian secularist ideal.

[114] Viswanathan, 'Literacy and Conversion in the Discourse of Hindu Nationalism' in A. Needham and R. Rajan (eds), *The Crisis of Secularism in India* (2007) 333, 335.

[115] Adcock, 'Debating Conversion' (n. 113) 365.

[116] Niyogi Report (n. 111) Vol. 1, Pt III, Ch. II, para. 9.

[117] Ibid. Vol. 1, Pt III, Ch. II, para. 10.

or incidental to, the exercise of certain liberties in matters of religion, they have done so not with a view to curtailing individual rights and freedom, but to the exercise thereof in a manner consistent with public order, morality and health. After all, the goodwill of the majority community in any country is the greatest and the safest guarantee for the fulfilment of Constitutional obligations, even more than law courts or executive authorities.[118]

The Report aligns public order, morality, and health with 'the goodwill of the majority community', subordinating individual rights to concerns for communal and national protection. In its model of religious freedom, or 'religious liberty', it utilizes a particular conception of religion: not just as the sphere of individual autonomy, but 'as the basis of political and communal identity... [which] needed to be preserved in order to preserve the unity of India itself'.[119]

The Report reveals a split self-awareness: it brings attention to the dominant position of Hinduism in India and yet presents Hinduism—and, by extension, national unity—as vulnerable to the threat of Christian missionary activity. It is clear from the Report that Christian missionary activity tapped into deep-seated colonial anxieties. The experience of colonization and the ongoing economic and cultural dominance of Western interests meant that Indian Hindus could conceive of themselves simultaneously as beneficiaries of the political rights of a majority and vulnerable (with entitlement to protection) as a minority.[120]

The Niyogi Report in many ways laid the groundwork for contemporary anti-conversion laws.[121] The overly broad and open-textured notions of public order and morality have been built into arguments for the justification of anti-conversion laws including by institutions such as courts with a mandate to protect individual rights. The Supreme Court echoed the Report's concerns about public order and morality in its landmark 1997 decision, *Rev. Stanislaus v. State of Madhya Pradesh*.[122] *Stanislaus* was an appeal against judgments from the High Courts of Orissa[123] and Madhya Pradesh[124] on the constitutionality of anti-conversion laws in those states. While the Orissa law was ultimately struck down on the basis that it was in excess of legal authority (*ultra vires*),[125] the Madhya Pradesh High Court upheld the right of the state to enact such laws by arguing that it fell within the category of 'public order', which, according to Article 246 of the Constitution, is within the jurisdiction of the state governments.[126]

118 Ibid. Vol. 1, No. 993, para. 4.

119 Bauman (n. 107) 208.

120 As Kenneth W. Jones puts it, 'as a result of centuries of foreign domination the Hindu community, in spite of its majority status, took on many of the attitudes that are typical of suppressed minorities'. Jones, 'Politicized Hinduism: The Ideology and Program of the Hindu Mahasabha' in R. Baird (ed.), *Religion in Modern India* (1981) 447. Quoted in Bauman (n 107) 194. See also Jaffrelot (n. 21) 19–25.

121 Viswanathan (n. 114) 336.

122 *Rev.* Stanislaus *v. State of Madhya Pradesh* AIR 1977 SC 908. See Jenkins (n. 86) 115–16.

123 *Yulitha Hyde v. State of Orissa* AIR 1973 Orissa 116.

124 *Rev. Stanislaus v. State of Madhya Pradesh* AIR 1975 MP 163.

125 Neufeldt, 'Conversion and the Courts', 13 *Journal of Hindu-Christian Studies* (2000) 1, 2.

126 The Constitution of India, Art. 246 sets out India's federal structure and defines the powers distributed between the federal (or Union) government and the state government, as well as powers that are to be shared by both. Public order is expressly reserved to the state governments.

In *Stanislaus*, the Supreme Court largely adopted the ruling of the Madhya High Court, relying on the public order clause to argue that such restrictions on efforts to convert are constitutional. The Supreme Court stated that public order 'contains a wide connotation',[127] reasoning that 'if an attempt is made to raise communal passions, e.g. on the ground that some one has been "forcibly" converted to another religion, it would, in all probability, give rise to an apprehension of a breach of the public order, affecting the community at large'.[128] The judgment ultimately concluded that the right to propagate religious tenets is subordinate to the preservation of public order, which it defined as 'the state of tranquility which prevails among the members of a political society as a result of internal regulations enforced by the government which they have established'.[129] In widening the scope and conception of 'public order' the Supreme Court placed the regulation of conversion under Entry I of list II of the Seventh Schedule, and therefore properly within the ambit of state regulation. Under this broad reading of 'public order', state legislatures could pass laws prohibiting forced conversions as such conversions would have 'created public disorder in the states'.[130]

The Supreme Court decision, read together with the unidirectional 'Freedom of Religion' laws it upholds, brings into sharp focus the underlying purpose and politics of anti-conversion laws in India. These laws are largely made and upheld to construct and protect the dominant position of Hinduism. As Gauri Viswanathan comments: '"Freedom of religion" came to be a euphemism for freedom *from* religion . . . the bills . . . were primarily intended to protect Hinduism against the incursions of other proselytizing religions, revealing the collusion of the state in the preservation of Hinduism.'[131] The state laws draw on religious freedom discourse to legitimize the subjection of religious freedom to public order—an interpretative move that is perhaps understandable when one considers that the indeterminate and restrained language of religious freedom is being interpreted through an unsettling legacy of colonialism. Like Malaysia, a type of double-speak facilitates the passage of anti-conversion laws: the laws rely on the discourse of religious freedom to authorize their cause, and simultaneously subvert the spirit of religious freedom by using it to perpetuate a politics of dominance in which public order or the 'state of tranquility' is understood as dependent on the privileged position of the Hindu population.[132]

[127] *Rev. Stanislaus v. State of Madhya Pradesh* (n. 122) 614, available at http://indiankanoon.org/doc/1308071/ (last visited). See also http://notacoda.net/2014/08/17/indias-anti-conversion-laws-the-right-to-propagate-and-the-mainstreaming-of-chauvinism/ (last visited 23 August 2018).

[128] *Rev. Stanislaus v. State of Madhya Pradesh* (n. 122) 617. [129] Ibid. [130] Ibid.

[131] Viswanathan (n. 114) 337.

[132] In an interesting recent twist, however, disadvantaged groups have threatened to convert *away* from Hinduism if their demands for better treatment are not met. These demands have been made in part in response to certain secular advantages that have been provided to encourage non-Hindus to convert to Hindusim. Lal, 'Ghar wapsi fallout: Meet our demands, else we'll convert to Islam, say UP Dalits', *Firstpost India*, 10 January 2015, available at http://www.firstpost.com/india/ghar-wapsi-fall-out-meet-our-demands-else-well-convert-to-islam-say-dalits-2039485.html (last visited 23 August 2018).

5. Restrictions on Religious Freedom under International Law

In his justification of the *Lina Joy* decision, Professor Shamrahayu A. Aziz turns to the public order limitation provisions in the Universal Declaration of Human Rights (UDHR)[133] and the International Covenant on Civil and Political Rights (ICCPR)[134] to explain and justify proselytism restrictions in Malaysia:

> Although these two international documents do not form the hard law of the country, many have actually looked at them as forming certain standards on human rights issues. The considerations or the grounds for the restriction include the importance of public safety or public order, which, in the context of the Malaysian social and political fabric imply a strong basis for the imposition of restrictions on the freedom to propagate a doctrine which is against the majority religion.[135]

Whatever the merits of his analysis, this line of reasoning raises some important questions: How would the public order arguments canvassed in the case studies be treated as a matter of international law? Would the public order restrictions placed on proselytism and conversion in Malaysia and India be protected under the human rights regime? A brief overview of religious freedom as it exists in international law reveals that traditional understandings of religious freedom cannot properly address or redress the problem of majoritarian oppression, particularly when it masquerades as legitimate public order restrictions on religious freedom.

The right to freedom of religion is enshrined in a number of international human rights instruments. Article 18 of the UDHR is the primary articulation of this right. It provides:

> Everyone has the right to freedom of thought, conscience and religion; this right includes *freedom to change his religion or belief*, and freedom, either alone or in community with others and in public or private, to manifest his religion or belief in teaching, practice, worship and observance.[136]

The rights contained in the UDHR are subject to the general limitation contained in Article 29(2) that:

> In exercise of his rights and freedoms, everyone shall be subject only to such limitations as are determined by law solely for the purpose of securing due recognition and respect for the rights and freedoms of others and of meeting the just requirement of morality, public order and the general welfare in a democratic society.

The wording of Article 18(1) of the ICCPR[137] is very similar to that of the UDHR. The most notable change is that the clear language of 'freedom to change' is replaced by 'freedom to have or adopt'. The ICCPR also includes in Article 18(2) a prohibition on 'coercion that would limit' the freedom of an individual to have or adopt a

[133] Universal Declaration of Human Rights, UN GA Res. 217 (III) A, 10 December 1948 (hereinafter 'Universal Declaration').

[134] ICCPR (n. 5).

[135] Aziz, 'Propagation of Religious Doctrines to Muslims: A Legal Perspective', 2 *Malaya Law Journal* (2010) cx, 5.

[136] UDHR (n. 133) (emphasis added).

[137] ICCPR (n. 5).

religion or belief. The right in Article 18 is subject to a limitation clause that is similar but not identical to the UDHR: 'Freedom to manifest one's religion or belief may be subject only to such limitations as are prescribed by law and are necessary to protect public safety, order, health or morals or the fundamental rights and freedoms of others.' The debates in relation to Article 18 revisited some of the controversies experienced in the drafting of the UDHR where the right to change religion was subject to some debate.[138] A number of Muslim states challenged the wording that allowed all individuals the right to 'maintain or to change religion'.[139] The issue of inclusion of the right to change religion was contentious in the debate with some Muslim states arguing that all reference to the right to change religion should be removed from the ICCPR.[140] These arguments were vigorously contested by Western states. The compromise position reached was to use the wording to 'have or adopt' a religion, with most delegates agreeing that such language encompassed the right to change one's religion.[141] However, this was the first step in the move to sideline the clear notion of the right to change religion, reflected in the Universal Declaration, from the international conception of religious freedom.[142]

It is important to note that neither proselytism nor the freedom to disseminate a religion is (directly) mentioned in international documents.[143] While teaching is included within the scope of Article 18(1), there is no clarity about whether this teaching might extend to include those who are not co-religionists in an attempt to convert them or whether it is simply an internal matter within the religion. However, the protection of freedom of expression in the ICCPR (which usually includes both the right to convey unpopular ideas and to be exposed to such ideas) provides an additional form of legal support for the right to proselytize. The issue, however, has never been without controversy in the international arena.

Compounding the lack of agreement around the scope of the international protection of freedom of religion and belief with respect to proselytism/conversion are the limitations contained in Article 18(3). Recognizing the capacity of these terms

[138] For a discussion on the controversies surrounding the drafting of the UDHR, see Clark, 'The United Nations and Religious Freedom', 11 *New York University Journal of International Law and Politics* (1978) 197, 200; B. Tahzib, *Freedom of Religion or Belief: Ensuring Effective International Legal Protection* (1996) 66–7; Lerner, 'The Nature and Minimum Standards of Freedom of Religion or Belief', *Brigham Young University Law Review* (2000) 909. For comments of the Saudi Arabian delegate, see UNGAOR, C.3, 127th mtg, 391, 392, A/C.3/SR. 127 (1948) 3(l). Cited in Evans, 'Chinese Law and the International Protection of Religious Freedom', 44 *Journal of Church and State* (2002) 749, 751–6.

[139] Aargaard, 'Proselytism and Privacy: Some Reflections on the Tantur Conference on Religious Freedom', 50 *The Ecumenical Review* (2009) 464, 465. 15 UNGAOR, C.3, 1021st, 1023rd, 1025th mtg, UN Doc. A/C.3/SR. 1021, 1023, 10295 (1960); the proposal by Saudi Arabia to delete the phrase was subsequently withdrawn, 15 UNGAOR C.3, 1026th mtg 222, A/C.3/SR.1026 (1960).

[140] S. Chowdhury, *Rule of Law in a State of Emergency* (1989) 221. Cited in Evans (n. 138) 755.

[141] 15 UNGAOR, C3, 1027th mtg, UN Doc A/C.3/SR. 1027 (1960); Scheinin, 'Article 18', in A. Eide *et al.*, *The Universal Declaration of Human Rights: A Commentary* (1992) 265. Cited in Evans (n. 138) 755.

[142] Scheinin cited in Evans (n. 138) 755.

[143] Danchin, *Of Prophets* (n. 3) 259. See also Stahnke (n. 11) 276 (footnote 66), citing Evans, *Religious Liberty and International Law in Europe* (1997) 194. (Quoting Report of the Working Group to the CHR, E/CN.4/56, art. 15).

to be used too broadly to restrict religious freedom, the Human Rights Committee has noted that:

Article 18.3 permits restrictions on the freedom to manifest religion or belief only if limitations are prescribed by law and are necessary to protect public safety, order or morals, or the fundamental rights and freedoms of others... The committee observes that paragraph 3 of article 18 is to be strictly interpreted: restrictions are not allowed on grounds not specified there, even if they would be allowed as restrictions to other rights protected in the Covenant, such as national security. Limitations may be applied only for those purposes for which they were prescribed and must be directly related and proportionate to the specific need on which they are predicated.[144]

Yet a range of issues remains around the scope and application of Article 18(3) limitations. Danchin explains that in order to understand the function of Article 18(3), we need first to appreciate the distinction between the freedom to hold beliefs (what is sometimes referred to as *forum internum*) and the freedom to manifest beliefs (the *forum externum*). While the former is considered to be absolutely protected from interference by the law, i.e. not subject to limitation by the state, the latter is subject to valid limitations—as can be seen by the language of Article 18(3) which applies only to the 'freedom to manifest one's religion'.[145] But even if we are able to draw a clear distinction between what constitutes *forum internum* and *forum externum* (and the divide is highly contested), the language used to describe the limitations placed on the latter—'prescribed by the law' and 'necessary to protect public safety, order, health or morals or the fundamental rights and freedoms of others'—are themselves open-textured and indeterminate.

The case studies demonstrate the need for a certain degree of indeterminacy in international law to accommodate the particularities of different national legal orders—particularities that 'also reflect a specific concept of the protection of public order'.[146] As Harold Berman argues, 'rights may properly be declared in universal terms, but their application in specific cases must always take into account the specific circumstances of those cases'.[147] But the case studies also suggest a need for placing checks on appeals to communal religious rights, especially when such arguments are used to advance majoritarian or state interests. Unchecked claims of the collective good 'threaten to eviscerate even a modest conception of the individual right to freedom of religion or belief', but they also threaten to eviscerate the collective rights of minority or dissenting groups. It is one thing to rely on public order restrictions to protect the existence of a dominant religious group; it is quite another to draw on those arguments actively to protect or maintain the very dominancy of

144 See Human Rights Committee, General Comment No. 22 (48) (art. 18), UN GAOR, 48th Sess., Supp. No. 40, para. 3, UN Doc. CCPR/C/21/Rev. 1/Add.1 (1989), reprinted in UN Doc. HR1/GEN/1/Rev.1 (1994) 26. Cited in Stahnke (n. 11) 260–7.

145 Danchin, *Of Prophets* (n. 3) 260.

146 Martinez-Torron, 'The Permissible Scope of Legal Limitations on the Freedom of Religion or Belief: The European Convention on Human Rights', 3 *Global Jurist Advances* (2003) 2, 12.

147 Berman, 'Religious Rights in Russia at a Time of Tumultuous Transition: A Historical Theory' in J. Witte and J. van der Vyver (eds), *Religious Human Rights in Global Perspective: Legal Perspectives* (1996) 285–6.

those groups, especially when such measures take place at the expense of individual and minority group rights. This structure leaves the notion of religious freedom 'vulnerable to far-reaching and potentially oppressive limitations',[148] allowing dominant religious groups to stake their claims with the language provided by international law, often obscuring the fact that such claims are advanced to promote a conception of the collective good that is closely aligned with the identity and the interests of the nation state.[149]

While space does not permit a full discussion of the issue, it is also worth noting that the issue of conversion/proselytism and public order becomes more complex in countries like India and Malaysia where there is some degree of recognition of personal religious laws. When being identified as a member of a particular religion gives rise to certain legal rights or obligations, there will be reasons for changing religion that might not be associated with personal faith (for example, to obtain the benefit of better access to rights on divorce). When the legal system itself is partially based on religious identity, the challenge to the state that is created by allowing fluidity, change, or ambiguity with respect to what religion a person belongs to is far greater than it is in a state where religion is not relevant to the applicable legal system.

6. Conclusion: The Public Order Argument

The United Nation's Special Rapporteur on freedom of religion or belief recently made the following observation about the pattern of religious conflict in India:

> There is a continued climate of fear, and maybe that's even the purpose. The acts of violence are part of a broader pattern of instigating fear into the minorities, sending them a message they don't belong to this country unless they either keep at the margins or turn to Hinduism.[150]

Both in India and Malaysia, (anti-)conversion and proselytism court rulings and state enactments themselves have occasioned violence and unrest.[151] In both states, the courts have pointed to episodes of religious violence to buttress their public order arguments. The Supreme Court in *Stanislaus*, for example, concluded its decision with the following statement:

[148] Danchin, *Of Prophets* (n. 3) 276. [149] See generally Hasson (n. 1) 81.

[150] Vishal Arora, 'UN Official: India's "Conversion" Laws Threaten Religious Freedom (2014), available at http://blogs.wsj.com/indiarealtime/2014/03/10/un-official-indias-conversion-laws-threaten-religious-freedom (last visited 23 August 2018).

[151] This pattern is in keeping with Grim and Finke's study, identifying a strong correlation between government restrictions on religious freedom and higher levels of religious persecution and violence. B. Grim and R. Finke, *The Price of Freedom Denied: Religious Persecution and Conflict in the Twenty-First Century* (2011). Discussed in Durham, 'Religious Freedom in a Worldwide Setting: Comparative Reflections', presented at the Seventeenth Plenary Session of the Pontifical Academy of Social Sciences, Rome, Italy, 29 April–3 May 2011, available at http://www.religlaw.org/content/blurb/files/Religious%20Freedom%20in%20a%20Worldwide%20Setting.pdf (last visited 23 August 2018). See also Hertzke, 'Religious Freedom in the World Today: Paradox and Promise' in M. Glendon and H. Zacher, *Universal Rights in a World of Diversity: The Case of Religious Freedom* (2011) 114–15.

[I]f an attempt is made to raise communal passions, e.g. on the ground that some one has been 'forcibly' converted to another religion, it would, in all probability, give rise to an apprehension of a breach of the public order, affecting the community at large. The impugned Acts therefore fall within the purview of Entry I of List II of the Seventh Schedule as they are meant to avoid disturbances to the public order by prohibiting conversion from one religion to another in a manner reprehensible to the conscience of the community.[152]

The Court of Appeal in the *Allah* case relied on a similar argument:

[T]he Minister in charge of home security and public order need not wait for violence to break out before exercising his discretion to prevent such violence that [is] likely to lead to lawlessness and public disorder... [E]vents that unfolded soon after the learned High Court judge pronounced her decision on the respondent's judicial review application showed that the concern of the first appellant on the potential harm to public order and safety had become a reality and not merely imaginary.[153]

This line of reasoning has attracted much criticism from legal experts and commentators in both jurisdictions. Writing about the *Stanislaus* decision, Bhairav Acharya notes that it wrongfully holds individual expressions of religious belief responsible for disruptions to public order, and 'excuses the lumpen mob that actually causes public disorder and violence'.[154] Dian A.H. Shah similarly observes of the *Allah* case: 'The upshot of these cases is that the religious rights of minorities should yield to the greater good, never mind that the threat to that "good" would actually emanate from the majority.'[155] Andrew Harding's criticism of the case is likewise biting:

If the Minister is allowed to restrict acts which may provoke a hostile reaction or create a hostile environment, then he is in effect surrendering his exercise of discretion to those who pose the greatest or voice the loudest threat to public order, i.e. those who hold the most extreme views on the matter, and are prepared to threaten public order in expressing them. No government, surely, can properly restrict the exercise of individual liberty on the ground that it is likely to provoke a hostile reaction?[156]

There is certainly something amiss and unintuitive about a constitutional rights system that, while not necessarily designed to do so, 'empower[s] the majority instead of restraining the will of the majority'.[157] Particularly in countries with deep religious tensions, constitutions 'are seen as important guarantees against government excesses of power and restraint on the will of the majority'.[158] At the international level, too, religious freedom discourse is meant, at least in part, to guarantee the 'rights of religious minorities to observe their traditions and to participate

[152] *Rev.* Stanislaus *v. State of Madhya Pradesh* (n. 122) 614. [153] *Allah* case (n. 74) 509.

[154] Acharya, 'India's "Anti-conversion" Laws, the "Right to Propagate", and the Mainstreaming of Chauvinism', available at http://notacoda.net/2014/08/17/indias-anti-conversion-laws-the-right-to-propagate-and-the-mainstreaming-of-chauvinism/ (last visited 23 August 2018).

[155] Shah, 'Constitutional Arrangements on Religion and Religious Freedom in Malaysia and Indonesia: Furthering or Inhibiting Rights?', 1 *The Indonesian Journal of International and Comparative Law* (2014) 260, 294.

[156] A. Harding, 'Language, Religion, and the Law', available at https://my.news.yahoo.com/blogs/loyar-burok/language-religion-law-andrew-harding-094116777.html (last visited 23 August 2018).

[157] Shah (n. 155) 262. [158] Ibid. 261.

equally in civic life'.[159] That public-order considerations enable a subversion of this guarantee in two vastly disparate legal landscapes gestures toward a crucial failing of religious freedom discourse. Proselytism and conversion are often the points at which religious freedom as a first principle of human rights law begins to unravel. The difficulties also present us with an opportunity or a challenge to return to first principles of constitutionalism and human rights theory, but to confront that challenge will entail bringing a critical eye to the postcolonial rhetoric of majoritarian-minoritism.

[159] Adcock, 'Debating Conversion' (n. 113) 363.

5

Too Much Secularism? Religious Freedom in European History and the European Court of Human Rights

Samuel Moyn

In January 1999, Belgin Dogru, an 11-year-old Muslim girl living in Flers, a small French town in lower Normandy, began wearing a headscarf to school. Her teacher ordered her to remove it for gym class, and the school expelled her because she refused to obey. Dogru invoked her right to manifest her religion, but found no relief from administrators or courts. She remained in Flers, finishing high school by correspondence as her case made its way through the French courts to the European Court of Human Rights (ECtHR), which agreed in a 2008 ruling that no violation of her religious freedom had occurred.[1]

The case was not an isolated one.[2] A series of decisions by the ECtHR in the era of the pan-European headscarf controversies has thrown open an important debate on the trajectory of the principle of religious freedom. The Court, most recently in the case of *Lautsi v. Italy* permitting crucifixes to be displayed in Italian schools, adopts a forgiving attitude towards Christian symbols and practices permeating the public sphere but does not offer comparable protection to Muslim symbols and practices suppressed by state legislation and administrative decisions.[3] This trend reached a crescendo in the striking case of *S.A.S. v. France*, which appealed to the importance of 'living together' (*vivre ensemble*) to justify a ban on Muslim religious attire in public spaces.[4] Together, these interlocking attitudes suggest that the renowned European devotion to a neutral state, existing above competing religions, is more image than reality.

[1] ECtHR, *Dogru v. France*, Appl. no. 27058/05, Judgment of 4 December 2008, paras 5–9. All ECtHR decisions are available online at http://hudoc.echr.coe.int/.

[2] Decaux, 'Chronique d'une jurisprudence annoncée: laicité française et liberté religieuse devant la Cour européenne des droits de l'homme', 82 *Revue trimestrielle des droits de l'homme* (2010) 251.

[3] ECtHR, *Lautsi v. Italy*, Appl. no. 30814/06, Judgment of 18 March 2011 (Chamber); ECtHR, *Lautsi v. Italy*, Appl. no. 30814/06, Judgment of 18 March 2011 (Grand Chamber). See Ch. 7 of this work, Lorenzo Zucca, 'Rethinking Secularism in Europe'.

[4] ECtHR, *S.A.S. v. France*, Appl. no. 43835, Judgment of 1 July 2014 (Grand Chamber). See Zucca (n. 3).

Too Much Secularism? Religious Freedom in European History and the European Court of Human Rights. First Edition. Samuel Moyn
Published 2019 by Oxford University Press.

Do the cases, then, reflect a Christian Islamophobia concealed in the principled garb of secularism? Many commentators see nothing wrong with the Court's decisions, nor with the norm of religious freedom in the European Convention on Human Rights (ECHR). At worst, there may simply be a mistake in the way in which the Court applies the norm. But it is worth paying attention to the more thoroughgoing criticism that insists that the decisions follow from a deeper syndrome that has existed for many years (if not centuries), in part because more uncompromising critics are right to resist ascribing the results to accident alone. One case can be an honest mistake, but an almost unbroken trend demands some other interpretation.[5] For both defenders and critics of the Court's mission to sustain a supranational human rights regime—indeed to be in the vanguard of such regimes and thus a model for the world to emulate—much is at stake in deciding how to interpret the history of religious freedom. Is it possible that it is poisoned at the root?

In several of the cases, the ECtHR worked with a historical narrative of the rise of secularism close to that which John Rawls offered in his late 'political liberalism'. In this story, the secular political space is the outcome of a bloody era of early modern religious warfare: what began with the nervous truce of a *modus vivendi* evolved into an overlapping consensus featuring not just peace but justice too.[6] In this narrative, religious freedom is a long-term companion of the creation of a secular political space, in which a transcendent state rises above the attempt by sects to infuse public matters with their private faith. That faith is protected in private on condition that it stays there. Ironically, those sceptical of European secularism see the same tight relationship between religious freedom and secular politics. They agree that, early on, the former became allied to and swept up in the rise of the latter. But for them, since secularism amounts to not much more than what Edward Said once denounced as 'orientalism' in particularly effective disguise, the bias against Muslims in the ECtHR cases is entirely unsurprising. On this view, precisely because of religious freedom's long-term links to the creation of a secular political space, it has proven discriminatory in practice.

In what follows, I begin by showing that it is largely wrong to assume a long-term alliance between religious freedom and 'secularism'. The actual history of the principle of religious freedom points in a very different direction from that which either the enthusiastic or the hostile account suggests. In understanding how the decisions have played out in the way they have, I do not rule out strategic assumptions by contemporary judges about the ECtHR's institutional viability and the interface of its role with the often roiling politics of Europe's religious and ethnic diversity today. But if the apparent discrimination is rooted in the principles of religious freedom that the Court has inherited and deployed, they are not principles that have been connected to an exclusionary secularism for long.

[5] Thus, Judge Françoise Tulkens, in a rare dissent in one of the cases, viewed the result merely as a misapplication of the norms, without asking, as this chapter will, why the Court would view the wearing of a headscarf as a threat to democracy. See ECtHR, *Şahin v. Turkey*, Appl. no. 44774/98, Judgment of 10 November 2005 (Tulkens, J., dissenting), esp. at para. 10, as well as the similar dissent in *S.A.S.* (n. 4) by Judges Helena Jäderblom and Angelika Nußberger.

[6] J. Rawls, *Political Liberalism* (1994).

Against this deeper background, I then turn to a closer analysis of the era when religious freedom was internationalized through the Universal Declaration of Human Rights (UDHR) and Europeanized in the form of the ECHR itself. As in its earliest origins, so also in its mid-twentieth century iteration, religious freedom was not part of a secularist enterprise, whether one defines it as the project of privatizing religious affiliation, creating a 'naked public square',[7] or—as suggested by the critics—concealing the Christian faith behind the mask of neutrality. On the contrary, religious freedom was historically a principle that was most often intended to marginalize secularism. Indeed, it was as part of such a campaign that the ECHR, including its Article 9 on religious freedom, first appeared, little more than a half century ago. If so, the secularism of the ECtHR's headscarf cases is a recent artefact, primarily resulting from the collapse of European Christianity which has been experienced in living memory. Even more ironically, I tentatively suggest, the headscarf cases actually owe part of their doctrinal rationale, and perhaps their exclusionary implications, not to the secularist associations of religious freedom but to the legacy of the religious struggle against communism, once feared as secularism incarnate. The Muslim has taken the place of the communist in the contemporary European imagination—and, above all, in the history of the religious liberty norm.

There are, evidently, many stories to tell about the history of religious freedom; mine summarizes innovative recent scholarship for a specific argumentative purpose. One of my main aims is to recall features of the long and contested relationship of religion and politics which are often overlooked. The familiar liberal story of the necessary transcendence by the state of the sphere of interfaith competition and fratricide is good at capturing some developments while failing to recognize the powerful and direct influence Christianity has had on European and transatlantic politics and law (including the ECHR itself) until recently. The postcolonial account, by contrast, has given us sobering reasons to be sceptical of secularism, while ignoring the fact that current interpretations of religious freedom may actually owe some of their defects to how embattled secularism was in European lands for many years. The guiding theme when exposing the limitations of both accounts is that religious freedom emerged long ago and until lately functioned for the sake of the continuation of Christianity's public dominance—not secularism's displacement of it. The historical reframing is allied to a normative goal: to afford contemporary European secularism a confrontation with a critical history that permits it to survive the encounter in some future and better form, instead of being cast aside altogether.

1. The Court, the Cases, and the Critique of Secularism

Article 9 of the ECHR has two clauses. Announcing the principle of religious freedom, it begins by closely following the UDHR: 'Everyone has the right to freedom of thought, conscience and religion; this right includes freedom to change his religion or belief and freedom, either alone or in community with others and in public

[7] See R.J. Neuhaus, *The Naked Public Square* (1984).

or private, to manifest his religion or belief, in worship, teaching, practice and observance' (Article 9(1)). But the ECHR also assumes that, unlike the inviolable right to the sanctity of the *forum internum* of conscience, the right to manifest internal beliefs can be overridden: 'Freedom to manifest one's religion or beliefs shall be subject only to such limitations as are prescribed by law and are necessary in a democratic society in the interests of public safety, for the protection of public order, health or morals, or the protection of the rights and freedoms of others.' (Article 9(2))[8]

Even before the '9/11' attacks in the United States, the ECtHR—which had not really taken up Article 9's promise of religious freedom until the 1990s—had shown itself willing to interpret that second provision in ways that treated Islam as a second-class religion, not entitled to the same sort of consideration as the Christian faith.[9] Since then, it has issued a series of decisions that have granted European states wide latitude to ban Muslim symbols. In *Dahlab v. Switzerland*, a Christian schoolteacher who had converted to Islam and began to wear a headscarf to work was told by authorities to choose between her headscarf and her job.[10] A Swiss federal court held that public safety and order justified the administrative decision. On her appeal, the ECtHR agreed that while Dahlab incontestably had an Article 9(1) claim, Article 9(2)'s list of exceptions justified the abridgment. '[T]he wearing of a headscarf', the Court reasoned, 'might have some kind of proselytising effect.'[11] But if *Dahlab* dealt with a teacher, allowing the court to emphasize the power of a role model in the classroom (even though no student or parent had complained), *Leyla Şahin v. Turkey*, like *Dogru*, and a series of cases testing France's 2004 law banning conspicuous religious symbols in public schools, concerned Muslim students.[12] The most visible and discussed of these cases, *Şahin*, involved a medical student who had worn the headscarf in her training in Vienna but was told she could not do so at her Turkish certification test. The *Dogru* case, following the *Şahin* ruling, emphasized 'the state's role as the neutral and impartial organiser of the exercise of various religions, faiths and beliefs'. The state's service as secular arbiter above the fray, a hard-won outcome of

[8] Convention for the Protection of Human Rights and Fundamental Freedoms 1952, 213 UNTS 222.

[9] Notably, the European Commission (parent body of the ECtHR, and in the original treaty scheme the sole source of the Court's cases) sided against a Muslim applicant from Great Britain claiming that Salman Rushdie's *Satanic Verses* violated the then-extant common law ban on blasphemy—though the Commission, like the Court later, was willing to uphold blasphemy prosecutions in cases of offence to Christian sensibilities. ECtHR, *X Ltd and Y v. United Kingdom*, Appl. no. 8710/79, Judgment of 7 May 1982; ECtHR, *Choudhury v. United Kingdom*, Appl. no. 17439/90, Judgment of 5 March 1991; ECtHR, *Otto-Preminger-Institut v. Austria*, Appl. no 13470/87, (ser. A), Judgment of 20 September 1994; ECtHR, *Wingrove v. United Kingdom*, Appl. no. 17419/90, Judgment of 25 November 1996. Prior to *Lautsi* (n. 3), the Court allowed a Swiss ban of minarets to proceed. See ECtHR, *La Ligue des Musulmans de Suisse v. Switzerland*, Appl. no. 66274/09, Judgment of 28 June 2011; ECtHR, *Ouardiri v. Switzerland*, Appl. no. 65840/09, Judgment of 28 June 2011.

[10] ECtHR, *Dahlab v. Switzerland*, Appl. no. 42393/98, Judgment of 15 February 2001.

[11] *Dahlab* (n. 10) 9 (official English translation).

[12] ECtHR, *Aktas v. France*, Appl. no. 43563/08, Judgment of 30 June 2009; ECtHR, *Bayrak v. France*, Appl. no. 14308/08, Judgment of 30 June 2009; ECtHR, *Gamaleddyn v. France*, Appl. no. 18527/08, Judgment of 30 June 2009; ECtHR, *Ghazal v. France*, Appl. no. 29134/08, Judgment of 30 June 2009; ECtHR, *J. Singh v. France*, Appl. no. 25463/08, Judgment of 30 June 2009; and ECtHR, *R. Singh v. France*, Appl. no. 27561/08, Judgment of 30 June 2009. These cases also involved Sikh boys wearing a *keski* or turban to school.

past conflict, remained 'conducive to public order, religious harmony and tolerance in a democratic society'.[13] The Court observed that though 'the wearing of religious signs was not inherently incompatible with the principle of secularism in schools', it 'became so according to the conditions in which they were worn and the consequences that the wearing of a sign might have'.[14] Similarly, in *S.A.S. v. France*, the Court concluded that the goal of creating the conditions for public interaction 'in a democratic society' permitted a ban on practices that one might (in fact, that some do) regard as a strike against pluralism rather than on behalf of it.[15]

Combined with the ECtHR's nonchalant attitude towards Christian symbols in public, its disposition of cases involving Muslim ones seems hard to understand.[16] Even as the Court tolerates a public space saturated by the historical residues and contemporary practices of Christians—most graphically in the recent and hotly contested *Lautsi* case—Europe's increasing number of Muslim citizens have not found a sympathetic hearing as their minority practices are banned by national laws, local regulations, and administrative decisions. A pretextual neutrality in the service of discriminatory results is precisely the syndrome that the thoroughgoing criticism of 'secularism', so influential today, has diagnosed as a glaring form of orientalism.

In her essay on the politics of the veil, to take one example, Joan Wallach Scott worries that the secularism of public authorities is simply:

> ... a mask for the domination of 'others,' a form of ethnocentrism or crypto-Christianity... Its claim to universalism (a false universalism in the eyes of its critics) has justified the exclusion or marginalization of those from non-European cultures (often immigrants from former colonies) whose systems of belief do not separate public and private in the same way.[17]

This line of criticism frequently attributes discrimination against Muslims, viewed as prevalent in Western societies and in international political relationships, to deep historical roots. According to Talal Asad, the entire concept of 'religion' is a modern Protestant one that tilts against Islam in its theoretical foundations and political deployments. Protestant modernity defined religion as internal faith (precisely the value most central to contemporary human rights regimes, including in the non-abrogable Article 9(1) freedom of belief).[18] According to the critique of secularism,

[13] *Dogru* (n. 1) para. 62.

[14] Ibid. para. 70.

[15] *S.A.S.* (n. 4) paras 137–59.

[16] For a range of legal comment, see D. McGoldrick, *Human Rights and Religion: The Islamic Headscarf Debate in Europe* (2006); Evans, 'The "Islamic Scarf" in the European Court of Human Rights', 7 *Melbourne Journal of International Law* (May 2006) 52; Langlaude, 'Indoctrination, Secularism, Religious Liberty and the ECHR', 55 *International and Comparative Law Quarterly* (October 2006) 929; Gibson, 'An Unwelcome Trend: Religious Dress and Human Rights Following Leyla Şahin vs. Turkey', 25 *Netherlands Human Rights Journal* (2007) 599; Rorive, 'Religious Symbols in Public Space: In Search of a European Answer', 30 *Cardozo Law Review* (June 2009) 2669; and Julie Ringejheim, 'Rights, Religion and the Public Sphere: The European Court of Human Rights in Search of a Theory?' in L. Zucca and C. Ungureanu (eds), *Law, State, and Religion in the New Europe: Dilemmas and Debates* (2010) 283. The literature on the larger European headscarf debate is by now endless. An especially insightful multinational treatment is C. Joppke, *Veil: Mirror of Identity* (2009).

[17] J. Wallach Scott, *The Politics of the Veil* (2007) 92.

[18] See T. Asad, *Genealogies of Religion: Discipline and Reasons of Power in Christianity and Islam* (1993) and *Formations of the Secular: Christianity, Islam, Modernity* (2003). The critique of secularism is very diverse, to be sure, including in the political sympathies of the sometimes strange bedfellows who

given these priorities, Islam with its emphasis on law and practice, and its refusal to privatize faith, is likely to lose out. When it comes to religious practices, Asad continues, Christianity naturalizes its own practices while making alternative ones seem like intolerable interferences. Churches litter the American and European landscape while mosques in Manhattan and minarets in Switzerland are viewed with concern, and Christian symbolism saturates public life even as Muslim practices are banned. From this perspective, even the hierarchy of belief and manifestation or faith and practice looks like a falsely neutral stratagem used to police Islam and to make Christianity normative by calling itself secularism. The ECtHR's Muslim headscarf cases, implicating manifestation, are simply further proof of Europe's orientalist shortcomings.[19]

Without justifying the arguable discrimination in the cases, I will suggest that this diagnosis is unpersuasive on both historical and normative grounds. A closer look at the cases shows that the Court offered two rationales for its decisions. The Court certainly did prominently refer to local interpretations and ingrained traditions (in France, Switzerland, and Turkey) of secularist political order. Invoking its well-known judge-made doctrine of 'margin of appreciation'—a perennially controversial principle of deference to national judiciaries—it found that these particular European countries might well have the latitude to forge especially stringent interpretations of secular space. But in doing so, the Court also developed its own interpretation of what democratic societies require; an interpretation that the headscarf offends. This 'democratic minimum' analysis, I will argue, proves to be a valuable clue to the legacy of history in the Court's cases.[20] In this connection, consider *Refah Partisi v. Turkey* (2003), a decision declining to uphold the claims of Turkish applicants whose Islamist political party had been banned. Though already strongly implied in *Dahlab*, the later case made it even clearer that, in the Court's judgment, Muslim practices can be plausibly viewed as threats to a democratic minimum, justifying state abridgment of rights to manifest; and it was cited again in *Şahin* and *Dogru* for precisely that proposition.[21] This complementary element of Article 9

adopt it. Cf., e.g., William Connolly, *Why I Am Not a Secularist* (2000) or Winnifred Fallers Sullivan *et al.* (eds), *After Secular Law* (2011) with S.D. Smith, *The Disenchantment of Secular Discourse* (2010).

[19] Danchin, 'Islam in the Secular *Nomos* of the European Court of Human Rights', 32 *Michigan Journal of International Law* (2011) 663. Another and deeper version of the critique of secularism, also drawing on Asad, focuses not so much on the crypto-Christianity of secularism as on the regulatory consequences of the very distinction between religion and non-religion. Cf. Anidjar, 'Secularism', 33 *Critical Inquiry* (Winter 2008) 52 with Danchin and Mahmood, 'Immunity or Regulation?: Antimonies of Religious Freedom', 113 *South Atlantic Quarterly* (Winter 2014) 63.

[20] This is my rationale for skirting more discussion of the margin of appreciation doctrine, which has received much critical commentary both in general and with respect to the headscarf cases. See, e.g., Kratochvíl, 'The Inflation of the Margin of Appreciation by the European Court of Human Rights', 29 *Netherlands Quarterly of Human Rights* (2011) 289. Of course, sometimes the two doctrines interact, because several countries have the protection of a democratic minimum built or inferred into their constitutional texts.

[21] ECtHR, *Refah Partisi (The Welfare Party) and Others v. Turkey*, Appl. nos 41340/98, 41342/98, and 41344/98, Judgment of 13 February 2003 (Grand Chamber), esp. at para. 93. Though the Court focused on Art. 11's right to assembly, it made clear that its permissive attitude towards a secularist democratic minimum covered the other rights, including Art. 9's protection of the right to manifest religion. For a powerful critique, see Boyle, 'Human Rights, Religion, and Democracy: The Refah Party

jurisprudence—in which the minimum 'necessary in a democratic society' (Article 9(2)) does not protect religious practices but is compatible with their suppression—is more important to evaluating the critique of secularism than the Court's deference to national judiciaries below. For this conceptual basis, on which the cases rest, had nothing originally to do with religion in general or Islam in particular. Instead, its source lies in Cold War anxiety that secularist communism would topple Christian democracy.

In the rest of this chapter, I will show, first from a long-range perspective on religious freedom and then through a focus on its Cold War internationalization, that the norm needs to be kept separate from 'secularism' precisely in order to understand their recent joinder in the European cases and in general. From its origins until a few decades ago, the ideal of religious freedom—including in its form as an international human right codified in the middle of the twentieth century—frequently served as a Christian principle of discrimination. Its purpose was to secure a social and global tilt not against Islam but against secularism. And in a Cold War against a Soviet Union, frequently treated orientalistically as Eastern barbarity, and a godless affront to a civilization which was still viewed as essentially Christian, religious freedom emerged as the keystone human right for which 'the West' stood—but against secularism. Cold War history, and most especially the early history of the ECHR and the ECtHR, indicates that the project of policing threats to a democratic minimum did not begin with the aim of discriminating against any religion but instead aimed to protect one.

The consequences of this finding—which speaks directly to the doctrinal maintenance of the democratic minimum the ECtHR now deploys in Muslim headscarf cases—are significant. What if the more historically accurate and normatively plausible objection to the current ECtHR cases is that they have inadvertently assigned to Muslims the frightening characteristics originally pioneered to cast secularist communism beyond the pale? If so, then the root difficulty in the cases is not so much 'secularism' but elements still persisting from the European regime's—and Europe's—original attempt to keep it at bay.

2. The Origins of Religious Freedom in a Non-Secularist Age

In the depths of Western history, before the Protestant Reformation, crucial steps had already been taken to wrest control of public matters from the church, opening many new possibilities. A state had to exist before anyone could propose the separation of church and state, just as 'politics' had to become, in a revival of classical ideas, an imaginable domain before anyone could hope to purge religion from it.[22]

Case', 1 *Essex Human Rights Review* (2004) 1. The moment in European Union relations with Turkey in which the case was decided has since passed; and Abdullah Gül, once a member of the very Islamist party whose ban the case upheld, was later able to become Turkish president, in a new era in which the political majority approved the lifting of the ban on the headscarf in the university (though the Turkish constitutional court then annulled the measure).

[22] For the longest range speculative narrative, see M. Gauchet, *The Disenchantment of the World: A Political History of Religion*, trans. Oscar Burge (1998), where the invention of political hierarchy after

The very notion of the 'secular' as a non-religious space, superimposed on the term's original temporal meaning (still preserved in the Virgilian motto of the American dollar bill), rose on the basis of medieval distinctions between property that belonged to the church and property open to seizure from it. Yet whatever the preliminaries were to distinguishing state from church institutionally or politics from religion imaginatively, long into modernity it remained possible not simply to have states with established churches but for religion to pervade politics in the most direct and intimate of ways. The central point of this analysis is that the formal split of authority between what belonged to Caesar and what did not hardly implied the decline of religion as a public force. Put differently, secular possibilities of long standing did not translate into secularism.

Perhaps the most important reason, therefore, to doubt that there was an age-old alliance between religious freedom and political secularism is that for a long time the former made its way as a Christian principle while the latter simply did not exist. Contrary to an older view, it is now obvious that promotion of something called 'liberty of conscience' was not an avowed end of the Reformation of Christianity.[23] The progress of this principle has been, over the long term, more a matter of a means becoming an end in itself, since toleration rose originally as a tool in regimes of religiosity and even persecution. In the beginning, freedom of conscience was not in any way a secularist ideal (let alone a religious one masquerading as secularist); it was born in an age in which the highest social premium still fell on collective achievement of some one true faith. It was a device to continue the struggle for the true Christianity, not to end that struggle.

Martin Luther argued for 'the freedom of the Christian man', and introduced some compelling reasons against state interference in the *forum internum* of the seat of conscience, the effects of which can still be seen in European human rights law. But Reformation-era battles, so frequently bloody, were often settled not by severing state and church in the name of individual choice but rather simply by coordinating them—as the renowned principle of the Peace of Augsburg, *cuius regio, eius religio*, demanded. Even in England, among the Puritans, liberty of conscience as a political value originally emerged through very restricted versions of toleration, at first between some antagonistic sects of Protestants (excluding not simply other versions of Protestantism, but also Catholicism, Judaism, Islam, and especially atheism).[24] This was true at the level of social practices, as well as later in the high theory of John Locke and others, even if Locke ultimately went further than some in making room for rival faiths—though perhaps not for Catholicism and definitely not for athe-

'primitive' equality is presented as the beginning of the state's autonomy, and Christianity for various doctrinal reasons proves to be 'the religion for leaving religion behind', establishing a separate domain of politics.

[23] For medieval roots, see Bejczy, '*Tolerantia*: A Medieval Concept', 58 *Journal of the History of Ideas* (1997) 365. Excellent guidance to recent literature on early modernity is to be found in Collins, 'Redeeming the Enlightenment: New Histories of Religious Toleration', 81(3) *Journal of Modern History* (September 2009) 607.

[24] Worden, 'Toleration and the Cromwellian Protectorate' in W.J. Sheils (ed.), *Persecution and Toleration* (1984) 199; cf. Coffey, 'Puritanism and Liberty Revisited: The Case for Toleration in the English Revolution', 41 *Historical Journal* (1998) 961.

ism.[25] Far from spelling a halt to interdenominational struggle or a move to 'the secular', liberty of conscience was invented primarily as a ground rule for further, and contained and non-violent, struggle. And that struggle continued indefinitely. Modern history is as much the attempted globalization of this struggle as it is its replacement by a thoroughgoing secularism. This should not be surprising, for Christianity—in an open, not hidden form—remained central to European lands until very recently.[26]

Of course, freedom of conscience as a 'secularist' ideal whereby a non-discriminatory state keeps religion in private did develop. But if Enlightenment historians have not resolved how far Benedict Spinoza's unusual (because full-blown) secularism paved the way for modernity, this is above all true with respect to the progress of the ideal of freedom of religion. The most plausible source of an expanding culture of toleration, in which freedom of religion became a candidate for a powerful public norm and religion became a more privatized affair than before, was not 'the Reformation' but raucous social interchange and coexistence in the midst of struggle in which appeals to state power remained extremely common.[27] Even theoretically, toleration advanced where and when it did, not through atheistic freethinking but through the slow acceptance by moderates of religious coexistence.[28] The same was certainly true of pre-revolutionary America, whose history shows that breakaway sects of Christians, including breakaway sub-sects like Roger Williams's Rhode Islanders, saw no contradiction between suffering discrimination in one place, then finding another in which to seek the dominance of their own sect—even when their sectarian religious faith called for religious premises for less state discrimination against rivals.[29]

The relaxation of the quest for certainty, an irenic or 'Erasmian' attitude that characterized many versions of the Christian Enlightenment, slowly eroded the zeal with which Christian sects called on the state for assistance in their proselytizing campaigns. It is well known that, to this day, many European countries have

[25] For a brilliant depiction of Locke in context, see J. Marshall, *John Locke, Toleration, and Early Enlightenment Culture* (2006).

[26] Ian Hunter has depicted a turn in German lands to a 'civil' approach that immunized the state against sectarian disputes of the populace, to which another 'metaphysical' school culminating in Immanuel Kant responded by seeking ways of infusing putatively secular reason with purposes that were in fact religious and redemptive. But this powerful story ignores how long straightforwardly religious approaches to governance prevailed. Cf. I. Hunter, *Rival Enlightenments: Civil and Metaphysical Philosophy in Early Modern Germany* (2001) with D. Sorkin, *The Religious Enlightenment: Protestants, Catholics, and Jews from London to Vienna* (2008). See also Bhuta, 'Two Concepts of Religious Freedom in the European Court of Human Rights', 113 *South Atlantic Quarterly* (Winter 2014) 9.

[27] B. Kaplan, *Divided by Faith: Religious Conflict and the Practice of Toleration in Early Modern Europe* (2007).

[28] In fact, some have gone so far as to argue that it was the 'Erastian' attempt to subordinate church to state that, paradoxically, became the main laboratory in which claims regarding freedom of religion were elaborated and tested as well as put into law. The emergence of atheism as a cultural option eventually widespread in Europe is a case study in unintended consequences. See, e.g., M. Hunter and D. Wootton (eds), *Atheism from the Reformation to the Enlightenment* (1992).

[29] Cf. M. Nussbaum, *Liberty of Conscience: In Defense of America's Tradition of Religious Equality* (2008) with Perez Zagorin's letter in response to the *New York Review of Books* discussion of Nussbaum's book: Roger Williams's 'animating conviction [was] that freedom of conscience and religion and the separation of church and state are absolutely essential to the spiritual welfare of Christianity'. Zagorin, 'Christianity and Freedom', *New York Review of Books*, 25 September 2008.

established churches, which (unlike the US Constitution's First Amendment) the ECHR does not forbid. Still, in these Christian lands the inroads of a 'secularism' which confined religion to the private sphere were very slight and halting. It is easy to overstate Enlightenment anti-clericalism, or to rewrite the history of the Enlightenment—as Jonathan Israel has done recently—around the ragtag forces that embraced libertine materialism and defended freedom of conscience for the sake of *libertas philosophandi*. Puzzlingly, secularism's contemporary critics often collude in a similar rewriting. But in fact the Enlightenment was primarily a religious phenomenon, and the political ideal of freedom of conscience made its way first within Protestantism and later in Catholic lands mainly as a religious principle and in slow and modest ways.[30] It continued to advance according to a familiar logic: restricted compromise in which modest inclusion and persistent exclusion were companions. And there was nothing built into the logic that guaranteed increasing inclusion, though in some places it slowly came about. The eighteenth century remained what Lucien Febvre has famously dubbed an earlier era: 'a century that wanted to believe'.[31] By the nineteenth century, it was clear to many analysts that the logic of restricted toleration might solidify rather than undermine a public Christian consensus. Thus, not only did freedom of religion not follow from secularism; in its dominant uses, it involved a rejection rather than an acceptance of indifferentism, or full-blown scepticism, or frightening relativism, which were all theological errors with which secularism was long tasked (indeed by the Catholic Church long into the twentieth century).

The thesis that the full privatization of religion as a matter of conscience rather than public meaning or collective practice is what early modern Christian developments were about, even determining what could count as 'religion', has gone very far in recent years, thanks to Asad's important work. But in spite of a kernel of truth, his suggestion is false. It not only leaves out the rather large number of Catholics on the European continent, who are so relevant here because they were only to embrace religious freedom in the later twentieth century—precisely when Christian Democracy, not secularism, became dominant on the European continent in the era of the drafting of the ECHR and the internationalization of religious freedom in general.[32] 'Conscience' was an important piece of St Thomas Aquinas's medieval philosophy long before Protestantism, and remains present in the preamble to the UDHR, which defines man Thomistically as a union of reason and conscience.[33] Far more

[30] J. Israel, *A Revolution of the Mind: Radical Enlightenment and the Intellectual Origins of Modern Democracy* (2008); for a similarly skewed portrait of American history, see S. Jacoby, *Freethinkers: A History of American Secularism* (2004). Cf. Sheehan, 'Enlightenment, Religion and the Enigma of Secularization', 108 American Historical Review (October 2003) 1061 Coleman, 'Resacralizing the World: The Fate of Secularization in Enlightenment Historiography', 82 *Journal of Modern History* (June 2010) 368, or Moyn, 'Mind the Enlightenment', *The Nation*, 31 May 2010.

[31] L. Febvre, *The Problem of Unbelief in the Sixteenth Century: The Religion of Rabelais*, trans. B. Gottlieb (1982).

[32] For a serious Catholic Enlightenment, however, see M. Printy, *Enlightenment and the Creation of German Catholicism* (2009).

[33] This phraseology was due to Charles Malik, on whom see later, in section 3. See the etymological history of 'conscience' through the American founding in Feldman, 'The Intellectual Origins of the Establishment Clause', 77 *N.Y.U. Law Review* (2002) 346.

important, Asad's story also omits the fact that Protestantism normally stigmatized secularism. It is, to be sure, true that it is due in part to Protestantism that the notion of inward conscience emerged as a regulatory zone separate from the body, which could be immunized against state interference. Liberal secularism is undoubtedly indebted to Protestantism in this sense. Yet Protestantism never meant giving up on religion as public meaning and collective practice, whether in early years when it intensified the desire for a godly city and could promote even more serious hunts for heresy than before, or later when freedom of religious exercise and even disestablishment of churches occurred in the name of consensual public—and very Christian—moral norms.

The French Revolution changed but did not abolish this situation; the secularism that it eventually pronounced has, so far, triumphed in world history only in a few locales after that revolutionary experiment imploded under pressure. First, after 1917 there was the communist Soviet Union and its satellites along, perhaps, with some other communist regimes. Later, and in much less aggressive form, there is today's Western Europe. In the nineteenth century, some social conflicts were indeed structured around the proposal that the principle of state non-interference with privatized belief must become a political end not an instrumental means.[34] And for some, toleration came to be not about the promotion of struggle for the true Christianity, but a genuinely post-Christian ideal, however selectively and ambiguously applied in practice. Yet, arguably, even in the most radical phases of the Enlightenment when French revolutionaries seized the property of the church and proclaimed a cult of the supreme being, at no point did anything called secularism come about as a truly pervasive social norm. Unlike in the aftermath of the Reformation, of course, by the era of the American and French Revolutions it was possible for religious freedom to be asserted as a call for a secular political space by actors who had never existed in prior phases of transatlantic history. And it is certainly the case that, in the form of conservative reaction, anti-secularism emerged as a possibility (in fact, reactionary Catholic 'enemies of the Enlightenment' may have done more to invent their secularist enemy than secularists themselves did on their own account).[35]

Nevertheless, through much of the nineteenth century Christianity remained publicly dominant, even if one or two freethinking pharmacists—like Homais in Gustave Flaubert's *Madame Bovary*—dotted the countryside. 'Liberal values' like freedom of religion were rooted by Protestant figures, such as pioneering liberal theorist Benjamin Constant, in the millennial evolution of Christianity, which Constant insisted was the essential crucible of liberty.[36] Publicly dominant Protestantism became central to American and British national identity, notably for the purposes of

[34] See C. Clark and W. Kaiser (eds), *Culture Wars: Catholic-Secular Conflict in Nineteenth-Century Europe* (2003).

[35] D.M. McMahon, *Enemies of the Enlightenment: The French Counter-Enlightenment and the Making of Modernity* (2001).

[36] H. Rosenblatt, *Liberal Values: Benjamin Constant and the Politics of Religion* (2008); Garsten, 'Constant on the Religious Spirit of Liberalism' in H. Rosenblatt (ed.), *The Cambridge Companion to Constant* (2009) 286. This supersedes an earlier literature portraying liberalism, much as in Ian Hunter's work, as based fundamentally on a *politique* response to Reformation struggle with a wholly neutral state

social norms and moral regulation; the same happened to Catholicism in France; and each version of Christianity had its zones of authority further east.[37] Whiggish politics in Britain developed a myth of progress to assert claims about 'Puritanism and liberty' that later historians have found to be mistaken, but practically no one proposed stepping beyond a British identity steeped in the dominance of Protestant ethical culture; the same applies to pretty much all of the rest of the North Atlantic world.

Historians of secularism are surely not wrong about the consequences of the polarizing experience of the French Revolution and its aftermath. French politics in modern times did indeed involve a visible struggle and seemingly wild oscillation between assertive anti-secularisms and secularisms. The former were epitomized by the Bourbon Restoration and Vichy authoritarianism; the latter by republicanism and the law of separation that followed the Dreyfus affair. Clearly, this historical dispute gave rise to the ideal of secular education so threatened a century later by Muslim children, at least in the eyes of its defenders.[38] And as the *Kulturkampf* of the 1870s, in which Catholics were targeted after unification of Germany under Prussian auspices, graphically demonstrated, secular-religious divides could also crop up in other places.[39] It is also true that, following the French Revolution, some broke with a formerly assertive Gallicanism in order to make Rome the capital of ultramontane reaction. As we will see, it was to be crucial that popes terrified by modernity associated religious freedom, which Protestants had in fact used to organize a strong public religiosity, with an apostate campaign to destroy the Christian faith.

Yet just as the anti-secularists of the counterrevolutionary tradition implausibly claimed that the large middle ground that many liberals (like Benjamin Constant and Alexis de Tocqueville) occupied could not exist, so secularists were occasionally prone to forget how much civil peace was based on the moral ambiance provided by religious uniformity in a Christian country, even when the state was accorded civil and educational functions. (Secularists and anti-secularists in France also found much common ground in various state programmes, including imperial expan-

above the religious fray; see S. Holmes, *Benjamin Constant and the Making of Modern Liberalism* (1984), which omits Constant's (and liberalism's) religiosity.

[37] D. Sehat, *The Myth of American Religious Freedom* (2011); L. Colley, *Britons: Forging the Nation, 1707–1837* (1992); C. Ford, *Creating the Nation in Provincial France: Religion and Political Identity in Brittany* (1993). Philip Hamburger even claims that the whole idea of a wall of separation really emerged not as a secularist campaign but as a device through which Protestants stigmatized Catholics. See P. Hamburger, *Separation of Church and State* (2002); cf. Moore, 'Common Principles, Different Histories: Understanding Religious Liberty in the United States and France', 7 *Modern Intellectual History* (August 2010) 468.

[38] P. Stock-Morton, *Moral Education for a Secular Society: The Development of 'Morale Laïque' in Nineteenth-Century France* (1988). For a vivid defence of the famous French veil law of 2004 as in effect forcing Muslims to be free, as the republic had done for Christians and Jews before them, see Weil, 'Why the French Laïcité Is Liberal', 30(6) *Cardozo Law Review* (June 2009) 2699.

[39] Of course, this does not mean that German Catholics would have been liberals and saved Germany from Nazism if they had not been driven into a confessional party with its own ambiguous history into the twentieth century. Cf. Anderson, 'The Kulturkampf and the Course of German History', 19 *Central European History* (March 1986) 82 and Anderson, *Practicing Democracy: Elections and Political Culture in Imperial Germany* (2000).

sion.[40]) In short, though it involves much ideological distortion, there is some factual basis for Nicolas Sarkozy's claims when he champions what he terms a *laïcité positive* that begins in the recognition of France's Christian heritage.[41] (The same, one might note in passing, is true of the United States, where John Rawls's own biographical trajectory from Christian thinker in the making to secularist liberal reveals the chronology of the social dominance of Christianity and its passing much more clearly than his own later philosophical narrative focused on the wars of religion.[42])

It was really the twentieth-century *crisis* of European liberalism, religious and secular alike, that set the stage for a novel equation on the continent. Mainly this was because European Christians frequently concluded that Christianity would benefit from the prospective rise of illiberal regimes. (Consider the early case of Christianity in Austria, where the formation of a powerful Christian social party around the turn of the century eventually led to a Catholic state before the invasion led by Adolf Hitler in 1938.[43]) It was only through this development, and then the rise of new regimes that were eventually to seem inimical to Protestant and Catholic ideals (mostly after the defeat of those regimes), that religious freedom became a cause central to European self-understanding. In pre-communist Eastern Europe, especially, liberal principles did not get very far in modern history—though they were imposed in interwar constitutions—before being simply overwhelmed by Christian nationalism, whether in Poland with its homogeneous Catholicism or Hungary with its considerable intra-Christian differences.[44] Though spats certainly developed once Adolf Hitler took power, Catholicism in and around Munich provided the mainstay of Nazism's earliest support.[45] In Germany in the twentieth century, Protestants did not prove immune to believing that the illiberal state could serve their faith, though after Nazism they could easily follow the long-established path of Anglo-American Protestants in seeking moral hegemony without state control.[46] For that reason, the central factor in the extraordinary symbiosis between Christianity and religious freedom in the mid-twentieth century, going beyond its familiar Protestant zone during that time, is that transnational Catholicism ultimately found its way onto the same path.[47]

[40] J.P. Daughton, *An Empire Divided: Religion, Republicanism, and the Making of French Colonialism, 1880–1914* (2006).

[41] Cf. Jean Baubérot, *La laïcité expliquée à M. Sarkozy* (2008).

[42] J. Rawls, *A Brief Inquiry into the Meaning of Sin and Faith* (1942) (B.A. thesis on file at Princeton University, rpt. 2009).

[43] See Cole, 'The Counter-Reformation's Last Stand: Austria' in C. Clark and W. Kaiser (eds), *Culture Wars* (2009) 285.

[44] See, e.g., B. Porter-Szücs, *Faith and Fatherland: Catholicism, Modernity, and Poland* (2011), esp. Ch. 9; P. Hanebrink, *In Defense of Christian Hungary: Religion, Nationalism, and Anti-semitism, 1890–1944* (2006).

[45] D. Hastings, *Catholicism and the Roots of Nazism: Religious Identity and National Socialism* (2009).

[46] See, in a vast literature, D. Bergen, *Twisted Cross: The German Christian Movement in the Third Reich* (1996) or R. Steigmann-Gall, *The Holy Reich: Nazi Conceptions of Christianity, 1919–1945* (2003).

[47] Perreau-Saussine, 'French Catholic Political Thought from the Deconfessionalization of the State to the Recognition of Religious Freedom' in I. Katznelson and G. Stedman-Jones (eds), *Religion and Political Imagination* (2010) 150; and E. Perreau-Saussine, *Catholicism and Democracy: An Essay in the History of Political Thought*, trans. R. Rex (2012).

Despite the significant diversity of Catholics on national scenes, the Catholic Church remained opposed to the idea of religious freedom until the fateful events of World War II transformed it into one of the principle's most vigorous defenders. Before this, Catholic popes in modern times had rejected the whole idea of rights, and most especially the right of religious freedom, favouring the church's freedoms (leaving open the possibility of recapturing the state in exigent circumstances). In his encyclical *Mirari vos* (1832), Gregory XVI denounced 'that absurd and erroneous proposition which claims that *liberty of conscience* must be maintained for everyone. It spreads ruin in sacred and civil affairs, though some repeat over and over again with the greatest impudence that some advantage accrues to religion from it'. In *Quanta cura* (1864), Pius IX added that liberty of conscience was nothing more than 'liberty of perdition'. In its scandalous indifference to truth, Leo XIII added in *Immortale Dei* (1885), freedom of religion is little more than slavery to falsehood. According to this encyclical on 'the Christian constitution of states', Catholic theology stood against the:

> ... theory that all questions that concern religion are to be referred to private judgment; that every one is to be free to follow whatever religion he prefers, or none at all if he disapprove of all. From this the following consequences logically flow: that the judgment of each one's conscience is independent of all law; that the most unrestrained opinions may be openly expressed as to the practice or omission of divine worship; and that every one has unbounded license to think whatever he chooses and to publish abroad whatever he thinks. Now, when the State rests on foundations like those just named... it readily appears into what and how unrightful a position the Church is driven.[48]

As late as the 1950s, such views remained dominant in Catholic thought.

Rather than the now obscure early modern developments to which the ECtHR and some of its commentators routinely refer, the way in which these views changed is probably the critical puzzle when trying to understand the trajectory of religious freedom between the European past and the European present. Very roughly, the solution to this puzzle has interlocking parts: World War II and the Cold War. The first—once the Axis lost—suggested that in modern circumstances the subordination of state to religion was unlikely, because of the failure of the Christian flirtation with the now defeated far-right regimes. The second featured a newly dominant anti-totalitarian politics according to which an ethic of religious freedom seemed to provide a plausible and powerful device to promote religious dominance in a struggle against a godless enemy. The war for Christian states against a liberalism whose secularism was partial and qualified, when it was not altogether imaginary, was reinvented as the war of Christian democracy against a Soviet Union whose secularism was, in fact, very real—and far more radical than the most emphatic European versions today.

[48] Leo XII, *Immortale Dei* (On the Christian Constitution of States), 1 November 1885, available at http:/ /w2.vatican.va/content/leo-xiii/en/encyclicals/documents/hf_l-xiii_enc_01111885_immortale-dei.html (last visited 15 August 2018).

3. How Religious Freedom Became an International Human Right

The Soviet Union was the first country founded to promote secularism, in a radical version aimed at stamping religion out altogether. Eventually, it also recognized religious freedom as a formal principle: the Soviet Union's 1936 'Stalin' Constitution, though propounded in an era of terror, includes the most extensive list of human rights ever recognized in history, including its Article 124 offering religious freedom. But the devotion of the Soviet Union to a thoroughgoing secularism to deprive the masses of their favourite 'opiate' prompted it to establish an unapologetic public tilt against religion, going far beyond the separation of church and state that remained neutral towards religion if kept as a private matter, even as churches remained to shepherd faith communities. The regime's Commissariat of Enlightenment was intended to take public re-education in hand in the name of a glorious secular future, and the League of the Militant Godless arose among civil society activists to promote scientific atheism.[49]

It was not least in view of the Soviet Union's avowed secularism that, in what remains one of the massive causes of non-governmental activism of the entire twentieth century, organized religion mobilized around depredations against Russian Orthodoxy and minority faiths (and later Catholics and Protestants in the Soviet Union's satellites). Prior to World War II, however, no one would have said that the attempt to internationalize the ideal of religious freedom seemed to be a central device in this campaign. The spectre of potential revolution at home in democracies which were still highly unstable, and with a shifting international system, meant a much more visible and fateful mobilization against liberalism, viewed as a stepping stone to communism. Compared to the spectre of communism, believers and churchmen viewed fascism and reaction not as a 'totalitarian' companion of communism, but as the lesser evil to choose (if not a positive good to embrace).

Subsequently, the Allies—the Americans in league with the Soviets—won the war and took political and often clerico-fascist reaction off the table as an option for postwar Europe, the Iberian Peninsula aside. In its wake, what was promoted was not secularism but rather religious freedom to ward secularism off. During the war, when the idea of 'human rights' began to circulate for the first time in the English language, American mainline Protestants responded to Franklin Delano Roosevelt's 'Four Freedoms' promises (the second of which promised freedom of religion everywhere in the world) by making human rights central to international activism for the first time in history. They outstripped any other non-governmental activists in this regard in the United States—and they made religious freedom the most important human right. These American Protestants put aside their internal disputes about whether Christianity demanded pacifism (and whether they should stay out of the European war). After the war's end, they were by any standard mainly responsible for

[49] See W.B. Husband, *'Godless Communists': Atheism and Society in Soviet Russia, 1917–1932* (2000); and D. Peris, *Storming the Heavens: The Soviet League of the Militant Godless* (1998). For post-World War II developments, see S. Luehrmann, *Secularism Soviet Style: Teaching Atheism and Religion in a Volga Republic* (2011).

the original move to the internationalization of religious freedom and, in fact, for the presence of the entire notion of human rights in international affairs.[50]

Their groups, spearheaded by the Federal Council of Churches of Christ (FCC) and its Commission of Churches on International Affairs (CCIA), always placed freedom of religion first among all other causes, as the foundation of all other rights, and the basic premise of their early struggle against the Soviet Union and on behalf of far-flung missionary activity.[51] During the war, an FCC group headed by John Foster Dulles, known as the Commission for a Just and Durable Peace, issued its widely circulated 'Six Pillars of Peace', incorporating early calls for an international bill of rights, which—it insisted—must prioritize freedom of religion as its essential linchpin.[52] Internationally, the FCC and its parts were also deeply connected to the so-called ecumenical movement. It had the same priorities, and after a series of false starts in the interwar period, it finally coalesced as the World Council of Churches (WCC) in Amsterdam in 1948. In the person of Frederick Nolde, the FCC and CCIA were deeply involved in ensuring that human rights were included in the UN Charter at San Francisco. Nolde's good friend, Lebanese philosopher Charles Malik, who was Eastern Orthodox but with strong Catholic leanings, considered freedom of religion to be the keystone of the UDHR, which he helped write (notably by inserting its preambular image of man as the site of reason and conscience). At the time, few serious non-Christian publicists were theorists or partisans of the new idea of human rights—or even rights generally.[53] It is true that Malik was not simply motivated by anti-communism in the goal of internationalizing religious freedom; he also held out hope for the conversion of the entire Mediterranean basin to Christianity, just as several of those most deeply connected to the promotion of religious freedom as a new international principle were animated by the desire to safeguard the premises of missionary activities in East Asia and elsewhere.[54] Nonetheless, the struggle against communism provided the essential unifying force for the campaign to internationalize religious freedom.

Primarily a federation of Protestants agreeing to put aside their once bitterly divisive differences in the name of common geopolitical interests, the FCC and its European allies were in the vanguard in perfecting 'freedom of religion' as the main principle with which to oppose communism, before the wartime alliance frayed or

[50] See D.A. Hollinger, *After Cloven Tongues of Fire: Protestant Liberalism in Modern American History* (2013).

[51] Cf. the relevant sections in A. Preston, *Sword of the Spirit, Shield of Faith: Religion in American War and Diplomacy* (2012).

[52] Commission for the Just and Durable Peace, *Six Pillars of Peace: A Study Guide* (1943) 72–81; and S. Moyn, *The Last Utopia: Human Rights in History* (2010) Ch. 2, whose presentation of human rights in the 1940s is extended in this chapter.

[53] See, e.g., Unesco, *Human Rights: Comments and Interpretations*, intro. Jacques Maritain (1948); and R.M. MacIver (ed.), *Great Expressions of Human Rights* (1950), with chiefly religious authors and contents, including famed American Catholic natural law theorist John Courtney Murray's appropriation of rights as part of praise for American traditions of fusing religious liberty and moral community.

[54] According to his cousin by marriage Edward Said, who sat at his feet in these years, Malik's devotion to rights as a proxy for Christianity flowed unacceptably into doctrines of 'the clash of civilizations, the war between East and West, communism and freedom, Christianity and all the other, lesser religions'. E. Said, *Out of Place* (1999) 265.

the Cold War even began. The work of the FCC's Joint Commission on Religious Liberty, founded during the war to survey the state of religious freedom and suggest avenues for its promotion after the war, makes this clear.[55] British and Continental European ecumenical groups were full participants in this discourse.[56] Many Anglo-Americans, it is true, eventually found the WCC too soft on communism, as Dulles's tutorial on the subject at the Amsterdam summit suggested, but the transatlantic coalition remained united in taking the individual right of religious freedom as the core right.[57]

Meanwhile, at home, mainline American Protestants were involved in an epoch-making renovation of national identity which, for the first time, brooked the admission of Catholics and Jews to the national project in the creation of a 'Judeo-Christian' or 'tri-faith' America that explained, in the eyes of a succession of presidents and their people, what the country stood for in its emerging struggle against the Soviet foe. Far more than ever before, Protestants relaxed confessional disputes and especially their anti-Catholicism, uniting with other Christians and even Jews, who were instrumental in accepting the bargain of inclusion in the 'Judeo-Christian West' on condition of stigmatizing secularism.[58] This episode has tended to be forgotten, not least because this move by mainline Protestant elites inadvertently set the stage for the destruction of their long-term dominance in the United States. The decision by the hitherto Protestant universities to diversify, for example, ended up driving rather than forestalling secularism, even as the Cold War promoted the boom of an evangelical conservatism away from so-called 'mainline' Protestant formations. But if America's mainline Protestant elites no longer have the dominance they once enjoyed, the same was not true in the years immediately after the end of World War II. One of the most important developments in Cold War historiography of late is to show, even as the US Supreme Court turned to impose a 'wall of separation' between church and state, how the country's self-avowed Christian statesmen viewed their

[55] M. Searle Bates, *Religious Liberty: An Inquiry* (1945), which ranks the Soviet Union first among all threats to religious freedom, followed by 'the Moslem countries', before turning to history and theory and concluding with a programme of embedding religious liberty in international law.

[56] H.G. Wood, *Religious Liberty To-Day* (1949), which extensively reviews violations behind the Iron Curtain (Ch. 4) before turning to a 'failure of left-wing intellectuals' for failing to see that their socialism was driving them into the arms of intolerant communism.

[57] Ironically, the FCC's rise and promotion of religious freedom internationally paved the way for what David Sehat calls a 'liberal moment' domestically during which, exceptionally in US history, religious freedom was not primarily understood as a device of Protestant public hegemony and moral control. In international affairs, however, it remained very much part of a campaign about the fate of Christianity in a world in which the Soviets had defeated Nazism, as well as a struggle for the continuation of the Christian cause in an age in which missionary proselytizing remained a major global enterprise. Sehat (n. 37) Ch. 11. For Dulles and Nolde at Amsterdam, see Dulles, 'The Christian Citizen in a Changing World' and Nolde, 'Freedom of Religion and Related Human Rights' in World Council of Churches, *Man's Disorder and God's Design*, vol. 4, *The Church and the International Disorder* (1948) 73–189. See also Stuart, 'Mission, Ecumenism, and Human Rights: "Religious Liberty" in Egypt, 1919–1956', 83(1) *Church History* (2014) 110–34.

[58] K. Healon Gaston, 'The Genesis of America's Judeo-Christian Moment: Secularism, Totalitarianism, and the Redefinition of Democracy' (2008) (Ph.D. dissertation on file with University of California-Berkeley); K.M. Schulz, *Tri-Faith America: How Catholics and Jews Held Postwar America to Its Protestant Promise* (2011).

task as a holy crusade against secularism. It was at this point that Americans pledged allegiance to a nation united 'under God' and therefore indivisible.[59]

With the Western powers dominating the United Nations for a few years, during the period when the UDHR was propounded, the immediate postwar trajectory of human rights in international politics shows how central religious freedom was to this anti-secularist venture. Of the few causes generally understood as human rights concerns in international politics at the time, the most prominent by any measure involved depredations of religion under communism, as UN attention to the once famous internment of Hungarian Cardinal Jószef Mindszenty—in the month when the UDHR was passed—shows.[60]

The new individual human rights, centring for so many on religious freedom, left the League of Nations minority rights regime behind, even though that regime was more effective in recognizing the collective, practical, and political dimensions of religious affiliation, given its protection of insular group minorities in Eastern Europe often living in relatively closed faith communities. Contrary to the critique of secularism, this interwar episode shows that few had trouble thinking about religious identity in terms that were collective and practical rather than individual and conscientious alone.[61] Instead, it was mainly due to the partnership of Malik and Nolde that Article 18 of the UDHR took on the form it did, strongly emphasizing the priority of individual conscientious decision and the right to change religion (which ultimately caused several abstentions in the General Assembly vote on the part of Muslim states). Far from following directly from a Protestant individualization of religion occurring centuries ago, the emphasis on the *forum internum* of the human being beginning with the UDHR's preamble, as determined by Malik, actually invoked the medieval Thomist formula of humanity's 'reason and conscience' but with one eye towards potential conscientious non-conformists suffering under communism. By contrast, the Soviets proposed that instead of giving special protection to conscientious choice of religion, law should focus instead on carving out a secular space for 'freethinkers' who, they said, were historically beset by the fanaticism of religion. (Obviously, their suggestion was rejected.[62])

Of course, the internationalization of religious freedom in wartime and after did not come out of nowhere. There had been clauses guaranteeing religious freedom in

[59] See W. Inboden, *Religion and American Foreign Policy, 1945–1960: The Soul of Containment* (2010) on presidential rhetoric and diplomacy; and J.W. Stevens, *God-Fearing and Free: A Spiritual History of America's Cold War* (2010) on culture; along with Jonathan P. Herzog, *The Spiritual-Industrial Complex: America's Religious Battle against Communism in the Early Cold War* (2011).

[60] See UN Gen. Ass. Res. 272 (III) (1949) and, later, 294 (IV) (1949) and 385 (V) (1950). Cf. Cornelis D. de Jong, *The Freedom of Thought, Conscience, and Religion or Belief in the United Nations (1946–1992)* (2000).

[61] Mazower, 'The Strange Triumph of Human Rights', 47 *Historical Journal* (2004) 379; Lindqvist, 'The Politics of Article 18: Religious Liberty in the Universal Declaration of Human Rights', 4 *Humanity* (Winter 2013) 429.

[62] See, e.g., UN Doc. A/C.3/SR.127–128. For a contemporary, and I assume independent, revival of this once commonplace Soviet position, see Leiter, 'Why Tolerate Religion?', 25(1) *Constitutional Commentary* (Spring 2008) 1; and B. Leiter, *Why Tolerate Religion?* (2012). See also Schwartzman, 'What If Religion Isn't Special?', 79(4) *University of Chicago Law Review* (Fall 2012) 1351; and Shea, 'Beyond Belief', *Chronicle of Higher Education*, 20 June 2014.

various European treaties after the Reformation settlement; indeed, they were the distant source of the contemporary norm of 'the responsibility to protect', albeit one forged by Christians for Christians.[63] It should also be acknowledged that in the most fledging steps in the internationalization of the norm of religious freedom before World War II, the targets were very much Oriental despotisms—especially the Ottoman Empire—where Christians and Jews were imagined as beset by backwards misrule.[64] In spite of these extremely modest antecedents, however, the internationalization (and Europeanization) of religious freedom in the 1940s took its historical 'quantum leap' under the auspices of a Christianity which was positioning itself geopolitically for anti-secularist struggle. By the interwar period, a large range of defenders of religious freedom existed, and the norm percolated in traditions of constitution-making across modern times and around the world. But in its mid-century internationalization and Europeanization, the secularist defenders of the principle who now supported it in many domestic circumstances were not the main agents. And to complete the picture, but above all to explain how this strategy defined the Western European human rights regime, Catholicism demands the lion's share of attention, since it was Catholicism's historically surprising, but geopolitically crucial, alliance with transnational Protestantism that deserves most credit for solidifying the international politics of religious freedom into its Cold War form.

4. The Catholic Transformation

As a preliminary to looking at the larger transformation of Catholicism, it may help to examine by far the most influential Catholic thinker of the era, and not by coincidence by far the most prominent philosophical defender of human rights in the world at the time: Jacques Maritain. In his youth, Maritain, a Thomist, had followed his philosophical master in his monarchist politics; but in the 1930s he moved to the position that the old hope of state capture was a superannuated medievalism not at all preferable to a modern Catholic alternative—one which featured limitation of the state for the sake of religious permeation of civil society. As late as his lectures *Man and the State*, published in 1951, Maritain remained surprisingly faithful to old

[63] B. Simms and D.J.B. Trim (eds), *Humanitarian Intervention: A History* (2011) Chs 2–3.

[64] The early, modest institutionalization of this norm occurred neither because of a Christian nor because of a secularist impulse in foreign affairs. Rather, Jewish notables and eventually Jewish organizations invoked religious freedom strategically on behalf of their foreign coreligionists to encourage the imperial policymaking France and Great Britain to take the rhetoric of the superiority of the tolerationist Christian West seriously—in order to commit Christian states to the defence of the Jewish people abroad. In fact, in several treaties and eventually at Versailles, internationalist Jews were able to embed the ideal of religious freedom in fledgling ways in the international order against 'backwards' sovereigns in Poland, Romania, and elsewhere, who were Christian rather than Muslim. This point seriously qualifies the otherwise sobering presentation of the history of international religious freedom as an orientalist crusade in Mahmoud, 'The Politics of Religious Freedom and the Minority Question: A Geopolitical Problem?', 54 *Comparative Studies in Society and History* (April 2012) 418. For doctrinal details, see M.D. Evans, *Religious Liberty and International Law in Europe* (1997) Chs 2–6. For Jewish politics, see the many references to religious freedom in L.M. Leff, *The Sacred Bonds of Solidarity: The Rise of Jewish Internationalism in Nineteenth Century France* (2006); and esp. C. Fink, *Defending the Rights of Others: The Great Powers, the Jews, and International Minorities Protection, 1878–1938* (2004).

papal pronouncements by underlining that freedom of conscience had to be theorized so as to avoid indifferentism, relativism, and secularism. If it was 'the most basic and inalienable of all human rights', it was because it was 'the right freely to believe the truth'. If 'error has no rights' (as the Catholic saying had it), Maritain insisted that this did not rule out the centrality of religious freedom now that a situation of religious unity and state subordination to a church characteristic of the Middle Ages had passed.[65]

Once the prospect of reviving the medieval solution, which had driven many Catholics in a reactionary direction, was rejected as either undesirable or unavailable, the idea of religious freedom could be reconsidered. And, Maritain insisted, the modern circumstance showed that religious freedom could strengthen Christian societies, as the Protestants that Catholics had so long blamed for secularism always believed. Of course, the considerable risk of secularist error, so important to Catholicism, had to be clearly recognized and fervently combated:

> The modern age is not a sacral, but a secular age. The order of terrestrial civilization and temporal society has gained complete differentiation and full autonomy, which is something normal in itself, required by the Gospel's very distinction between God's and Caesar's domains. But that normal process was accompanied—and spoiled—by a most aggressive and stupid process of insulation from, and finally rejection of, God and the Gospel in the sphere of social and political life. The fruit of this we can contemplate today in the theocratic atheism of the Soviet Union.[66]

For such reasons, in a secular age religious freedom had to be invoked against secularism—theocratic secularism!—in order to safeguard a Christian society through 'a sanctification of secular life'. As Maritain put it in 1943 in his first exposition of human rights, and cited again in *Man and the State*, 'the world is done with neutrality. Willingly or unwillingly, States will be obliged to make a choice for or against the Gospel. They will be shaped either by the totalitarian spirit or by the Christian spirit.'[67] While providing space for the tolerance of minorities and even unbelievers, religious freedom not only would promote a Christian society with its moral order but would also provide the essential bulwark against the risk that a secular age would give rise to secularist totalitarianism. Religious freedom meant a Christianity that, forsaking medievalist statism, infused society, immunizing it from a secularist and materialist tilt by ensuring that it had a religious and spiritual one.

When he came to them in the 1930s, Maritain's arguments were radical because so many Catholics would vote with their feet in favour of explicitly Catholic states in crisis circumstances (in Austria, Portugal, and Spain before World War II and then Croatia, Vichy France, and Slovakia during it), and fascist states when this first best option was not available (in Germany and Italy before World War II and most of Europe during it). Indeed, forsaking state capture still seemed radical in the 1940s, when a powerful current of opinion in the Vatican remained stalwart in its

[65] J. Maritain, *Man and the State* (1951) 150. [66] Ibid 159.

[67] Cited in ibid at 159. For the inception of Catholic anti-totalitarianism, see Chappel, 'The Catholic Origins of Totalitarianism Theory in Interwar Europe', 9 *Modern Intellectual History* (November 2011) 561.

defence of the older view that an endorsement of religious freedom made sense only as a 'hypothesis' in those situations in which Catholics were in the minority—as in the United States—rather than a general principle or 'thesis'. Through the 1950s, and in fact through Vatican II, the Church opposed religious freedom, standing against a strong set of dissidents such as Maritain and others. After the war, critical figures such as Cardinal Alfredo Ottaviani (last head of the millennial inquisition) inveighed against religious freedom, offering Spain, where clerico-fascism in a majority Catholic country had survived, as the ideal model.[68]

But even though Ottaviani and his allies, in a once dramatic set of events, nearly derailed it, Vatican II finally adopted a declaration on religious freedom, the most high-profile and visible part of its work, significantly framed as a necessary consequence of its first principle, the dignity of the human person.[69] If one asks why this startling change occurred when it did, fewer than 50 years ago, the geopolitical context of the Cold War has to be a significant part of the answer. The text of the declaration makes clear that it seemed that endorsement of the principle of religious freedom undermined global secularism more than it risked encouraging it. 'Men of the present day want to profess their religion freely in private and in public', the Declaration states, before turning this novel Catholic view against the Soviet Union. '[But] there are forms of government under which, despite constitutional recognition of the freedom of religious worship, the public authorities themselves strive to deter the citizens from professing their religion and make life particularly difficult and dangerous for religious bodies.'[70] This move went along with a very marked transformation among Catholics in the direction of 'Judeo-Christianity', one likewise resisted by the conservatives, as the history of Vatican II's declaration *Nostra aetate* on the Jews shows. As with religious freedom, when one asks how and why the church could put a traditional hatred of the Jews behind it after so many years, including the recent history of much spilled blood, once again the answer is that the Cold War with its novel enemy encouraged the shift.[71] In this situation, certain principles like freedom of conscience, once denounced by a reactionary church, were reappropriated. Once tasked in Catholic political thought as a catalyst of secularism, religious freedom found itself recuperated as a crucial tool to be used to stave secularism off.

[68] See, e.g., C. Santamaria, 'L'Église et les libertés dans l'histoire' in *L'Église et la liberté* (1952); and, for commentary, A.F. Carrillo de Albornoz, *Roman Catholicism and Religious Liberty* (1959).

[69] Ottaviani and his faction succeeded in postponing consideration of the declaration in 1964, which caused a major international uproar. Doty, '1,000 Bishops Balk at Moves to Drop a Vote on Liberty', *New York Times*, 20 November 1964; Doty, '1,000 Bishops Fail in Plea to Pontiff on Liberty Draft', *New York Times*, 21 November 1964. The pope then sided against the reactionaries the next year, saving the proposal. Doty, 'Italian [Cardinal Ottaviani] Assails Church Liberty', *New York Times*, 18 September 1965; Doty, 'Pope Intervenes on Liberty Text, Backs Liberals', *New York Times*, 22 September 1965; Cogley, 'Freedom of Religion: Vatican Decree Supplants Ancient Doctrine that "Error Has No Rights"', *New York Times*, 8 December 1965.

[70] 'Dignitatis humanae (Declaration on Religious Freedom)', in A. Flannery, O.P. (ed.), *Vatican Council II: The Conciliar and Post-Conciliar Documents* (1975) 811.

[71] Cf. J. Connelly, *From Enemy to Brother: The Revolution in Catholic Teaching on the Jews, 1933–1965* (2012).

This point suggests that the most general way to interpret the incorporation of religious freedom as a crucial anti-secularist principle in Catholicism is to connect it to the formation of Cold War Christianity generally, in which America became the model of the promotion of religion precisely through its commitment to disestablishment and the ideal of religious freedom. For the transformation of Catholicism enabling its embrace of religious freedom was also its Americanization, as defenders and critics of the transformation well understood at the time.

As noted earlier, for Catholics the American situation had been the chief example of the 'hypothesis', not a generally defensible model of the relation between a tolerant state and religious truth, from the first papal encyclical on the American church, Leo XIII's *Longinqua oceani* (1895). After 1945, American Catholics joined their Protestant brethren in promoting religious liberty as the 'first freedom' of the Constitution, warning sternly against its interpretation in mistakenly secularist ways by the US Supreme Court of the day.[72] Catholics like Maritain promoted America on the grounds that it showed how religious freedom promoted rather than undermined Christianity; he went so far as to claim that his philosophical hero, St Thomas, would have endorsed America as his utopia if he had lived another half-millennium.

In the nineteenth century, Catholic thinker Alexis de Tocqueville's attitude towards Protestant America was that it had discovered, by disestablishing the church, how to make Christianity more publicly powerful than ever. His message to Catholic reactionaries at home who denounced America as godless was that they needed to know how strong Christianity can become precisely among those who have given up the campaign to capture the state. ('I shall wait until they come back from a visit to America', Tocqueville wrote of his reactionary opponents, noting that his fellow Catholics in the United States were if anything more favourable than Protestants towards religious freedom American-style.[73]) Maritain, who had also formerly denounced America, spent World War II there, forging alliances with theologians like John Courtney Murray who followed him in marginalizing the thesis/hypothesis model. Murray, under Maritain's influence, became the pivotal figure in Vatican II's work on religious freedom.[74] The rise of the American model, on the premise that religious freedom was the best tool to hold secularism at bay, thus meant that even European Catholics joined the tendency to craft narratives of teleological victory that 'reductively credited liberal democracy—and particularly its Anglo-American variant—with the achievement and perfection of toleration, which was thus defined

[72] See, e.g., W. Parsons, S.J., *The First Freedom: Considerations on Church and State in America* (1948).

[73] A. de Tocqueville, *Democracy in America*, trans. G. Lawrence (1966) 294.

[74] Murray, 'Current Theology: Freedom of Religion', *Theological Studies* (March 1945) 85; Murray, 'Governmental Suppression of Heresy', *Proceedings of the Third Annual Meeting of the Catholic Theological Society of America* (1948); Cogley, '"The American Schema": Vatican Text on Religious Liberty Derives from U.S. Tradition', *New York Times*, 27 October 1965; Murray (ed.), *Freedom of Religion: An End and a Beginning* (1966); J. McGreevy, *Catholicism and American Freedom* (2003) Ch. 7 on 'Democracy, Religious Freedom, and the *Nouvelle Théologie*'. It was on this basis that later American Catholics, such as Father Robert Drinan, could champion religious freedom as 'a new global right'. See R. Drinan, *Can God and Caesar Coexist?: Balancing Religious Freedom and International Law* (2004). For Maritain's attempt to update Tocqueville, see J. Maritain, *Reflections on America* (1958).

as a positive civilizational virtue'.[75] This was not for the sake of secularism against religion, but just the reverse. It was also a shocking development given the political situation of Catholic Europe in the first half of the twentieth century.

5. The ECHR and Christian Democracy

Ultimately, even as the UDHR was finalized, the idea of human rights as a set of international legal principles, including a principle guaranteeing religious freedom, survived nowhere in the cacophony of world ideology except in what became its West European homeland, in an era of Christian political and social dominance based on a reformulated conservatism. Dulles may have inspired some Europeans, but soon made rather clear, as Dwight Eisenhower's Secretary of State, that the United States no longer stood for the internationalization of human rights as a diplomatic and legal matter. Meanwhile, if Western Europeans turned to human rights and experimented with federalism, it was on the basis of newly ascendant Christian parties, which experienced unprecedented success and whose statesmen and party apparatuses connected across borders to establish a decades-long dominance.[76] Just as ecumenical Protestantism drove the transatlantic ascent and internationalization of religious freedom, transnational Catholicism undergirded its Europeanization—and provided the deepest foundations of the European human rights regime.[77]

As Marco Duranti and others are beginning to demonstrate, the origins of the ECHR reflect a striking degree of influence by Christians critical of secularism, even more than in the case of the UDHR itself.[78] In retrospective appraisals, the UDHR and the ECHR are frequently seen as complementary projects—or successor ones, with the UN's failed move towards legalization creating the origins of a principled community's insistence on enforcement. The reality is wholly different. While eclectic in its supporters, the ECHR involved a stark departure from the welfarist premises of the UDHR, led by those interested in using Europeanization as a way to combat domestic socialism, in the era of the greatest popular and ideological appeal of both social democratic and communist ideals. Meanwhile, mechanisms for

[75] The hallmark cases are the histories of religious freedom most prominent during the Cold War in America and Europe respectively: R.H. Bainton, *The Travail of Religious Liberty: Nine Biographical Studies* (1951); J. Lecler, S.J., *Histoire de la tolérance au siècle de la Réforme*, 2 vols (1955), available in English as *Tolerance and the Reformation*, 2 vols, trans. T.L. Westow (1960). The quotation is from Collins (n. 23) 609.

[76] Wolfram Kaiser, *Christian Democracy and the Origins of the European Union* (2007).

[77] It was ultimately Christian democracy that solved the tenacious 'German problem'. See, e.g., Granieri, 'Thou Shalt Consider Thyself a European: Catholic Supranationalism and the Sublimation of German Nationalism after 1945' in M. Geyer and H. Lehmann (eds), *Religion und Nation, Nation und Religion: Beiträge zu einer unbewältigten Geschichte* (2004) 336.

[78] See M. Duranti, *Human Rights and Conservative Politics in Postwar Europe* (forthcoming). On the Cold War framework, see earlier literature including Cohen and Madsen, 'Cold War Law: Legal Entrepreneurs and the Emergence of a European Legal Field (1945–1965)', in V. Gessner and D. Nelken (eds), *European Ways of Law: Towards a European Sociology of Law* (2007) 175. Often the right of parents to choose their children's education in the ECHR, First Protocol, Art. 2, which some took to imply state funding of religious schools, was the truly contentious site around which the relationship between state and religion was fought.

enforcement were made close to inaccessible; they were not used for decades, and then mostly after being updated. (For instance, the ECtHR set in motion by the treaty decided its first religious freedom case in 1993.[79]) The ECHR's purposes were, in the beginning, didactic and expressive. As the social and economic rights still prominent in the UDHR were dropped, the right of religious freedom—along with that of private property—surged, forming some of the central symbols of what made Western Europe distinct from the encroaching communist foe.

Especially after the communist takeover of Czechoslovakia, and the internment of Mindszenty as well as that of Czech Cardinal Joseph Beran, much of the rhetoric turned on how the ECHR would symbolize the essence of Western civilization against eastern criminality (and its local avatars). 'All over Europe, Socialism is proving no defence against Communism's attack on the triple European heritage of Christianity, mental freedom and even-handed justice', as David Maxwell-Fyfe, conservative British politician (and lead British prosecutor at the Nuremberg trials) declared in 1948, in defence of the Convention project.[80] Anxious not to be outmanoeuvred, Labour Party politicians in Great Britain, whether they had any interest in Christianity or not, went along with the Europeanization and 'spiritual union' for which Winston Churchill and fellow conservatives called in the fight against communism. (For its part, the Left in France simply blocked the ratification of the ECHR for more than 20 years, in part out of concern that it was primarily a weapon of the local Right.[81])

More generally, Christian Democracy was the single most defining feature of the post-World War II European political settlement, of which the ECHR was an extremely minor feature. Soon enough, the Cold War featured a saturation of politics by Christianity in non-communist Europe as well as transatlantically, in a common project uniting 'Western' politicians and churches. Indeed, in certain respects Western Europeans went far further in blurring the line between publicly dominant Christianity and political life than Americans have ever done. After all, if not only having explicitly Christian political parties but having them dominant over much of the continent for most of postwar European history is not a blurring of the divide between religion and politics, what is?[82] From the 1940s through the 1960s, a time of growing religiosity and great public presence of Christianity across Europe as measured by several metrics, this blending included the promotion in European and Christian history of 'human rights', notably the international right of religious freedom.

The drafting of Article 9 of the ECHR deserves a different brand of scrutiny to capture the impact of these forces, rather than the doctrinal analysis it has received

[79] ECtHR, *Kokkinakis v. Greece*, Appl. no. 14307/88 (ser. A), Judgment of 25 May 1993.

[80] Duranti, 'Curbing Labour's Totalitarian Temptation: European Human Rights Law and British Postwar Politics', 3 *Humanity* (Fall 2013) 361.

[81] See earlier Coupland, 'Western Union, "Spiritual Union", and European Integration, 1948–51', 43 *Journal of British Studies* (2004) 366; and A.W.B. Simpson, *Human Rights and the End of Empire: Britain and the Origins of the European Convention* (2001).

[82] Cf. Whitman, 'Separating Church and State: The Atlantic Divide', 34 *Historical Reflections/Réflexions historiques* (Winter 2008) 86. See also T.A. Howard, *God and the Atlantic: America, Europe, and the Religious Divide* (2011).

so far.[83] But it is clear that, given who was in the room, the formulation and passage of the provision was largely uncontroversial, as the treaty took over Article 9(1) essentially verbatim from the UDHR, and what debate there was focused on Article 9(2)'s restrictions. Main speakers such as Maxwell-Fyfe and Mouvement républicain populaire (Christian Democrat) representative Pierre-Henri Teitgen were entirely 'overt about the role they saw for the *Christian* religion in assisting with the development of human rights', simply equating Western Europe with Christian civilization in many speeches.[84] Whatever persisting lack of clarity there may be about the 'original intent' behind various clauses—as in most such cases—there is none at all about this general point.[85] Evidence teems in the *Travaux préparatoires* of the treaty that a number of delegates viewed religious freedom as the keystone right, one for which Europe must stand up vigorously against the persecutory spirit of political secularism: 'We must make it clear that our concepts of human dignity and human rights are something different from what we see in Eastern Europe', the Irish delegate William Norton remarked, for example. 'An effort is being made there to put out the light of the Church—not only of one church of almost all churches.... We here in this Council of Europe can be a rallying base and a beacon light to men and women struggling against persecution of that kind.'[86]

After a certain point in the negotiations, Article 9(2) came to be annexed to the general vision that the drafters adopted for the entire treaty, which was widely called the 'democratic minimum' approach. Hence as an omnibus provision in Article 9(2), the considerations that might lead to the abridgement of the right of freedom of religion were ones 'necessary in a democratic society', the phrase whose interpretation continues to be at stake in the current case-law.[87] But the most striking event of the original negotiations for the history of religious freedom shows even more conclusively how mistaken it would be to attribute secularism to the treaty. Turkey, the sole non-Christian power involved, proposed that the treaty explicitly should make the democratic minimum a secularist one, anticipating Islamist threats. In response, the Western European states unceremoniously rebuffed a proposal to have Article 9(2) mention religion as a potential threat to the democratic minimum. In the late 1940s, it was not the Western Europeans who were the secularists. It is fascinating and instructive—and perhaps the most revealing piece of evidence for my proposal here—that the result the Court reached in *Refah Partisi* 50 years later, as a matter of judicial interpretation, was one that the original drafters of the treaty explicitly declined to take up.[88]

83 For a start, see M. Evans, *Religious Liberty and International Law in Europe* (1997) Ch. 10.

84 Evans, 'Religious Freedom in European Human Rights Law: The Search for a Guiding Conception' in M.W. Janis and C. Evans (eds), *Religion and International Law* (1999) 388.

85 By a founding figure, see Modinos, 'La Convention Européenne des Droits de l'Homme: ses origines, ses objectifs, sa réalisation', 1 *Annuaire Européenne* (1955) 141. Recently, see Nicol, 'Original Intent and the European Convention on Human Rights', *Public Law* (2005) 152, or E. Bates, *The Evolution of the European Convention on Human Rights: From Its Inception to the Creation of a Permanent Court of Human Rights* (2011), which views the ECHR as a 'safeguard against totalitarianism' but does not mention how religious freedom figured in this project.

86 Council of Europe, *Collected Edition of the 'Travaux Préparatoires'*, 5 vols (1975) 1: 130.

87 Cf. similar phrases in the treaty's Preamble as well as Arts 6, 8, 10, and 12.

88 Cf. C. Evans, *Freedom of Religion under the European Convention of Human Rights* (2001) 42–4.

As noted previously, there was no case-law involving Article 9's right of religious freedom before our own time. However, this absence did not simply follow from the fact that there was so little ECHR case-law of any kind. For there is one early Article 9 decision suggesting strongly, as for the treaty itself, that 'secularism' was not a significant aim of its parties or interpreters. Upholding and importing the German constitutional court's new doctrine of 'militant democracy'—a homegrown version of the democratic minimum approach enforced against enemies of the constitution—the first European Commission Article 9 decision (1957) was one allowing the Federal Republic's ban on the Communist Party to proceed. That Party's publicly announced platform was to seek to scuttle the liberal regime currently in place, the commissioners concluded; and if so, then the preservation of the democratic character of the regime allowed the Article 9 rights invoked by party members to be overridden.[89] That the first decision in which ECHR Article 9 rights were restricted in the name of the preservation of democracy had nothing to do with religious freedom provides more evidence for the novelty of current interpretations. Doctrinally, put bluntly, one template for the current Muslim headscarf decisions was drawn up in policing the threat of secularism rather than religion. And whatever one thinks of the expansive concern about extremist political views on a post-fascist continent facing down a communist enemy (or indeed in Turkey today where Islamism is often regarded as a comparable danger), the migration of the Article 9(2) 'democratic' rationale for abridging rights from political to religious freedom, and from a perceived threat revolving around ideology to one linked to religion, is anything but a natural or logical extension of early views.[90] At the very least, such an evolution cannot be ascribed to the original secularism of the treaty—whose original negotiation and first use were on behalf of a Christian Europe struggling against secularism. The European human rights regime has enforced the democratic minimum for many years, but no one would have seen secularism as essential to that minimum until recently.

Though the template for their later judicial interpretation was drawn up at an early stage, Article 9's religious freedom clauses in particular were a dead letter for more than four decades, as if born in a time before the current conditions for their

[89] *Kommunistische Partei Deutschlands c. Allemagne, European Commission* Requête No 250/257 (1957). The notion of 'militant democracy' had emerged thanks to émigré legal theorist Karl Loewenstein and was adopted first by the German Constitutional Court and then followed by the European Commission on Human Rights in the above case. Loewenstein, 'Militant Democracy and Fundamental Rights I/II', 31 *American Political Science Review* (June 1937) 417 and 31(5) (August 1937) 638; KPD-Verbot, Entscheidungen des Bundesverfassungsgerichts, 85(5) *BVerfGE* (1956); for recent commentary, see Markus Thiel, *Wehrhafte Demokratie: Beiträge über die Regelungen zum Schutze der freiheitlichen demokratischen Grundordnung* (2003); for English language comment, see, e.g., D.P. Kommers, *The Constitutional Jurisprudence of the Federal Republic of Germany*, revd edn (1997) 217; or Müller, 'Militant Democracy' in M. Rosenfeld and A. Sájo (eds), *Oxford Handbook of Comparative Constitutional Law* (2012) 1253. The only discussion I have found of militant democracy in the ECtHR is Eiffler, 'Die "wehrhafte Demokratie" in der Rechtsprechung des Europäischen Gerichtshofs für Menschenrechte', 36 *Kritische Justiz* (2003) 218, but this does not focus on its legacy as seen in the headscarf cases.

[90] Indeed, after the Cold War, the Court was willing to find an Art. 11 freedom of assembly violation in the Turkish suppression of a communist party. (Art. 9 claims were not reached.) ECtHR, *United Communist Party of Turkey and Others v. Turkey*, Appl. no. 19392/92, Judgment of 30 January 1998 (Grand Chamber).

uses, and potential abuses, were even conceivable. What happened in between the two eras? The answer is straightforward: to a wholly remarkable and unanticipated extent, Western European Christianity collapsed. Along with it, the original rationale for the international and European priority of religious freedom, and indeed the very meaning of the principle, had to change.[91] It is this transformation, together with unprecedented Muslim immigration, emotional disputes over whether Turkey counted as a European country, and the ramifications of 9/11 across the Atlantic that did most to set the stage for the contemporary politics of religious freedom, including in the ECtHR.[92]

6. Conclusion

It is only in very recent times, with the collapse of European Christianity since the 1960s, that it has become possible for the ideal of religious freedom to become so closely associated with secularism in the continent's human rights regime and beyond. There certainly were secularists in modern history, but it seems graphically clear that throughout the Cold War—and particularly in the internationalization and Europeanization of religious freedom—they were not in the driver's seat. Instead, the ideal of religious freedom originated in, and long remained tethered to, a self-conscious attempt to preserve an explicitly and pervasively Christian society, most especially, after a certain point, against the threat of secularism. Though European secularism now attracts criticism for its covert Christianity, most often the ideal of religious freedom served the project of overt Christianity—which left secularism a seriously embattled ideal.

None of this saves or should save the ECtHR from the criticism it has properly attracted regarding its religious freedom cases. A minimum required in a democratic society should not simply provide high principles for a bias against Islam, even in self-declared secularist countries, especially when Christian practices are not subject to the same scrutiny.[93] But my analysis should clear away the historical distortions

[91] It may not have changed wholly for some, of course, especially in the US which experienced no comparable collapse. After 9/11, the Supreme Court case *Elk Grove Unified School District v. Newdow* 542 U.S. 1 (2004), provided a focal point in domestic debate, and the country considered adding Islam to Judeo-Christianity. Others saw strong continuities with Cold War Christianity in foreign policy. Though these matters are beyond the scope of this chapter, consider the following sources: Castelli, 'Praying for the Persecuted Church: U.S. Christian Activism in the Global Arena', 4 *Journal of Human Rights* (2005) 321; Chicago Council on Global Affairs, *Engaging Religious Communities Abroad: A New Imperative for U.S. Foreign Policy* (2010); Boorstein, 'Agency that Monitors Religious Freedom Accused of Bias', *Washington Post*, 17 February 2010.

[92] For a good summary of debates about the nature and causes of Europe's religious change, see H. McLeod, *The Religious Crisis of the 1960s* (2007) esp. Ch. 1. For a comparative study of Catholic countries, see Jean-Louis Ormières, *L'Europe désenchantée: La fin de l'Europe chrétienne? France, Belgique, Espagne, Italie, Portugal* (2005). For a recent pope's plea to remember the Christian roots that Europeans now barely deign to recognize, and his insistence on the need for re-evangelization of the Continent, see John Paul II, *Ecclesia in Europa* (2003).

[93] Promisingly, the ECtHR has now found an Art. 9 violation in a headscarf case from Turkey in which the applicants merely wanted to wear religious attire in a public square, rather than in an institutional setting in which its precedents might have led it to demand 'neutrality' of the sort enforced in

of a totalizing critique that leaves no room for alternative secularisms—precisely, in my view, what is most needed today.[94] If this recourse to the past is convincing, the historiographical implication that follows is that religious freedom became annexed to an exclusionary secularist agenda not in the mists of time but, relatively speaking, only yesterday. The theoretical implication of my finding is that since secularism is far from the dominant mode in the trajectory of the principle of religious freedom, both secularism and religious freedom are in fact considerably more ambiguous and promiscuous than either their current uses or the critiques of those uses suggest. It also means they could have other and new forms.

Let me close by contrasting my view with two other prominent views. In a provocative recent book, Ran Hirschl has coined the phrase 'constitutional theocracy' to describe legal regimes that distinguish between political and religious authority but nonetheless allow religious norms to pervade public life.[95] If I am right, this is a good description of much of modern politics, including—with due allowance for its originally non-constitutional status—the European human rights regime at its beginning.[96] Strangely, however, Hirschl groups Europe today with the rest of the world in a drift further towards theocracy. I have not discussed the *Lautsi* case here, which may seem to bolster Hirschl's contentions. But from my perspective, it is contemporary Europe's *departure* from 'constitutional theocracy' in recent decades that deserves emphasis. The ECtHR's headscarf cases are troubling not because European secularism is marginal today, but because it is the wrong kind of secularism.

Joseph Weiler looks at the situation somewhat differently. Having warned Europeans at the time of the debate over the abortive European constitution against what he termed a 'Christophobic ghettoization' of its Christian heritage, Weiler intervened as an advocate in the *Lautsi* appeal to warn Europe against a worrisome secularist drift.[97] Confusingly, Weiler invoked the United States as an example of the secularist society that Europe must not become, going so far as to complain, like some American conservatives, that a profane America in which the 'public square' is 'naked' has to be avoided at all costs.[98] Yet the real contrast between contemporary

Dahlab, *Şahin*, and *Dogru*. ECtHR, *Affaire Ahmet Arslan et autres c. Turquie*, Appl. no. 41135/98, Judgment of 23 February 2010, esp. at paras 44–52 for its 'democratic society' analysis.

[94] Cf. Moyn, 'Hannah Arendt on the Secular', 35 *New German Critique* (Fall 2008) 71, a paper that pursues a similar agenda in a different way.

[95] R. Hirschl, *Constitutional Theocracy* (2010).

[96] Scholars debate whether to consider the ECHR treaty regime a constitutional one (and how best to theorize the relationship between constitutionalism and pluralism). Cf. Sweet, 'On the Constitutionalisation of the Convention: The European Court of Human Rights as a Constitutional Court', 80 *Revue trimestrielle des droits de l'homme* (2009) 923 with N. Krisch, *Beyond Constitutionalism: The Pluralistic Structure of Postnational Law* (2010) esp. Ch. 4.

[97] J.H.H. Weiler, *Un'Europa cristiana: Un saggio esplorativo* (2003), Part I and *passim*, as well as 116–21 for a 'Christian historiography of European integration' radically different from the one I have suggested here. For some reason, only a small portion of this book has been published in English, as Weiler, 'A Christian Europe?: Europe and Christianity: Rules of Commitment', 6 *European View* (2007) 143.

[98] A transcription of Weiler's oral pleadings as lawyer representing various intervening states can be found at http://www.ilsussidiario.net/News/Politics-Society/2010/7/1/EXCLUSIVE-Oral-Submission-by-Professor-Joseph-Weiler-before-the-Grand-Chamber-of-the-European-Court-of-Human-

Europe and contemporary America, contrary to those who pine for a bygone Europe of more than minimal Christian affiliation and observance, is that Europeans have moved fundamentally to pioneer—rather starkly against the background of human history so far—an unprecedented form of collective life in which religion has lost its hold. And in this context, the more plausible concern is that Europeans seem tempted to discriminate against Muslims, who are a living presence, than that they risk 'ghettoizing' a Christianity that has already departed to such a great extent and so quickly. The ECtHR's headscarf cases are troubling not because Europe should return to the public Christianity it has largely given up, but because its version of secularism is discriminatory rather than inclusionary.

Western Europe today is perhaps the equivalent for human politics of the 'non-religious ethics' that Derek Parfit once claimed to be 'at a very early stage.... Since we cannot know how Ethics will develop, it is not irrational to have high hopes.'[99] I have argued that the discriminatory secularism of today's European rights regime is far from written in the stars. Indeed, the ECtHR's religious freedom decisions, too consistent now to be random missteps, follow doctrinally not from a long-range secularism but rather from an inheritance of an anti-secularist past with which secularist judges need to break. Of course, to say that the Court's doctrines have allowed it to describe Muslims as threats to the minimal requirements of democracy, much as it once did with communists, is not to say its actions are not due to other factors too, including strategic deliberation about institutional standing and political judgment about the likely impact of its decisions. But if European secularism goes further—as one may legitimately hope it does, if only to illustrate an interesting and novel way to organize human community—perhaps it will need to overcome a discrimination against Muslims brought about not because Europe is too committed to secularism but because it is not committed enough.

Rights/96909/ (last visited 20 April 2016); and a video at http://dotsub.com/view/65bc5332-aa10-4b8c-bc50-d051e8f4fcc7 (last visited 20 April 2016). See also Weiler, 'Editorial: Lautsi: Crucifix in the Classroom Redux', 21(1) *European Journal of International Law* (February 2010) 1 and Weiler, 'Editorial: State and Nation; Church, Mosque and Synagogue—The Trailer', 8 *International Journal of Constitutional Law* (April 2010) 157. The rhetoric of the pleadings originates in Neuhaus (n. 7).

99 D. Parfit, *Reasons and Persons* (1984) 454.

6

US Exceptionalism in the Regulation of Religion

Winnifred Fallers Sullivan

1. Introduction

The legal regulation of religion is a complex and changing area of the law in the US, as it is everywhere today. But the US has a distinctive religious landscape and a distinctive regulatory regime with respect to religion, one which is often misunderstood both inside and outside the US. While continuing to be formally founded in the shifting interpretation of the first 17 words of the First Amendment to the US Constitution: 'Congress shall make no law respecting an establishment of religion, or prohibiting the free exercise thereof', the extent to which US law in this area is profoundly affected by the peculiar nature of both American federalism and American religious disestablishment is rarely acknowledged. In other words, while religion worldwide is increasingly dispersed and de-centred, and more and more people understand themselves as being in charge of their own religious lives, in the US that 'DIY' quality has been present in religion from the beginning, constantly subverting efforts to control it, even while ordinary law shapes religion in countless ways.[1] 'We, the people' govern religion as well as politics.

The US has a strong unitary narrative regarding its founding era myths, including its myth of religious freedom—a narrative which includes the inevitability of continental expansion, as well as the sources of its particular political arrangements and commitments. A different story can be told about the legal regulation of religion in North America if one starts not with those myths, but if one starts before European settlement. Before European settlement in North America, more than 500 Indian nations were present in what is now the continental US, each with its own political, legal, and religious culture; these cultures continued after the Europeans arrived, and even today they continue to structure the lives of native communities and to influence majority cultures.[2] Early European immigrants to North America came from a Europe where the political and legal landscape was changing. Seventeenth-

[1] For classic descriptions of the effects of this process on religion, see M. deWolfe Howe, *The Garden and the Wilderness* (1963); W. Herberg, *Protestant Catholic Jew* (1955); and R. Wuthnow, *The Restructuring of American Religion: Society and Faith since WWII* (1990).

[2] For an introduction to Indian law in the US, see C. Goldberg, K. Washburn, and P. Frickey, *Indian Law Stories* (2010).

US Exceptionalism in the Regulation of Religion. First Edition. Winnifred Fallers Sullivan

and eighteenth-century Britain, in particular, was characterized by profound religious disagreement; this upheaval distracted the Empire from attempting to force its established church on its colonies. Toleration in the Empire was more practical than idealist.[3] African slaves were taken from a variety of kingdoms and brought indigenous traditional religions with them as well as Islam; colonial and subsequent federal and state governments severely restricted their capacity to practise those religious traditions.[4]

The various North American colonies each had distinct religious demographics and distinct political arrangements. At the time of independence there was no clear religious majority or legally established church throughout the original 13 Atlantic colonies; the religious landscape was already complicated. There were Baptists, Congregationalists, Dutch Reformed, Presbyterians, Catholics, Anglicans, Quakers, and a small number of Jews and Muslims, as well as practitioners of African and native religions and of European folk religions. There was also a low level of church membership at the time of the Revolution, probably the lowest level of 'churched' population in US history—partly because of displacement by revolutionary religion (as in the French Revolution) and also because of the low number of clergy serving a widely dispersed population. Before the Revolution, Presbyterians and Congregationalists were the largest Protestant denominations; after the Revolution—with revival and the growth of evangelical religion, westward expansion, and evangelization—Baptists and Methodists came to dominate. These social facts underlying US religious and legal diversity affect how efforts to manage through constitutional means have been received.

This chapter will consider the remarkable diversity of American religion from the beginning, the constitutionalizing of religion, the reasons for the delayed implementation of the First Amendment religion clauses, the evolution of the free exercise and establishment clause doctrine, and the ongoing difficulty in defining religion.

2. Constitutionalizing Religion

The main body of the US Constitution was completed in 1787. During the ratification process, opponents of the proposed Constitution complained that it contained no protection for individual liberties, including religious liberty.[5] Federalist defenders of the Constitution, including James Madison, argued that the proposed federal government, as constituted by the Constitution, was a government of such limited powers that it possessed no authority whatsoever to legislate beyond the areas enu-

[3] See E. Haefeli, *English Tolerance and Overseas Expansion between Renaissance and the Early Enlightenment, 1497–1688* (forthcoming).

[4] A. Raboteau, *Slave Religion: The 'Invisible Institution' in the Antebellum South* (1978).

[5] For descriptions of the history of the drafting of the religion clauses of the First Amendment, see McConnell, 'The Origins and Historical Understanding of Free Exercise of Religion', 103 *Harvard Law Review* (1990) 1409; and T. Curry, *The First Freedoms: Church and State in America to the Passage of the First Amendment* (1986). For a comprehensive introduction to the religion clauses of the US Constitution, see K. Greenawalt, *Religion and the Constitution*, vols I and II (2009).

merated in the Constitution; a bill of rights was therefore unnecessary. According to this view, because no provision in the Constitution permitted the federal government to legislate with respect to religion, no amendment protecting religious freedom was needed. Madison's views, and those of the other Federalists, changed, however, as it became clear that, as a practical political matter, support from those advocating such amendments was necessary first for ratification and then, more particularly, for Madison's electoral prospects. Political support from religious dissenters to existing state establishments, including Baptists, was particularly salient in this campaign.

The legislative record as to the choice of the actual wording of the religion clauses is sparse. Various possibilities were considered. The final version was adopted on 25 September 1789, as the third of a proposed package of amendments. (The third became the first with the defeat of the first two. No significance can thus reasonably be attributed to the religion clauses appearing first in the Bill of Rights, although the primacy of place is often mentioned today as a reason for their foundational importance.) Madison proposed that a protection against violations of rights of conscience by the states should also be inserted into the new Bill of Rights, although such protection was not added. Legal protection for religious liberty at the state level was left to the individual state constitutions. Thus the religion clauses, as originally drafted, are directed at the federal government: '*Congress* shall make no law . . .' and should be understood to be primarily jurisdictional. Individual state constitutions gradually adopted their own provisions protecting religious liberty.

The religion clauses of the First Amendment were little litigated before the twentieth century because they applied only to the federal government and federal authority was weak; disputes regarding religion were mostly decided under state constitutions which gradually ended formal state 'establishments' of various kinds. The Constitution is not the whole story, of course. There has always been pervasive regulation of religion in the US at the municipal, state, and federal levels, most of which has not been constitutionally tested. These laws both privilege and disable religiously motivated individuals and groups, shaping the form that religion takes in the US through, for example, laws of incorporation, zoning laws and building codes, tax exemptions, health and safety regulation, and noise ordinances.

In the early federal period, Americans worked, in a sense, on a blank slate as far as many of their institutions were concerned, not just religion. Religious and business leaders worked, often together, to enable the formation of legal corporate forms under which they could do their work.[6] The result by the mid-nineteenth century was what has been termed a de facto Protestant establishment, even in the midst of great religious diversity.[7] There was both a culturally strong Protestant establishment and a fissiparous ferment of religious fragmentation and innovation.

[6] See Barringer Gordon, 'The First Disestablishment: Limits on Church Power and Property before the Civil War', 162 *University of Pennsylvania Law Review* (2014) 307.

[7] For a description of the effects of that establishment on the regulation of sexuality, see J. Jakobsen and A. Pellegrini, *Love the Sin: Sexual Regulation and the Limits of Religious Tolerance* (2003).

3. Religion and Law in the Nineteenth Century

Although Catholics were present in the US before the Revolution, in Maryland as well as in the former French and Spanish colonies, large-scale Catholic immigration began in the 1840s, first from Ireland and Germany and then from Southern Europe. By World War I 25 per cent of Americans were Catholic. Reactions to Catholic immigration profoundly affected the law regarding religion in the US. Non-denominational Protestant practices that had been developed to broker among Protestant differences were discarded in favour of a harder-edged separationism—one that eventually, and ultimately unsuccessfully, attempted to exclude all religion from public spaces.[8]

Also over the course of the nineteenth century, the logic of manifest destiny, Indian removal policy, and the experience of the American Civil War, divided religious communities in ways that persist today. There are many religio/legal stories to be told in the US: north/south, east/west, Protestant/Catholic, black/white, indigenous/settler, conservative/liberal. Each religious community's story is specific, even while they all faced similar circumstances and learned political and legal strategies from one another. The Mormons have played, and continue to play, a starring role, however.[9]

The 1820s and 1830s were a time of religious experimentation in the new country; many new religious movements emerged, especially in the 'burned-over district' of upper New York State; most were short-lived. In 1827 Joseph Smith reported a new revelation, eventually published as the Book of Mormon. The fledgling Mormon community made a trek to Salt Lake in 1847, founding the state of Deseret. Smith also received a special revelation requiring plural marriage for Mormon men who were able to support more than one wife. The founding of the Mormon Church, officially called the Church of Jesus Christ of Latter-Day Saints, challenged American political, economic, and religious orders because it was theocratic, communalist, and heterodox. The Mormon Church was actively persecuted by the federal government. Unionist political ideology during the Civil War spoke of the 'twin evils of slavery and polygamy'. This challenge eventuated in an iconic constitutional case, *Reynolds v. US*,[10] decided by the US Supreme Court in 1871.

Reynolds was the first major 'free exercise' case. Mr Reynolds, prosecuted for bigamy in a federal court in what was then the Utah territory, defended himself on the ground that he would be damned if he failed to follow his religious duty to marry a second time. Justice Waite, writing for the majority, looked to the religious liberty campaigns of Thomas Jefferson and James Madison in colonial Virginia for guidance in interpreting the free exercise clause of the First Amendment,[11] concluding that 'Congress was deprived of all legislative power over mere opinion, but was left

[8] See P. Hamburger, *Separation of Church and State* (2002).

[9] See S. Barringer Gordon, *The Mormon Question: Polygamy and Constitutional Conflict in Nineteenth Century America* (2002).

[10] *Reynolds v. US*, 98 U.S.145 (1878).

[11] M. Peterson and R. Vaughan (eds), *The Virginia Statute on Religious Freedom: Its Evolution and Consequences in American History* (1988).

free to reach actions which were in violation of social duties or subversive of good order'. Because 'Polygamy has always been odious among the northern and western nations of Europe, and, until the establishment of the Mormon Church, was almost exclusively a feature of the life of Asiatic and of African people', it was not a violation of the Constitution to prohibit it even though it was arguably an 'exercise of religion'.

Reynolds continues to be important because of the legal salience of the Virginia experience, its articulation of the opinion/act distinction, its selective use of 'social science' evidence, and because the Church continued to exist while being radically reformed by law. In 1887 the federal Edmunds-Tucker Act annulled the act of incorporation of the Mormon Church and expropriated Church property, disenfranchised women, and made the vote for statehood conditional on disavowing polygamy. The Act was held constitutional in *The Late Corporation of the Church of Jesus Christ of Latter-Day Saints v. US*.[12] In 1890, Wilford Woodruff, then President of the Mormon Church, issued a manifesto ending the practice of polygamy, explaining the decision as based on a divine revelation to him as the head of the Church. Utah was granted statehood in 1890. Polygamy was thereafter prohibited by the Church and gradually died out except among some dissenting Mormon groups, including the Fundamentalist Latter-Day Saints who continue to live today in the intermountain west and in Texas.

During this same period—while the Mormon Church was being forcibly 're-formed'—the federal government used law to convert Indians to Christianity by granting the right to found Indian schools to various churches and religious orders, requiring Indians to own property individually rather than communally, and formally outlawing Indian religious practices, among others. Religious changes over the course of the nineteenth and early twentieth centuries also included the growing influence of Catholic and Jewish immigrant cultures, the resulting creation of institutions parallel to majority Protestant ones, and an important division in American Protestantism between conservatives and liberals. This division is usually marked by the publication of the *Fundamentals* in 1910, the Scopes trial in 1925,[13] and the subsequent political retreat of conservative protestants, on the one hand, and the social gospel movement, liberal embrace of science, and progressive protestantism, on the other. Asian immigration (until the borders were closed in 1920) also changed the religious demography of the US. After the Civil War, growth in federal power relative to states, the continued rise of capitalism, US imperialism, and the passage and delayed implementation of the reconstruction amendments (13th, 14th, 15th) and the rise of the Jim Crow laws, profoundly affected religion and the regulation of religion in the US. Today, however, the ways in which US religion has been legally shaped over its history are often masked through recourse to an imagined unifying jurisprudence, one that in fact was the short-lived result of the federalizing of the clauses in the 1940s through the doctrine of 'Incorporation'.

[12] *The Late Corporation of the Church of Jesus Christ of Latter-Day Saints v. US*, 136 U.S. 1 (1890).

[13] See M. Lienesch, *In the Beginning: Fundamentalism, the Scopes Trial and the Anti-evolution Movement* (2007).

Until 1940, the First Amendment had applied only to acts of the federal government. It was the doctrine of incorporation, developed by the US Supreme Court in the early twentieth century, that inaugurated US Supreme Court administration over the activities of state and local governments.

4. Incorporation

The Fourteenth Amendment to the US Constitution reads, in relevant part:

Section 1. All persons born or naturalized in the United States, and subject to the jurisdiction thereof, are citizens of the United States and of the State wherein they reside. No State shall make or enforce any law which shall abridge the privileges or immunities of citizens of the United States; nor shall any State deprive any person of life, liberty, or property, without due process of law; nor deny to any person within its jurisdiction the equal protection of the laws.

With the enactment of these words, former slaves were declared to be full citizens of both the US and of the individual states in which they resided. But what precisely did it mean to be a full citizen? Which privileges and immunities could not be abridged? What process was due? What did equal protection mean? To whom exactly did these words apply? States were then, and still are, jealous of their rights and jurisdiction. For 50 years, the guarantees of the Fourteenth Amendment were not fully enforced by the US Supreme Court. But, beginning in 1905, the Supreme Court began to fulfil the promise of the Civil War amendments by using the enumerated rights of the Bill of Rights to detail the obligations of the states to their citizens—with respect, first, to freedom to contract, freedom of speech, and freedom to educate one's children. As to religion, two cases federalized and unified US religion policy: *Cantwell v. Connecticut*,[14] in which religious proselytizing in the streets by Jehovah's Witnesses was held to be protected by the 'free exercise' clause; and *Everson v. Board of Education*,[15] in which public funding for the bus fares of schoolchildren attending private Catholic schools was found not to be an establishment of religion. Decided as the country was only just beginning to come to grips with the need to enforce civil rights for black Americans, equality became an important value for the regulation of religion as well as in the eradication of racist law.

Although US constitutional cases concerning religion are often denominated as free exercise or establishment clause cases, all US constitutional religion cases have both free exercise and establishment clause aspects, creating a persistent tension between the clauses: free exercise clause cases ask when religiously motivated persons are exempt from laws that apply to everyone else, and establishment clause cases ask what limits exist on government support for religion. With incorporation these questions became national questions. The mid to late twentieth century was a period during which the Court made a sustained—if uneven and ultimately unsuccessful—effort to both thoroughly dis-establish religion and robustly protect free

[14] *Cantwell v. Connecticut*, 310 U.S. 296 (1940).
[15] *Everson v. Board of Education*, 330 U.S. 1 (1947).

exercise, attempting to achieve what was termed 'neutrality' of the law with respect to religion.[16] The *Everson* and *Cantwell* decisions set the terms for this effort.

In *Everson*, Mr Everson sued to have a New Jersey law declared an unconstitutional establishment of religion. The law reimbursed parents for the cost of bus fare for schoolchildren between their home and school, whether they attended public or private schools (including religious private schools). For the first time, the US Supreme Court considered what exactly was 'an establishment of religion' under the Constitution. Justice Black, in his opinion for the Court, announced that:

> The 'establishment of religion' clause of the First Amendment means at least this: neither a state nor the Federal Government can set up a church. Neither can pass laws which aid one religion, aid all religions, or prefer one religion over another. Neither can force nor influence a person to go to or to remain away from church against his will or force him to profess a belief or disbelief in any religion. No person can be punished for entertaining or professing religious beliefs or disbeliefs, for church attendance or non-attendance. No tax in any amount, large or small, can be levied to support any religious activities or institutions, whatever they may be called, or whatever form they may adopt to teach or practice religion. Neither a state nor the Federal Government can, openly or secretly, participate in the affairs of any religious organizations or groups, and vice versa. In the words of Jefferson, the clause against establishment of religion by law was intended to erect 'a wall of separation between church and State.'

These ringing categorical words have been repeated countless times, yet rarely applied. Even in *Everson*, which upheld the statute as constitutional, New Jersey was found to be aiding children, not the Catholic Church!

5. 'Incorporating' American Religion

As the Court worked through how it would enforce *Everson*, the dominant standard for determining whether the establishment clause has been violated by an action of the state or federal government became the *Lemon* test, named for another school case. *Lemon v. Kurtzman*[17] held that state laws providing salary supplements for teachers in private religious schools were an unconstitutional establishment of religion, because supervision of the aid would involve the government in religious matters. Under the *Lemon* test a law must be secular in purpose and effect with no entanglement between government and religion in order to pass constitutional muster. *Lemon* has also been very unevenly applied, and is understood by many now, as is *Everson*, to have been motivated by anti-Catholicism. Most cases under the *Lemon* test involved locally popular legislative efforts to provide government aid of various kinds to Catholic schools, such as free textbooks and teacher supplements.

[16] For a description of that litigation, see S. Barringer Gordon, *The Spirit of the Law: Religious Voices and the Constitution in Modern America* (2010).

[17] *Lemon v. Kurtzman*, 403 U.S. 602 (1971).

Separationist readings of the establishment clause led to the creation of a separate Catholic school system and eventually, by analogy, in response to racial integration, of Protestant religious academies. The perception that the Court and the federal government were working to secularize education has also contributed to the rise in popularity of the homeschool movement in the US in the past couple of decades. Public schools in the US are funded and governed at the local municipal level, paid for by local property taxes, and run by local school boards. Religiously affiliated schools have, until recently, been privately funded. This policy has caused huge disparities in the quality of education and differences in what education for citizenship means. More broadly, efforts to enforce the establishment clause have revealed the impossibility of separating religion from American culture. Today, new voucher and charter school movements, part of a larger privatization of government services, are creating new opportunities for government funding of religious schools, opportunities largely approved by the Supreme Court.

The 1984 *Lynch* case[18] shows the Court's majority at its most religiously irenic—endorsing a broadly Christian American public culture—but it also illustrates the always surreal representation of religion that underwrites constitutional jurisprudence.[19] In 1983 several citizens of Pawtucket, Rhode Island, supported by the American Civil Liberties Union, brought an action against the mayor demanding that a city-sponsored Christmas display in a downtown park be declared an establishment of religion in violation of the First Amendment. Chief Justice Warren Burger, writing for a five-member majority, found the display, which featured a centrally placed crèche, to be a permissible recognition of a now secularized holiday. While analysing the display under the *Lemon* standards, the Chief Justice suggested that there were a set of public practices historically connected to religion that have been constitutionalized—and, in effect, secularized—through their long historic acceptance. These practices include token ceremonial references such as 'In God We Trust' and 'God Save This Honorable Court', as well as the display of religious paintings in public museums, annual Thanksgiving proclamations, and the celebration of Christmas. Justice Sandra Day O'Connor, in her concurring opinion, argued that the Court's majority and the *Lemon* test were insufficiently attentive to the risks of majoritarian imposition. She argued that the appropriate question is not whether a particular government practice is religious or not but whether the practice can reasonably be perceived as an endorsement of a particular religious position, dividing citizens into groups of favoured and less favoured. Characteristically, however, having attempted to shift the terms of the debate towards issues of democratic inclusion, she agreed with the majority, finding the Pawtucket display to be unproblematic because it could not reasonably be perceived as endorsing Christianity. Justice William Brennan for the four dissenting justices argued that the crèche remained a potent sacred object, that the establishment clause required a privatization of reli-

[18] *Lynch v. Donnelly*, 465 U.S. 668 (1984).

[19] For an extended consideration of the *Lynch* case, see W. Fallers Sullivan, *Paying the Words Extra: Religious Discourse in the Supreme Court of the United States* (1994).

gion, and that government display of a crèche scene was an impermissible establishment of religion.

The opinions in *Lynch* display different understandings of religion and different views of what counts as evidence in such cases, with Burger seeing display of the crèche as non-religious, O'Connor seeing it as religious but benign, while Brennan saw it as intensely and exclusively religious—being the representation of a central doctrine of Christian belief, the incarnation of the deity in the person of Jesus Christ—and its display by government as offensive to non-Christians and non-believers. The Constitution, like other laws mandating separation, gives little hint as to how one might adjudicate among these positions.

Subsequent cases testing the placing of religious symbols in public spaces—whether displays relating to religious holidays, or the erection of monuments of the Ten Commandments or Christian crosses—continue to ring the same changes, along a spectrum from seeing them as inoffensive cultural references to seeing them as an intentional and exclusive identification of government with Christianity and a consequent marginalization of non-Christian Americans. The trend, however, since the decision in *Lynch*, has been away from the separationism of Brennan's *Lynch* opinion towards a broad acceptance of the public sponsorship of Christian cultural symbols.

Free exercise also underwent changes under incorporation, but it too has been haunted by the problem of proving religion. The rule in *Reynolds*, the Mormon polygamy case, was held to be that the free exercise clause only gives you a right to your opinion, not a right to act on that opinion. No accommodation or exemption from the law would be given to you if you were religiously motivated to violate that law. That was federal law for almost a hundred years. Yet, after incorporation, in a series of cases beginning in the 1960s, the Court held that there were times when the free exercise clause did give you constitutional protection for your acts as well as your opinions. The most impressive of these cases from the second half of the twentieth century was *Wisconsin v. Yoder*,[20] decided in 1972.

Mr Yoder, a member of the Old Order Amish, was prosecuted for violating the mandatory schooling laws. He had kept his children out of high school so that they could learn Amish ways of life. This case set up a clear conflict between an important public policy—mandatory schooling—and an important private religious value—collective life as an intentional religious community. Indeed, Yoder had a very low opinion of high schools and claimed that the Old Order Amish would ultimately be destroyed if their children were sent to them. Unlike Reynolds, Yoder won. The Court held that the free exercise clause provided a defence to the law. The Amish in Wisconsin did not have to send their children to high school; the survival of their community was deemed to be more important than training future citizens. The Court's opinion was very admiring of what it took to be Amish values. *Yoder* is arguably the high water mark of constitutionally mandated accommodation. The Court retreated after that.

[20] *Wisconsin v. Yoder*, 406 U.S. 205 (1972).

6. The World *Smith* Made

The mid-century regime of constitutionally mandated accommodations for religiously minded folk ended abruptly in 1990 when Justice Scalia, speaking for the majority in *Employment Division v. Smith*, returned the Court to its position in *Reynolds*, affirming once again the distinction between opinion and act.

Alfred Smith and Galen Black were substance abuse counsellors working for the State of Oregon. They had been dismissed from their jobs for violating the state's narcotics laws when they ingested peyote, a cactus fruit with hallucinogenic properties, as a part of a ceremony of the Native American Church, of which they were members. They were subsequently denied unemployment compensation on the grounds that they had been fired 'for cause'. Smith and Black challenged this decision, citing *Yoder* and arguing that they should be exempt from the narcotics laws for reason of religious motivation. Scalia's opinion reinterpreted the previous free exercise cases, including *Yoder*, which seemed to allow for such exemptions, announcing that those earlier cases had been misunderstood, and that they had actually relied on hybrid rights combining free exercise with other rights independent of religion, such as, in *Yoder*, the right of parents to control schooling.

Smith thus held once again that the free exercise clause of the First Amendment to the US Constitution does not mandate a religious exemption, or accommodation, from neutral laws of general application when they impinge on the activities of religiously minded people, even if such laws effectively outlaw acts that are understood by those people to be significant, non-negotiable, religious obligations—even, in the *Smith* case, what were termed sacraments. Such accommodations, Scalia announced, should be subject to the political process. Otherwise, he said, echoing the Court in *Reynolds*, every man would be a law unto himself. Disestablished US religion was simply too diverse and messy to support exemption from the law.

Importantly, however, although *Smith* ended religious exemptions as a *constitutional* matter, both specific and general statutory exemptions and accommodations have proliferated, as Scalia anticipated. Narcotics laws, for example, now specifically exempt the use of peyote by members of the Native American Church. Employment discrimination legislation mandates religious accommodation in the workplace. But, most significantly, immediately in the wake of the *Smith* decision, a coalition of more than 60 religious groups, liberal and conservative, joined by the American Civil Liberties Union, came together and quickly and successfully lobbied Congress to overrule *Smith* with near-unanimous passage of the federal Religious Freedom Restoration Act (RFRA). The coalition included groups from across a very broad American spectrum, politically and theologically speaking, all appearing to agree that, whatever divisions existed between them, religion was under threat.

The purpose of the new law was explicitly to 'restore' what Congress took to be the pre-*Smith* rule. Passage of RFRA created a constitutional showdown between the two branches of government: Congress and the Supreme Court. In 1997 RFRA was declared unconstitutional as applied to the states.[21] Congress responded with a raft

[21] *Boerne v. Flores*, 521 U.S. 507 (1997).

of other, more carefully drafted, legislation, including the Religious Land Use and Institutionalized Persons Act at the federal level—legislation specifically intended to salvage some of the intended reach of RFRA. Exemptions were also built into other legislation such as employment and civil rights law. And dozens of states passed their own laws in response to *Smith*—sometimes known as mini- or state RFRAs—all designed to provide robust and broad protection for religious accommodation. The aftermath of *Smith* also saw the development of a vigorous and well-funded specialized bar devoted to promoting the rights of religion in the US and elsewhere. We now live in the world that *Smith* made, a noisy world of religious freedom advocacy. It is a world that has become increasingly contentious as various visions of religious freedom seem to be at war with each other, both within the US and elsewhere.

Among other things, in my view, what we are seeing is why *Reynolds* and *Smith* were rightly decided, and why RFRA laws cannot work, however they are drafted. We are seeing why religious freedom is impossible. It is impossible because we have no way of resolving our differences as to what religion is, even in fairly uncontroversial cases, let alone controversial ones. Religion in the US is disestablished and fragmented. No one is in charge, and the proliferation of RFRA laws has only magnified this situation. We have been reduced to competitive cherry-picking and proof-texting from the writings of various founding fathers, bits of history, and judicial opinions. There are a variety of ways of illustrating the impossibility of religious freedom. I will focus next on the problem of 'proving' religion in law.

7. Proving Religion

Any talk of a need for special legal accommodations for religiously motivated persons, or of a need for the legal separation of religion from government, presumes a capacity to give a precise account of what religion is, where it can be located, and what effects it has. Such an account, for legal purposes, might take various forms depending on the nature of the conversation. If the account is to be given in court in the US, the account is subject to the rules of evidence. For example, in the US federal courts, Rule 402 of the Federal Rules of Evidence provides that, with some exceptions, relevant evidence is admissible while irrelevant evidence is always inadmissible. 'Evidence is relevant if: (a) it has any tendency to make a fact more or less probable than it would be without the evidence; and (b) the fact is of consequence in determining the action.'[22]

With respect to religion, legally relevant evidence arguably does not exist in the US because the word religion lacks a commonly agreed-upon referent; the US, unlike most countries, lacks either an established legal order whose responsibility it is to define orthodox religion or an academic establishment whose specialized work it is to produce such knowledge for law. Religion is singularly underdetermined as a legal matter. Further complicating the matter is the fact that courts are increasingly sceptical of a range of forensic and other expert evidence offered in courts, ranging

[22] Federal Rules of Evidence 401.

from the identification of fingerprints to various different computer modelling products, often produced for a commercial market. Such scepticism increasingly extends to expert evidence about religion. The instability of the term and the failure to distinguish between what the law appears to demand and what we actually know is resulting in the further accumulation of what is already a serious problem in the US courtroom—that is, the accumulation of 'junk science'.

To illustrate the difficulties with proving religion in the contemporary American courtroom, it is worthwhile focusing on the expert evidence in two cases which are termed, in US constitutional terms, a free exercise case and an establishment clause case: one case about whether an individual should be exempt from the force of law because the law burdens her exercise of her religion, and the other a case about whether what the government is doing is an unconstitutional 'establishment' of religion. These are lower court opinions, not Supreme Court opinions. They do not make new law but they do illustrate the troublesome challenge of 'proving' religion.

In 1999, in the case of *Warner v. Boca Raton*,[23] five experts on religion were called to give opinions as to whether the burial practices of the plaintiffs in a federal lawsuit—a group of families whose relatives had been buried in a municipal cemetery in Boca Raton, Florida—were 'religious' and therefore entitled to legal protection.[24] Cemetery regulations had limited gravesite memorialization to small flat plaques, flush with the ground; these regulations were designed, it was said, to facilitate lawn maintenance and the movement of heavy equipment for grave-digging, but they were also consistent with contemporary trends in cemetery design. Over a couple of decades in the 1980s and 1990s, however, city cemetery workers had allowed several hundred families—ordinary American Protestants, Catholics, and Jews—to install small home-made assemblages on the graves, including Christian crosses, statues of saints, and the Star of David, among other items, in apparent violation of the regulations.

In 1998, the City abruptly changed its policy and decided to start enforcing the rules by removing existing grave decorations. After a period of political lobbying and protest, the plaintiffs sued in federal district court, claiming that both the cemetery rules and the City's enforcement of the rules violated the free exercise clause of the First Amendment to the US Constitution, the Florida Constitution, and the then brand new Florida Religious Freedom Restoration Act. Because the constitutional claim was fairly clearly foreclosed by the *Smith* decision, the principal issue at trial was whether what the plaintiffs had done was a 'practice of religion' within the meaning of the new Florida statute prohibiting government from 'substantially burden[ing] the practice of religion'. The City argued that the installations were not religious because they were not formally and explicitly 'mandated' by the respective religions to which the plaintiffs belonged, that is, they said, Judaism, Catholicism,

[23] *Warner v. Boca Raton*, 64 F. Supp. 2d 1272 (S.D. Fla. 1999).
[24] See W. Fallers Sullivan, *The Impossibility of Religious Freedom* (2005).

and Protestantism—as if one could isolate a single burial practice attached to each of these deeply problematic, world-historical categories.[25]

The five religion experts who testified had five different theories of what constituted religion and whether the plaintiffs' activities should be so described. In the end, the judge rejected the plaintiffs' claim; he constructed his own theory of religion in his opinion, which he synthesized using habits of mind cultivated in his own conservative Presbyterian Church as well as by picking and choosing among the views of the courtroom experts. All of the theories were intellectually defensible on some ground; arguably, none were *legally* relevant in a formal sense. Indeed, there was no way of ascertaining the statutory meaning of the word 'religion' with sufficient certainty as to underwrite the admission of the testimony. What little evidence there was of legislative intent suggested a desire by the Florida legislature to be broadly inclusive.

What the plaintiffs needed the experts to say was that the plaintiffs' practices were religious and that they had been substantially burdened. The experts testified, each from a different academic perspective, as to why the plaintiffs' practices would or would not be considered religious by religious scholars; the three experts who testified for the plaintiffs testified that, although not explicitly mandated by religious law, the practices were rooted in, and consistent with, the broad social practices within these traditions and with the narratives expressed by the plaintiffs in their own testimony. These experts offered what might be called an endorsement of vernacular religion as morally significant, while ignoring the tautological nature of their assertions about religion.

The two religion experts for the defendant, the City of Boca Raton, offered formal structured models of religion that would permit the judge to locate the plaintiffs' practices along a spectrum from 'high' or 'central' religious practices (defined as institutional, textual, and male) to 'low' or 'peripheral' religious practices (defined as home-based, oral, and female); each of them concluded that the popular religious practices evident in the cemetery 'shrines' were 'low' or 'peripheral', and therefore did not rise to a level that deserved legal protection. Each offered an abstract hierarchical model of religion to be used to test what should count as legal religion in the US notwithstanding the non-existence of any constitutional or statutory grounds for such a hierarchy.

The judge in the *Warner* case revealed a deep and very Protestant scepticism about the relevance of the history of early Christian burial offered by the Church historian as well as of the methods of Jewish legal practice employed by the Orthodox rabbinical expert, substituting instead his own lay evangelical understanding of how scripture should be read, and finding no mandate in the Bible for the little shrines constructed by the plaintiffs. The religious evidence in the *Warner* case revealed the gap that often opens in these cases between the academic study of religion, on the one hand, and the version of a particular religious tradition experienced by the judge and the witnesses. The capacity of a court to adjudicate the orthodoxy of a witness' practices is deeply troubling in a country in which religion is constitutionally

[25] See T. Masuzawa, *The Invention of World Religions* (2005).

disestablished and the free exercise of religion is guaranteed. Indeed, the judge himself announced his respect for the sincerity of the plaintiffs' religious practices and celebrated US religious freedom. But he could not see his way clear simply to endorse such a broad definition. One might say that the judge refused to implement the evident intent of the Florida statute to protect all religiously motivated persons from laws that might impinge on their religious practices, however peripheral or unattested to in the tradition. The result, as the City lawyer frequently announced, would be 'cemetery chaos'.

Cases brought under the establishment clause address the question as to when government is prohibited from acting because its actions constitute an unconstitutional 'establishment' or favouring of religion. Academic experts in establishment clause cases testify as to the religiousness or secularity of activities of the government (or of agents of the government), rather than of individuals as in free exercise cases.

In a highly publicized case in 2005, *Kitzmiller v. Dover School District*,[26] a federal district court in Pennsylvania held that a local school board's recommendation to its students that they should consider 'Intelligent Design' (ID) as an explanation for the fossil record was an unconstitutional establishment of religion.[27] Again, many expert witnesses were mobilized to testify concerning the nature of ID. Judge Jones found for the plaintiff families who objected to the School Board's recommendation on the ground that ID is not science because it lacks an empirical foundation in the scientific method. Because he had determined that ID was not science, he decided it must be religion. Science and religion were the only options he considered; in effect, if not science, then religion.

The facts in the case suggest that the situation was less clear-cut. The Dover School Board had announced that, beginning in January 2005, teachers would be required to read the following statement to students in the ninth grade biology class at Dover High School:

> The Pennsylvania Academic Standards require students to learn about Darwin's Theory of Evolution and eventually to take a standardized test of which evolution is a part.
>
> Because Darwin's Theory is a theory, it continues to be tested as new evidence is discovered. The Theory is not a fact. Gaps in the Theory exist for which there is no evidence. A theory is defined as a well-tested explanation that unifies a broad range of observations. Intelligent Design is an explanation of the origin of life that differs from Darwin's view. The reference book, *Of Pandas and People*, is available for students who might be interested in gaining an understanding of what Intelligent Design actually involves. With respect to any theory, students are encouraged to keep an open mind. The school leaves the discussion of the Origins of Life to individual students and their families. As a Standards-driven district, class instruction focuses upon preparing students to achieve proficiency on Standards-based assessments.[28]

The legal question presented was whether the City of Dover had established religion when it required reading of the statement.

[26] *Kitzmiller v. Dover*, 400 F. Supp. 2d 707 (M.D. Pa. 2005).

[27] See W. Fallers Sullivan, 'Being Human: Negotiating Religion, Law, and Science in the Classroom and the Courtroom' in E. Mertz, W. Ford, and G. Matoesian (eds), *Translating the Social World for Law* (2015).

[28] *Kitzmiller* (n. 26) 708.

While ridiculed by many liberal commentators, the statement, taken at face value, seems a genuine effort, if somewhat untutored and unscientific—in the professional sense—to explain to students how science education works and how the School Board intended to handle local concerns about the role of government, the teaching of evolution, and the prerogatives of families in child raising. There is no mention of God or of religion either in the statement or in *Of Pandas and People*.[29]

Rather than starting with a definition of religion, Judge Jones' opinion in *Kitzmiller* used the evidentiary rules respecting expert scientific testimony to determine what constitutionally counts as religion. He found that ID is not science, and that it is, instead, a deliberate fraud. While it markets itself as science, he found that it is really 'stealth' religion. ID, and the question of its 'real' purpose, an artefact of American populism and of the US culture wars, became a test case for delineating the boundary between what the judge and the expert witnesses contended are two mutually exclusive domains, science and religion: a boundary whose boundedness and stability was assumed.

Proponents of ID are anti-establishment, in the sense of viewing themselves as being against both big government and big science. Some of them are striving to make space for a biblical account of human origins. But ID itself arguably has no specific religious content. Its proponents have learned that lesson from the fate of efforts to teach creationism. What evidence was offered to prove that the Dover School Board's statement constituted an establishment of religion? As with the *Warner* case, Judge Jones' decision in the *Kitzmiller* case was authorized by various experts who testified at the trial. Among them was a Christian theologian, John Haught, professor of theology at Georgetown University, who described ID as bad theology—the product, he said, of religious ignorance. ID was not just bad science, he claimed, it was also bad religion:

> ID tries to squeeze what is undeniably a supernatural cause, intelligent design, into an explanatory slot where only natural causes are methodologically permissible... Throughout the modern period scientific method has refused to use categories such as purpose, God, intelligence, value, meaning, importance, etc., and has attempted to understand all phenomena in a very limited impersonal and indeed physical way... Theologically, moreover, major traditions maintain that if God influences and interacts with the created world it cannot be in the same way that physical causes operate. From the point of view of the most prominent theologians, therefore, not only is ID poor science, it is also appalling theology.[30]

'Major' traditions and 'the most prominent' theologians have worked it out, according to Haught. No 'good scientist' would indulge in professional speculations on 'purpose, God, intelligence, value, meaning, or importance'. No good theologian would believe in miracles or assert that God intervenes in history. Furthermore, genealogy, according to Haught, establishes the essential nature of things. ID is tainted by its forbearers.

[29] P. Davis and D.H. Kenyon, *Of Pandas and People: The Central Question of Biological Origins* (1989).

[30] *Kitzmiller v. Dover School District*, Haught Expert Witness Report 2005, 6.

Haught is a liberal theologian. The practice of having 'liberal' theologians either testify or be cited in American courtrooms as experts in religion is longstanding. Their role is to debunk folk knowledge. In another evolution case, *McLean v. Arkansas*,[31] the well-known liberal Protestant theologian, Langdon Gilkey, served as an expert witness against the creation science statute in Arkansas. He used the Protestant Christian theology of Paul Tillich to define religion and to critique creation science. Haught, Gilkey, and Tillich have all been enlisted in service of what might be described as an anti-democratic liberal political theology. The fit between liberal theology and science is very cosy.

8. Conclusion

Together, American populist politics and disestablished religion have created a context in which either separating religion or accommodating it has become impossible as a practical matter, given the difficulty of resolving the question of what counts as religion. The pressure on the word 'religion' has become more than it can carry. What makes the US regulation of religion stand out among national legal orders is the dual commitment to federalism and to disestablishment. With a low 'statism' and a strong commitment to equality, theological, as well as political, academic expertise has little purchase on the national mind. Religion is what the people say it is. That is a very old story in the US.

How different is the US from other countries today? Its ongoing refusal to participate in the international legal order gives US law in this area a distinctive cast. Protection for 'religion *and belief*' is not an American project. For most of US history, to be American is to be religious. Religion is regarded as less suspect in the US than elsewhere because of the lack of a past history of a formal church–state alliance. The American difficulty with defining religion is somewhat modulated in the international context by the gesture of including non-religious belief. But that gesture solves some problems and creates others. What about religion which is not founded in belief?[32] Recent decisions from constitutional and international courts on religious freedom suggest that the problem of definition is not just a US problem. The critique of secularism, the declining authority of religious elites, and the claiming of authority to govern one's own religious life, mixing and matching from different sources, is widespread today, undermining the stability of definition necessary to support these laws.[33]

[31] *McLean v. Arkansas* 529 F. Supp. 1255 (ED Ark. 1982).

[32] For a comparative exploration of the law and politics of religious freedom, see W. Fallers Sullivan, E. Shakman Hurd, S. Mahmood, and P. Danchin (eds), *Politics of Religious Freedom* (2015).

[33] See R. Hirschl, *Constitutional Theocracy* (2010).

7

Rethinking Secularism in Europe

Lorenzo Zucca

1. Introduction

A spectre is haunting Europe—the spectre of secularism. All the powers of old Europe have entered into a holy alliance to exorcise this spectre: Pope and Putin, Merkel and Macron, French intellectuals, and the European Court of Human Rights.[1] Everywhere the secular state is under threat. One obvious threat comes from the revival of religion in Europe, and in particular its extremist manifestation.[2] The recent tragedies of Paris, London, and Brussels show the cleavage between European states and extremist minorities. A second threat comes from the spread of negative secularism: religion is regarded as an enemy of the secular state. This kind of secularism is historically dated, legally inapplicable, and politically inadequate. The view I am rejecting is exemplified by the standard French position of ideological *laïcité*, which gave rise to the recent statute banning the wearing of the burqa in public streets. This ideological interpretation of *laïcité* suggests that religion can only be free as a purely private and inward-looking practice: instead of understanding religion, ideological forms of secularism attempt to deny its social role and meaning and confine religious practices to private spaces.

Europe needs to fundamentally rethink secularism and freedom of religion. To be sure, freedom of religion in a secular age is a paradox: why single out for special protection something that is no longer special? Courts are central players in this paradox. They decide when a claim is deep enough to be a claim of conscience.[3] They are asked to discriminate between what is religion and what is not.[4] The second paradox flows from the first: in a secular age, religion does not have a stable definition; as a result, secularism is much harder to define—it turns out to be a denial of whatever happens to be identified as religion. But since no legal definition of religion is neutral, the denial of an ideological position is itself also an ideological position.

[1] This paraphrases K. Marx and F. Engels, *The Communist Manifesto* (2015).

[2] See, e.g., S. Mancini and M. Rosenfeld (eds), *Constitutional Secularism in an Age of Religious Revival* (2014).

[3] J. Maclure and C. Taylor, *Secularism and Freedom of Conscience* (2011).

[4] See Zucca, 'A Marriage Made in Heaven? The Relationship between Religious Pluralism and Secularism' in F. Requejo and C. Ungureanu (eds), *Democracy, Law and Religious Pluralism in Europe: Secularism and Post-Secularism* (2014).

Rethinking Secularism in Europe. First Edition. Lorenzo Zucca © Lorenzo Zucca 2019.
Published 2019 by Oxford University Press.

This is what characterizes negative secularism, namely the view that the secular state should focus on the denial of religion's place in the public sphere.

I suggest, instead, that secularism should be thought of as a positive attitude towards all forms of diversity in society, including religious views. I call this positive secularism; its point is not to deny the place of religion in the public sphere, but to promote diversity of worldviews.[5]

European courts, I shall argue, have a special responsibility: to promote diversity of worldviews and pluralism throughout Europe. Courts have an expansive role to play here. They define religion when they are asked to protect freedom of religion. And, negatively, they also define secularism. Moreover, they also shape the relations between political institutions and religions. Finally, they have to make sure that diversity does not threaten political unity. For the moment, they have abdicated their responsibility and oscillate between two positions that can be illustrated through two recent landmark cases of the European Court of Human Rights (ECtHR): *Lautsi and Others v. Italy*[6] and *S.A.S. v. France*.[7] In the first case, the crucifix is held to be a passive symbol and therefore acceptable in the public classroom. In the second case, the full-face veil is considered as a bar to living together and therefore prohibited as a form of private clothing. Such a glaring double standard points to the existence of inbuilt biases in favour of majority religions and against minority beliefs. European secular states do not know how to cope with religious diversity. Their secularism oscillates between a negative attitude towards minorities and a positive attitude towards traditional majorities.

European courts have to be bolder: in order to address the deleterious problem of the double standard, the point is to move beyond the negative conception of secularism that they assume. In section 2, I will illustrate the ways in which the ECtHR is stuck in a negative conception of secularism. To go beyond it, one needs to develop a new conception of secularism, which I call positive secularism. Section 3 will present two possible variants of positive secularism and illustrates how positive secularism could inform the practice of the ECtHR so as to nudge European states into being secular in a way that is compatible with religious pluralism.

2. Negative Secularism

Negative secularism is defined in opposition to religion. It carves out a domain for religion and one for secular politics. It was simple to understand what secularism was and why it was needed when European states were culturally and religiously homogeneous. Christianity and secularism were two sides of the same coin. The Christian religion was not contested either as a metaphysical doctrine or as an ethical standpoint. This was Europe after the Treaty of Westphalia: religious homogeneity was

[5] A similar distinction is offered by Taylor, 'How to Define Secularism' in A. Stepan and C. Taylor (eds), *Boundaries of Toleration* (2014).

[6] ECtHR, *Lautsi and Others v. Italy*, Appl. no. 30814/06, Judgment of 18 March 2011. All ECtHR decisions are available online at http://hudocl.echr.coe.int/ (last visited 28 August 2018).

[7] ECtHR, *S.A.S. v. France*, Appl. no. 43835/11, Judgment of 1 July 2014.

engineered in order to avoid conflicts between Catholics and Protestants. *Ejus regio, cujus religio* (to each kingdom its own religion) was the formula behind the birth of European nation states. From this viewpoint, secularism was just a compromise between each state and its own religious majority.[8] Today's Europe has changed beyond recognition since 1648. Three centuries later, and after two World Wars, the European system of nation states has had to be reconsidered. The Universal Declaration of Human Rights, which inspired the European Convention on Human Rights (ECHR), and the Treaty of Rome that lays the foundation of the European Union, regard human rights as the necessary limitation of state sovereignty. European human rights protect a diversity of worldviews over homogeneity and European courts have to act accordingly.[9] Negative secularism was formulated in a historical context where the secular state had to free itself from one dominant religion: the French state had to distance itself from the interference of the Catholic Church and did so with the statute of 1905, which formulated the legal principle of *laïcité*.[10] Today, *laïcité* is interpreted as denying religion any place in the public sphere, and securing its liberty only in the private sphere. Such interpretation is an ideological distortion of the principle of legal *laïcité*, which simply requested a separation between church and state. In what follows I will criticize the position of the ECtHR for embracing a negative idea of secularism that portrays secularism in turn as (a) a private conviction, (b) an ideology, or (c) a biased stance against minority religions. These three mistakes are part of (d) a negative project of secularism that needs to be abandoned.

A. Secularism as Private Conviction

Secularism is not in fashion in Strasbourg. In the *Lautsi* saga, the ECtHR had to decide whether Italy was violating the right of parents to have their children educated in a way that was compatible with their convictions. Mrs Lautsi complained, in particular, that the presence of the crucifix interfered with the secular education expected in a state school.

After an appeal by Italy, the Grand Chamber of the ECtHR concluded that Italy has the freedom to decide whether to hang a crucifix in public school classrooms without infringing the right of parents to have their children educated according to their own religious or philosophical convictions.

Previously, at the Chamber level, the decision had gone in the opposite direction. Secularism featured prominently and determined the outcome of the case in favour of the applicants, the Lautsi family: the Court decided that the state has an obligation of neutrality in light of its secular nature. As a consequence, classroom walls had to be blank, since the presence of any symbol would breach the state commitment to neutrality and the parents' right to educate their children according to their own religious or philosophical convictions. The Chamber presented secularism as Mrs

[8] L. Zucca, *A Secular Europe: Law and Religion in the European Constitutional Landscape* (2012).

[9] E. Brems (ed.), *Diversity and European Human Rights: Rewriting Judgments of the ECHR* (2015).

[10] O. Roy, *Secularism Confronts Islam* (2009).

Lautsi's philosophical conviction; a view which should be criticized as it portrays secularism as radically subjective: one of the many beliefs that can be held by people. This will be seen to be a major conceptual and strategic mistake. It is a conceptual mistake because it confuses the secular nature of the state with the individual preferences of the parents. Secularism as a conviction is at best a by-product of state secularism; it should not be boxed into the language of Article 2 of Protocol 1 ECHR, which reads as follows:

> No person shall be denied the right to education. In the exercise of any functions which it assumes in relation to education and teaching, the state shall respect the rights of parents to ensure such education and teaching in conformity with their own religious and philosophical convictions.

The Court linked parental secular convictions to secularism, thereby creating a basic confusion that still lingers on: that is, that secularism may be considered as one of many possible individual convictions, rather than the most important political project that Europe has embraced since the end of the wars of religion. Secularism in European constitutional history is a political project according to which the state should be run independently from the dominant religion in a given society. To present it instead as a philosophical conviction of the parents leads people to believe that secularism is an optional way of conducting the state's business.[11] There is not a single European state that is not secular to a greater or lesser extent. The converse of being a secular state would amount to being a theocratic state.

The Chamber's judgment makes a strategic mistake as well: by insisting that the classroom walls should respect parents' convictions, the Court is preparing the scene for a perfect storm. Why would the secular convictions of some parents be preferable over the religious convictions of other parents? Put this way, it becomes impossible to defend state neutrality. The state has no ability to choose between two convictions in a neutral manner. It is either one or the other. The problem here is that the state's default secular position as a guarantee of all convictions has been undermined by the Court which unwittingly put religious convictions and secular convictions on a par, as if the two were mutually exclusive and addressed the same set of beliefs. Herein lies one of the great weaknesses of negative secularism: it tends to simplify reality into two polar opposites. By the same token, it equalizes them. Religious convictions and secular convictions have the same value in the eyes of the court.

The opponents of secularism raised their glasses. The Catholic Church, together with Russia and other intervening states, banqueted on the corpse of secularism. The political battle began and it aimed to assert the Christian roots of the European project. The Chamber decision in *Lautsi* gave an opportunity to religious people to call for more representation of religion at the national and supranational level. The Grand Chamber of the ECtHR tried to limit the damage but the *faux pas* had already been made. To present secularism as an individual conviction empowered those holding religious convictions to claim equal treatment before the law and in

[11] Even theocracies cannot do away with a minimum commitment to secularism.

the court. The alleged neutrality of the secular state had been compromised in the quest to protect the secular views of the Lautsi family.

Some of the concurring opinions—in particular Judge Bonello's—went a long way towards delegitimizing secularism as the defining trait of European states and of Europe as a whole. In his colourful concurring opinion, Bonello claimed that 'in Europe, secularism is optional, freedom of religion is not'.[12] This is a highly controversial claim. As pointed out, the converse of secularism is theocracy. It is hard to find examples of theocratic societies where freedom of religion is upheld. We can try to be charitable towards Bonello: he may be suggesting that secularism is a defining trait of constitutional democracies, but not of an international system of human rights. However, even that claim is highly controversial. There is a minimal sense in which an international system of human rights is necessarily secular in so far as it has to refrain from taking the viewpoint of any given religion so as to be capable of protecting all religions equally.

So the question is not whether secularism is optional or not; the question is which secularism is best suited to an international system of human rights. Moreover, it is hard to imagine how freedom of religion could be protected in a non-secular political space. Let us imagine—this time it is not hard to do—a state that is run on religious precepts taken from one religion. In this case, the majority's religion does not need freedom, since it has power. Those practising other religions in this non-secular framework will enjoy freedom only to the extent that the majority's religion is willing to give it to them as a concession that can always be withdrawn. It follows that, contrary to Bonello's claims, freedom of religion as a human right can only truly exist in a secular framework that does not discriminate between religions. Bonello's mistake is to believe that freedom of religion and secularism can be easily detached one from another. Interestingly, Bonello also acknowledges: 'I believe anyone could persuasively try to argue that the presence of the crucifix in Italian State schools might possibly offend the doctrine of secularism and that of the separation between Church and State.' At this point, Bonello's opinion has changed tone: he recognizes that secularism is not an option. But he would like to suggest that the task of the Court does not include the review of a measure that is incompatible with the principle of secularism. The Court's job in this case, according to Bonello, is simply to protect the right to freedom of religion of the parents. Again, there is a distortion taking place here: the Lautsi family is not complaining about their right to freedom of religion, but about their right to have an education for their children in a non-religious environment. The question is whether the crucifix, which is a religious symbol, gives the environment a religious connotation. To answer this question one has to engage with the boundary that lies between a religious and a secular environment. The Grand Chamber, by deciding that Italy is free to display the crucifix in an Italian state school, is implicitly asserting that the presence of that symbol is compatible with the principle that a state school should by law be a secular space.

[12] *Lautsi and Others v. Italy* (n. 6) 40, para. 2.5.

B. Secularism as Ideology

Part of the blame for this predicament should be laid at the door of secularism as a political project. Secularism is the product of historical events that pitted church against the state and produced a series of ready-made doctrines to cope with such a problem: the most famous, and the most controversial, is the doctrine of the separation of church and state. The wall of separation has been exposed as a deficient metaphor in the US, Europe, and India.[13] When we look at the reality of the relationship between church and state, it can hardly be described as a form of mutual segregation. Religious symbols, practices, and beliefs enter the political realm as much as state laws enter the religious domain.

Originally, secularism was thought of as a good faith attempt to resolve a conflict; the idea was to allow the state to free itself from the bonds of one religion (or of many religions) in order to be the state of all its citizens. In order to treat everyone equally, the state had to be blind to religious symbols and deaf to religious beliefs. One can readily see, however, how good intentions can be transformed into discriminatory plans. From a legal-constitutional project, secularism was turned into a social ideology according to which religion should be relegated to the private sphere. This is what happened in France with the *Loi* of 1905 on *laïcité*: the statute did not originally claim that religion should be silenced in the public sphere. It simply intended to draw a line between church and state, but over time it was taken to represent a negative indictment of religion's presence in public.

In a separate concurring opinion, Judge Power stabbed secularism in its ideological back: 'To my mind, the Chamber Judgment was striking in its failure to recognize that secularism (which was the applicant's preferred belief or world view) was, in itself, one ideology among others.'[14] I believe, instead, that Judge Power's concurring opinion is striking in its failure to recognize that secularism is not only another ideology, but also the backbone of any modern state. I readily recognize that that backbone has been used with negative effects upon religion, and I also recognize that it is high time to rethink secularism for an entirely new world. The historical context has changed beyond recognition, and the chief aim of the secular state is not to deny religion a place in the public sphere as the French conception of *laïcité* does.[15] Rather, the secular state has the task of protecting religious and non-religious ways of thinking as part of a plural and diverse society. To do so the secular state needs a framework that guarantees that no particular view can be imposed on people.

Secularism does not have to be an ideological stance against religion. It is fair to say that that might have been the interpretation of Mrs Lautsi, but that should not be the way in which the state interprets secularism. If and when the state interprets it that way, it is fair to criticize the state for not giving religion its due and for unduly burdening it. A different, possible, interpretation of secularism brings us back to secularism as a collective political project to guarantee the coexistence of different

[13] L. Sager and C. Eisgruber, *Religious Freedom and the Constitution* (2010); R. Bhargava, 'Should Europe Learn from Indian Secularism?', available at http://www.india-seminar.com/2011/621/621_rajeev_bhargava.htm (last visited 28 August 2018).

[14] *Lautsi and Others v. Italy* (n. 6) 44–5.

[15] Roy (n. 10).

beliefs and ideologies. Judge Power chastised the Chamber for elevating secularist ideology over all other ideologies. But my point is that secularism properly conceived is not an ideology at all; it is the necessary precondition for beliefs and ideologies to coexist in the same space. Secularism should be conceived of as a normative requirement to respect any kind of diversity of a religious or non-religious nature. It does not merely amount to a position reached through an (overlapping) consensus amongst people who live in the same space. In Europe, such consensus would be hard to formulate against the background of a set of political societies that have been based on homogeneity rather than diversity.

Judge Power would like to salvage neutrality from the damning criticisms issued against the Chamber's decision. She attempted to do so by severing neutrality from secularism, and by suggesting instead that neutrality is better served by a general commitment to pluralism: 'Neutrality requires a pluralist approach on the part of the State, not a secularist one. It encourages respect for all world views rather than a preference for one.'[16] It is very difficult to conceive of a non-secular state that would promote respect for all religions. The European experience teaches us precisely that when one religious view is dominant, other religious views can, at best, expect toleration. In the same vein, it is hard to imagine how a non-secular state could promote pluralism without having to deny the primacy of the religious views in which it believes. If we were to believe the Court, secularism is just another ideology. It is a partial view of the world that is on a par with many other political ideologies, including religious views. It is undeniable that French secularism based on the *Loi* of 1905 was first conceived of as a legal separation between church and state, but then became an ideological stance that relegated religion to the realm of private life. However, the fact that *laïcité* was transformed into an ideological stance does not mean that secularism is an ideology like any other. If we were to replace secularism with any other religious ideology, the result would not be the automatic protection of religious pluralism. The link between pluralism and secularism is hard to deny: secularism may be an ideology, but it is crucially an ideology that promotes diversity above homogeneity. This is not true of other ideologies, in particular of religious ideologies which happily maintain a privileged status for one religion.

C. Secularism and Islamophobia

The paradoxical consequence of the decision in *Lautsi* is Strasbourg's neutrality vis-à-vis national arrangements that are paradigm cases of negative secularism: France and Turkey spring to mind. How is the ECtHR protecting freedom of religion in the case of *S.A.S. v. France*? France decides to criminalize the wearing of the full-face veil in public places and the Court decides that the ban is compatible with freedom.[17] What could justify such a ban? The Court suggests that the individual right to freedom of religion can be limited on the grounds of the rights of others.[18] But in this case, what are the rights of others that are at stake? Why should I have a right against someone who decides to cover their face? I may want to wear a carnival mask on a

[16] *Lautsi and Others v. Italy* (n. 6) 44. [17] *S.A.S. v. France* (n. 7). [18] Ibid.

daily basis—would that violate the rights of others? There is very little that can fit the bill: there is no tangible right of others that can be singled out. Compare with *Lautsi*: the readily identifiable 'right of parents to ensure such education and teaching in conformity with their own religious and philosophical convictions' (Article 2 of Protocol 1 ECHR) is treated as not having been infringed because Mrs Lautsi cannot prove the impact of the presence of the crucifix on her children.

In *S.A.S.*, the Court argues that the wearing of the full-face veil in public places has a sizeable impact on the French republican principle of 'living together'. Wearing the full-face veil, according to the French government, would prevent people from forming the necessary bonds in a society. While it may be correct that a full-face veil creates an obstacle to immediate socialization, it is unclear why it would violate the rights of others. 'Living together' does not provide the necessary content. More importantly, it is impossible to understand why secularism in *Lautsi* is presented as an abstract doctrine that has no connection with the rights contained in the ECHR, while 'living together' is accepted as a meaningful position that gives content to the rights of others. There is a strong presumption here that the Court uses abstract principles to suit its political preferences. In the case of *S.A.S.*, 'living together' appears to be a pretext to impose the views of the majority as to which symbols and clothing are considered to be conducive to stronger social bonds. If anything, the principle of 'living together' should encourage greater understanding of alternative ways of life rather than being used aggressively to single out those people who are deemed to be unacceptable.

There you can see the difficulty of the French legislation banning the full-face veil in public places. A confusion that lingers on in this debate has to do with the distinction between private and public. Is walking down the street a public act? More importantly, to insist on the idea that religion is free in the private realm, but that people should strip themselves of religious clothes and symbols when in public creates an extra burden for religious people when compared to non-religious people. In other words, non-religious people are the model citizens, while religious people have to behave as if they were non-religious when they step into the public sphere. Another source of doubt comes from a sociological analysis of the wearing of the full-face veil in France. The number of women wearing the veil is extremely limited: two thousand women out of a minority of four million people.[19] Interviews have been carried out with a great number of those women, revealing that their motivation is largely individual and not requested by the practices of the religious group.

France asks us not to take offence if religion is ridiculed. But then it takes offence if someone wears the symbols of their own religion while walking down the street. This is another double standard that needs to be unravelled and discussed. In both cases, offence does not seem to be sufficient to regulate the relevant behaviour. Behind the benign face of neutrality hides the dark face of double standards: the Christian religion can be embraced by a secular state as a form of tradition, but when other religious traditions claim freedom of religion they are silenced in the

[19] E. Brems, 'Introduction' in Brems (ed.), *Diversity and European Human Rights: Rewriting Judgments of the ECHR* (2015) 1.

name of the requirement of living together. The irony (and the deep sadness) lies in the fact that *Lautsi* allows the display of the majority's religious symbol in a classroom, pointing out that secularism is just an individual conviction like any other. In *S.A.S.* a minority's religious symbol is prohibited in the public sphere, on the grounds that it is incompatible with an ideological understanding of French secularism. The point is that freedom of religion amounts to the protection of whatever the majority happens to believe, be it religious or secular ideology. It is high time to rethink secularism and freedom of religion in a way that truly promotes living together—minority and majority alike.

D. Secularism as a Negative Project

Secularism is associated with disenchantment: from a world full of religious meaning, we come to a world emptied of its spiritual and magical content.[20] Some feel nostalgia for a world that has disappeared and that will not come back.[21] Secularism is not so much to blame here, but it is regarded as the empty alternative that has come to the scene. It does not make up for the loss incurred. It does not propose anything. It lacks the vision or the teleology that was provided by religion. How can we possibly subscribe to a negative project that does not offer any substantive value to guide society—a view that requires taking a negative stance towards religion?

The first step in that quest is to separate the concept of secularism from the concept of religion. If the two are too tightly linked, then secularism can only be understood as the denial of religion. There are many problems with such a negative approach, but the most daunting lies in the fact that there is no definition of religion in the first place. Thus, it is also impossible to define secularism; if anything it will be identified with whatever opposes religious beliefs and practices. But what if some of those religious beliefs and practices are part and parcel of the constitution of a society? To oppose them would amount to opposing the very identity of that society. Does secularism amount to a denial that some political societies define themselves in relation to religious beliefs or practices?

Needless to say, it would be detrimental for secularism to do so. In fact, it seems unavoidable to detach the concept of secularism from that of religion. In particular, it is impossible to take theology as a starting point for a definition of religion. More precisely, any type of monotheistic religion that comes with a theological apparatus has to be put aside in order to make space for non-monotheistic concepts of religion. Religion cannot be defined in relation to the presence of one God. It is equally clear that there is no secular definition of religion from an external viewpoint to religion: endless attempts have been made without success.[22] Religion defines itself from within. The problem arises when religion needs the official stamp of the state in order to take advantage of a number of benefits or exemptions.

[20] Taylor, 'Disenchantment–Re-enchantment' in G. Levine (ed.), *The Joy of Secularism* (2012) 57.
[21] Taylor is amongst those who are nostalgic for a Christian past, regarded as a more meaningful past.
[22] See, e.g., B. Leiter, *Why Tolerate Religion?* (2012).

It is interesting to note that judges are now required to reconsider their narrow assumptions as to what qualifies as religious. Once the monotheistic definition is swept under the carpet, it is hard to think of what could replace it to provide a stable yardstick with which to draw the boundary between religion and non-religion: that is to say, for many, between religion and the secular. It seems that judges are slowly moving towards a more empirical approach, which takes into account actual social and cultural practices.[23] The challenge for all judges is to come up with a legal definition of religion that is truly reflective of the religious diversity in Europe. This is a Herculean task that will transform into a Sisyphean struggle. A secular court cannot define religion because it is required to refrain from engaging with internal theological arguments. The seeming impasse can be dealt with by accepting that courts cannot provide a bright-line rule between religion and non-religion. At best, they can gather evidence from all parties involved and attempt a case-by-case approach that remains open to revision.

The ECtHR attaches great importance to liberal neutrality, while being very deferential to the way in which nation states define it. In the landmark cases discussed in this chapter, the Court approves of the status quo: France is neutral when banning the burqa on public streets; Italy is neutral when defending the crucifix in public schools. Today, the status quo is particularly problematic given the deep changes taking place in the social context. The role of the ECtHR should be more positive: to question nation states on their commitments rather than subscribe to, and rubber-stamp, them. The Court's position vis-à-vis negative secularism can be understood, but this does not mean that secularism is altogether incapable of providing a sound basis for the interpretation of human rights.

3. Positive Secularism

Positive secularism is not defined in opposition to religion.[24] It is not about separation of church and state, nor is it about privatization of religion. Crucially it does not attempt to define religion from the standpoint of secular reason. Positive secularism is about the protection and promotion of diversity of worldviews. There are two ways of creating these conditions: Charles Taylor's political secularism suggests that liberal democracies have to cope with diversity by seeking to uphold consensus wherever possible;[25] the other option, which I defend here, is to show that diversity is ethically superior to homogeneity. My account can be called ethical secularism, and can be contrasted to Taylor's political secularism.

The two accounts have, nevertheless, many points in common.[26] Neither account defines secularism in opposition to religion. But Taylor's account of secularism is political in the Rawlsian sense: it works along the lines of public reason, and defines it as that set of reasons that would be followed by reasonable people.[27] My account

[23] Zucca (n. 4). [24] Taylor (n. 5). [25] Ibid.

[26] Perhaps they even share the same intentions, but they differ as to the means necessary to achieve them.

[27] Taylor (n. 5) 61.

takes as its starting point an acknowledgement that even reasonable people have inbuilt biases that are part of their beliefs and practices. The double standard applied by the ECtHR, exemplified by its different treatment of Christian and Islamic symbols, is an example of such bias, and it affects the decisions of allegedly reasonable judges and all other policy-makers. It is not possible to ask the state, or its officials, to be neutral in relation to their own biases and other religious views.

The first difference between these two positive accounts is a practical concern: how does one remove the bias? Taylor's political account would trust the state to be a neutral arbiter between reasons that are public and reasons that are not. I believe, instead, that the state cannot be neutral at least as long as it has not freed itself from those inbuilt biases. First, it has to unravel the buried biases and tackle the negative emotional reactions to diversity. Then it has to reformulate its own secular commitments. In the process, the secular state is likely to realize that it can hardly rely on a political account, but must rather provide an ethical account of positive secularism. Thus, my account of positive secularism is ethical in that it claims to be normatively superior to any other alternative on comprehensive grounds, as opposed to Rawls' and Taylor's framework which is supposed to be grounded on overlapping consensus that does not appeal to any comprehensive views.

A. Political Secularism

Taylor's account of political secularism is divorced from his account of a secular age.[28] Taylor shows that the secular age has ushered in a great diversity of individual conceptions of the good that cannot be squared one with another.[29] As a result, there are various secular dilemmas that arise in modern society. It is therefore puzzling that Taylor advocates state neutrality as the tool with which the state should deal with those dilemmas: what would it mean to be neutral between two competing values or goods that clash with each other? Taylor's position seems to oscillate between taking neutrality as a regulative principle and taking it as one of the values to be balanced. For example, he claims on the one hand that 'the point of state neutrality is precisely to avoid favoring or disfavoring not just religious positions but any basic position, religious or non-religious. We can't favor Christianity over Islam, but also religion over against nonbelief in religion or vice versa.'[30] But on the other hand he criticizes French *laïcité* for being fixated on one single principle: 'the dilemma and its resolution remain hidden under the illusion that there is only one principle here, say, laïcité and its corollary of the neutrality of public institutions or spaces'.[31] The first quote treats neutrality as a regulative principle, while the second quote treats it as one principle amongst others. This illustrates the point that Taylor oscillates between those two conceptions of neutrality without taking a clear position.

Taylor bemoans the disappearance of a comprehensive Christian view of the world: he displays nostalgia towards an enchanted world that has disappeared, an age that has gone and that will not return: the age of religious monism. Taylor is clear

[28] Cf. C. Taylor, *A Secular Age* (2007) with Maclure and Taylor (n. 3). [29] Taylor (n. 5).
[30] Ibid. 60–1. [31] Ibid. 60.

that western secularism has been so far obsessed by the quest to divide religion from power through a single, simple-minded formula such as the wall of separation.[32] But things are more complex than that, Taylor insists, and this is particularly so in plural societies where the point of secularism should be completely redefined: it should deal with religious and metaphysical diversity of all kinds; it should not focus on the control of religion as orthodox secularism has done.[33]

If secularism is meant to protect diversity, then how do we define religion so that no belief is left behind? Taylor and Maclure argue in favour of a conception of freedom of religion that is radically subjective.[34] In order to know what counts as religion one has to examine individual conscience. Each individual will be able to express a claim of conscience in a way that captures its depth and vulnerability. Religion is collapsed into the wider category of conscience. But by collapsing religion into conscience, Taylor puts at the centre of his political doctrine a Christian Protestant bias in favour of individualistic forms of religion based on conscientious claims.[35] Thus, Taylor's subjective definition of religion does not fully escape the problem of a Christian bias.

If religion is radically subjective, then religious claims are likely to multiply. How does Taylor's account deal with them? Taylor's secularism deals with diversity by searching for equilibrium between the French trinity of values: liberty, equality, and fraternity.[36] In this context, liberty means that no religious view should be coerced to change or that different beliefs should be adopted. Equality means that all religious and metaphysical views should be treated equally and none should be privileged. Fraternity means that all views should be heard in matters of the constitution of society as well as on its policies to obtain the desired goals. The fundamental rethinking of secularism requires from the state a neutral position that relies on overlapping consensus as far as the general fundamentals are concerned, but with no preconception as to how the fundamentals will be balanced with each other. The trinity of values will bring inevitable conflicts, and will result in a set of dilemmas, which our societies are bound to face. To cope with such dilemmas, the secular state cannot adopt a 'one size fits all' solution, but should be patiently engaged in the negotiation of a collective identity that can only be achieved through a good faith attempt to always secure the three or four goals mentioned earlier.

We can single out two competing understandings of secularism from Taylor's account. The former is historical secularism, a project shaped in the dark ages of church and state conflict. The latter is a positive, substantive secularism that attempts to respond to the present age of diversity at the metaphysical and political level. Taylor believes that the context in which secularism has been formulated has changed beyond recognition, and it is now time to reformulate the content of that concept in light of the profound changes of context.[37]

[32] Ibid. 61. [33] Ibid. 59. [34] Maclure and Taylor (n. 3).

[35] For a similar point, see C. Laborde, 'Protecting Freedom of Religion in the Secular Age', *The Immanent Frame* (23 April 2012), available at http://blogs.ssrc.org/tif/2012/04/23/protecting-freedom-of-religion-in-the-secular-age (last visited 18 March 2016).

[36] Taylor (n. 5) 61. [37] Ibid. 63.

I agree with that distinction: political and ethical secularism agree so far. It is high time to rethink secularism, and even to rescue it from its own negative reputation. It is not about religion any longer. But the two secular accounts part company over the concept of conscience. Is it possible to be neutral if we start our analysis of freedom of religion from a concept such as conscience? The idea of conscience has a clear western root and, more precisely, it has an obvious Christian connotation, and its interpretation divides Protestant and Catholic Christianity.[38] Can such a notion be the starting point of a neutral evaluation of freedom of religion? Instead of focusing on conscience as a source of moral knowledge and moral action, as Taylor does, I focus instead on thought, and suggest that religious belief is an expression of diversity of thought.

The second point of disagreement concerns the French trilogy of values. By suggesting that the French trilogy provides the content for secularism, Taylor does not address the problem of what to do when secular dilemmas arise. Secularism, to have a bite, should be able to give guidance as to the management of secular dilemmas that will have to be dealt with by political actors and judges. What can be done in those cases? What kind of compromises can be found if secular dilemmas are genuine? Taylor defends neutrality as a desirable regulative principle. Even if Taylor is cautious as to how the balance can be achieved, he nevertheless leaves ample power to secular institutions to come up with a good faith balance of those values. But what does it mean to balance competing values in a way that preserves them all? This is, of course, the central question, but Taylor does not really provide a method to answer it. So it is not clear what would qualify as a good faith attempt to balance competing values.

Taylor's new conception of secularism is more inclusive than negative secularism, but it is not immediately apparent where its values originate. The French trinity constitutes a venerable wish list, but it is more of a stipulation than the realization that those values are constitutive of secularism. Taylor's secularism wants to present itself as a practical response to the problem of managing diversity. It does not aim to fill the gap left by the decreased role of the comprehensive religious view, as pointed out in Taylor's *A Secular Age*.[39] There is a hiatus between Taylor's genealogical explanation of the move towards a secular age, and his pragmatic secularism defended in the context of Canadian politics.[40] In fact, Taylor's political secularism runs the risk of simply upholding traditional Christian views in the garb of secular values.[41] This is the case in particular when he defends freedom of conscience as the central tenet of any conception of religious freedom.[42] Conscience is hardly a uni-

[38] R. Sorabji, *Moral Conscience through the Ages. Fifth Century BCE to the Present* (2014).

[39] See n. 28. [40] Maclure and Taylor (n. 3).

[41] The false assumption is that there is a sharp distinction between secular values and religious values. Secular values have been shaped and defined in relation to religious ones: thus 'secular' is often a negative property of that which is not religious. But then again, this implies that there is a stable definition of what qualifies a religious argument as well as a clear method to strip an argument from its religious garb. I find this disingenuous. Take, for example, the principle of sanctity of life. It is used by religious and non-religious people in countless arguments on euthanasia, abortion, and other issues. But who exactly holds the copyright to the understanding of sanctity of life, given that it is a religious idea to begin with?

[42] Maclure and Taylor (n. 3).

versal concept that includes all forms of religious diversity. It is, rather, a Janus-faced concept with religious and secular facets.

To conclude, there are two main problems with Taylor's political secularism. First, it defines religion by collapsing it into conscience. This move seems to be neutral and impartial, but it is not. Conscience is the expression of a Christian Protestant understanding of what religion should amount to, namely a private engagement with the divine that is not mediated by social institutions. Second, it acknowledges the existence of deep secular dilemmas, but does not offer a convincing way of dealing with them; to suggest that a good faith attempt to balance competing values might be enough to deal with secular dilemmas does not take those dilemmas seriously. In order to cope with secular dilemmas we have to recognize that secularism is an ethical doctrine that defends the superiority of diversity over homogeneity; religious worldviews are but one expression of diversity and they can be protected as such but not more than that nor less. The idea is not to work towards an overlapping consensus, but to defend the necessary primacy of ethical secularism.

B. Ethical Secularism

Ethical secularism takes secular dilemmas seriously. To suggest that it is possible to reach a compromise, as political secularism does, amounts to a denial of dilemmas, and to the silent entrenchment of the majority's views on the place of religion in the public sphere. The fact that we face secular dilemmas must be taken as a sign of vitality of the political society. The conflict between the majority and the minorities of a society should not be swept under the carpet. It must be acknowledged and dealt with in a way that promotes a genuine exchange.

Ethical secularism makes a non-neutral choice in favour of diversity and against homogeneity. Diversity works as an interpretive device of all other values: whenever a conflict between values is at stake, diversity works as a tiebreaker. Take, for example, the *Lautsi* case: does the presence of the crucifix contribute to a more diverse environment or does it promote homogeneity? Diversity clearly militates against the presence of the crucifix. Diversity of worldviews is superior to homogeneity, which has been the European default position since the Treaty of Westphalia. After all, the very homogeneity that characterized Europe after the Peace Treaty of Westphalia was an explicitly value-laden political decision taken at the international level in order to put an end to religious wars.[43] It is time to replace homogeneity with diversity as a non-neutral choice. The compromise entrenched by the Treaty of Westphalia can be rejected: we reject the idea that we have to carve religiously homogeneous nation states out of a broader European political space. To be sure, Westphalia engineered homogeneity to cope with religious conflicts. An evil was certainly removed, but with it the Westphalian political arrangement also removed the richness of sociocultural and religious diversity. Post-war Europe regained a robust degree of diversity very quickly, and that contributes to a richer and more interesting environment; it is also a non-artificial environment. To be sure, it also contributes to a

[43] Zucca (n. 8).

challenging political situation and the task of the secular state is to deal with diversity in a way that preserves its contribution and limits its risk. Ethical secularism has a strong instrumental component and a thin epistemological commitment.[44] It is instrumental in the sense that it is the value with which European states can be nudged away from state homogeneity. It has a thin epistemological commitment in the sense that diversity does not stand for a fully fledged substantive commitment. It simply challenges received ideas and works as a comprehensive worldview of worldviews, enabling rather than silencing them.

It is necessary to move towards an affirmation of the secular age, something that Taylor is not prepared to do. Ethical secularism displays no nostalgia for our religious past: the secular age is presented as being superior to the prior religious age. As an illustration of this superiority we can take freedom of religion: religious freedom can only be realized in a secular framework where all religious and non-religious views can live and thrive one next to another. To do so, there must be at least a minimum core of unity that is common to all religious and non-religious people alike. Since religious ethical views cannot comprehend other views—because by definition one religious truth excludes other religious truths—we have to look for a secular view that promotes diversity. Religious freedom is not protected where one religion is able to dictate the rules of the game for everyone else.

The secular age is affirmed at three different levels. At the political level, ethical secularism is affirmed as the limitation of the authority of the state in matters of religious and non-religious diversity. In this sense, ethical secularism makes ample room for freedom of religion. At the moral level, it is a vision of how to live together that promotes genuine respect for religious and non-religious diversity. At the metaphysical level, it holds that diversity amounts to free thought. Thought is free when it is able to question itself constantly, but it is not necessarily without presuppositions: it cannot be reduced to pure logic. Any thought starts from an assumption, and then goes on to examine it under the light of reason. Unconstrained thought can be both religious or non-religious. Free thought is the ultimate and most basic element of ethical secularism; in turn, this profoundly changes the conception of religion that we are working with.

Ethical secularism is ultimately severed from any conventional understanding of religion since it regards religion as one particular expression of free thought. Free thought is compatible with the idea of starting from a set of assumptions. The fact that religion begins with an assumption about faith singles it out as a special form of thought, which is different from other forms of thought that postulate natural reason as the sole guiding light. Religious and non-religious thought are equally protected and equally open to further inquiry. Of course, beliefs will be open to challenge and when they are not able to withstand those challenges, they will not be able to form the basis of any policy decision. Ethical secularism is positive in that it is not defined against religion, but is rather an affirmation of diversity of thought. Religion as a result is not central to the definition of ethical secularism. Religion is one of the

[44] Enoch, 'Political Philosophy and Epistemology', in D. Sobel, P. Vallentyne, and S. Wall (eds.), *Oxford Studies in Political Philosophy*, Vol. 3 (2017).

worldviews protected by it. Ethical secularism promotes a genuine exchange about all basic values and practices in our societies. The exchange does not require shedding one's own assumptions, but it does ask every participant to bring those assumptions to the forefront and to be prepared to accept all the challenges that free thought can bring to various ethical views of religious and non-religious origin.

It is a mistake to think that diversity of thought calls for legal pluralism. It is also a mistake to think that value pluralism is associated in any meaningful way with legal pluralism. Diversity of thought can be best realized within a unitary political framework. Human beings set up political institutions to maintain a certain degree of stability despite human irrationality due to the natural primacy of emotional reactions. Human beings come together and form political communities as a matter of necessity: they know that to form bonds with others is much more likely to serve their interest in survival and it is also likely to increase their own control over the external world. Political institutions are thus created to protect those basic human interests and as long as they are capable of serving those interests, they protect their existence; if political institutions start behaving in a way that undermines those basic human interests, then they become exposed to the risk of failure and, ultimately, extinction.

Political institutions can develop an instrument to deal with religious diversity: I call that instrument the 'marketplace of religions', which is a subsystem of the marketplace of ideas.[45] The link between the ethical and the instrumental is not straightforward, so some clarifications are in order. First, the connection is not direct; human beings have no access to the full knowledge of their biases; they only have a very fragmentary knowledge of human nature and of its own causal laws. Second, the impossibility of knowledge of human nature points to the inherent limits of human rationality that can at best work under less-than-ideal conditions of limited knowledge. Third, limited rationality means that human beings reach practical decisions on the basis of emotional reactions to the natural world. This means that prescriptive human laws have to engage with psychological motivations and provide appropriate answers to them. Fourth, the success of a rule-maker will be measured by the ability to grasp the overarching interest of the community, while at the same time motivating people to strive together in that direction.

From an epistemological perspective, secular political institutions can hardly be bound by the idea of an overlapping consensus amongst reasonable people. That presupposes too much about our possibility to know where the consensus lies and our ability to maintain it despite inevitable conflicts of worldviews. If it is correct that the actual possibility of consensus on religious matters amongst reasonable people is out of reach, the commitment to neutrality put forward by political secularism becomes problematic;[46] neutrality assumes that the secular state is completely separate and detached from any religion. But that is obviously not the case, and the existence of the double standard highlighted earlier shows the extent to

[45] See Zucca (n. 8) Ch. 5.

[46] Both Rawls and Taylor insist that liberal neutrality should be understood against the background of the overlapping consensus.

which that is not true. The existence of an inbuilt double standard makes neutrality impracticable and secularism weak. Neutrality is impracticable because European states automatically give preference to their own traditions, which are inevitably rooted in one form of Christianity. Secularism is weak because it depends on its relationship with one dominant religion. Neutrality would only make sense if biases could be completely removed. But this is unlikely to happen. And even if it could happen, until this has materialized, it is necessary to suspend talk of neutrality and start with the work of removing biases. The marketplace of religions removes biases by giving more space to all religions, while subordinating all religions to the paramount requirements of free thought.

The marketplace of religions has the following features. First of all, the state is not neutral towards religions. Historically, it treats some religions with great regard and distributes specific benefits and burdens to those practising those religions; to improve on that record, the secular state has to eliminate the barriers of access to the marketplace of religions. So, for example, a state with an established religion is likely to be creating undue burdens on other religions; it therefore has to improve its relations with non-established religions. It is important to understand that the marketplace of religions does not depend on the separation between religion and state. On the contrary, the marketplace of religions is there to organize collaboration between the state and religions. Collaboration does not require neutrality: the secular state collaborates with all the religions that offer goods and services to the society. In exchange for those goods and services, the secular state may grant some privileges to religions as long as they agree to exercise those privileges in accordance with the ordinary laws of the state. If a religious institution accepts a privilege, such as favourable tax treatment, it agrees to act as a provider of public services and cannot be exempted in any manner from the regular application of the law.

The marketplace of religions is a subcategory of the marketplace of ideas. To this extent, it recognizes the place of religion in the public sphere as an expression of an idea; if the idea conflicts with basic values of a liberal democratic society, then religion has an explanatory burden to overcome in order to be an acceptable ground of exemption from ordinary laws. In this way, religions open themselves up to rational scrutiny of their ideas and accept robust exchange between religious and non-religious people. Freedom of religion is protected as a form of free thought. Its protection is lowered when free thought turns into expression and action. The marketplace is the instrument through which the secular state can make sure that no religion curtails other freedoms or engages in discrimination.

To move from religious conflicts to peace and stability, one has to have a double account. On the one hand, ethical secularism affirms the superiority of diversity over homogeneity. On the other, it offers an instrument—the marketplace of religions—that treats religions as part of the unofficial public sphere[47] and as partners of the

[47] See J. Habermas, *The Structural Transformation of the Public Sphere: An Inquiry into a Category of Bourgeois Society* (1991). See more specifically, Habermas, 'Religion in the Public Sphere', 1 *European Journal of Philosophy* (2006) 1.

state, while at the same time subjecting them to the constraints of freedom and equality that apply to all other public actors.

C. Cashing out Ethical Secularism

Ethical secularism does not ask states to show neutrality at the political level; instead it promotes one comprehensive view that prioritizes diversity over homogeneity. Ethical secularism requires a rethinking of political identity in light of the change of social identity. For example, Italy's social homogeneity along Catholic lines is no longer true; as a consequence Italy's political identity should also be rethought: it must become a secular state that caters for all its religious and non-religious citizens. In other words, Italy in particular and Europe more generally must become self-consciously secular, rather than being secular by default. Italy can be further criticized from the viewpoint of ethical secularism. A society with a very homogeneous population and a strict relationship between church and state can hardly make space for a genuine diversity of worldviews. In such a context, ethical secularism, with its instrumental marketplace of religions, is going to have a deeper impact because it has to assist a mono-religious society to move towards becoming a religiously plural one.[48] Europe needs to examine its psychological biases before turning to regulation and limitation of freedom and equality. France, for example, erred very badly when it presented the prohibition of the wearing of the burqa on public streets as a defence of freedom and equality. It is neither. Moreover, it entrenches a psychological bias against Muslim minorities.

The stakes are very high. In order to remove one's own psychological biases, external help is needed. The ECtHR can provide some help by leading the national state to reconsider its own biases in a dialogic manner. Judicial institutions in Europe are the place where a discussion of that kind can begin. For the moment, unfortunately, the ECtHR is simply reinforcing the status quo. *Lautsi v. Italy* and *S.A.S. v. France* illustrate the problem of inbuilt biases and double standards. Majority religious symbols (the cross) are taken for granted. Minority religious symbols are contested everywhere, including when someone would like to display them privately. It is therefore not enough to ask the state to be neutral politically or legally if it works on the basis of assumptions according to which Christian symbols are passive, while Islamic symbols are threatening.[49] Those assumptions cannot withstand robust scrutiny. Until the biases have been unravelled, the change needed to make neutrality work in any meaningful way will not take place. To unravel a bias will require a systematic evaluation of one's political commitments. The existence of biases is incompatible with any talk of legal or political neutrality.

What then can the ECtHR do? The first step is to help nation states to unravel their own biases. The second step is to help to create instances of genuine rethinking

[48] For a similar point, see Urbinati, 'The Context of Secularism: A Critical Appraisal of the Post-Secular Argument' in S. Mancini and M. Rosenfeld (eds), *Constitutional Secularism in an Age of Religious Revival* (2014) 14, 15.

[49] Zucca, '*Lautsi*: A Commentary on a Decision by the ECtHR Grand Chamber', 11 *International Journal of Constitutional Law* (2013) 218.

about one's own identity. If a nation's identity happens to be biased towards one religious identity, then these legal cases are the best starting point for a genuine exchange. I confess to have inbuilt biases myself. I was a schoolchild in Italy and I never felt the presence of the crucifix in the classroom to be unusual. It was literally like any other piece of furniture: that was the point of the fascist decree that still defines what a classroom should look like in Italy. In 1929, when the decree was made, it was not even a matter for discussion. Courts, classrooms, administrations would display a crucifix. Who was there to object? The Italian society was still religious and homogeneous. Today, Italy's homogeneity is waning, but there is no sign of a rethinking of the unilateral privileged relationship between church and state.[50] It is also less religious, and in any case the post-war Constitution introduces the notion of secularity of the state; that is to say that, at least in principle, the Constitution entrenches legal secularism as a fundamental tenet. The ECtHR could have helped Italy to reflect on the implications of its changing sociocultural context as well as on its commitment to legal secularism.

Italy has to respond to the changes of its society in order to remove the barriers and thus to make coexistence between religious and non-religious people possible. The state has to engage in a serious and thoughtful debate about its identity and its symbols. The crucifix saga was the perfect moment to engage in such a debate: is Italy laic or is it religious? And more importantly, if it is laic, as the Italian Constitutional Court maintains, what does that imply? Ethical secularism as I defend it requires the state to be active and not merely neutral. Being active means first and foremost engaging in the debate wholeheartedly, which Italy has not done. Being active also means coming up with an official position that explains the principles of the state, as well as the decisions that flow from those principles. Italy has not done that; it simply reacted against change. It did not explain its position.

The ECtHR had the chance to ask Italy to be a grown-up and mature state; a state that treats its people as citizens, and not as children. But it did not do so. The result, therefore, is that Italy lives with the paradox of being constitutionally laic, while supporting Christian symbols. Here lies the problem of modern Europe: it is not serious about digging up the inbuilt biases that will inevitably result in more discrimination towards non-Christian symbols and practices. To fail to do so is to put one's head in the sand and avoid talking about the psychological problems of intolerance and hatred towards immigrants of different cultural and religious background. The inability to tackle those emotions results in the success of populism, which by definition gains political advantage by rousing negative emotions.

Populism is rife in France. When France banned the full-face veil, it was clear more than in any other case that the state was acting on a populist basis.[51] It was encapsulating in legislation the fears of French people towards Islam.[52] The legislation is purely symbolic and has limited effect on individual behaviour: as highlighted earlier, it only concerns two thousand women out of a Muslim population of over

[50] Urbinati (n. 48) 17–18.

[51] Weil, 'Headscarf v. Burqa: Two French Bans with Different Meanings' in S. Mancini and M. Rosenfeld (eds), *Constitutional Secularism in an Age of Religious Revival* (2014) 195.

[52] For a masterful fictional account, see M. Houellebecq, *Soumission* (2014).

four million people.[53] France is sending a message to the French electors and to the rest of Europe. The actual behaviour of people is not important: those women that wear the veil are typically doing so for highly personal motives, and the full-face veil is not even supported by the French Muslim community. By limiting the freedom of expression and freedom of religion of the few women who want to wear a controversial form of dress, France has given up on its secular commitments rather than upholding them. Even worse, France has embraced a populist attitude and transformed it into national legislation. The risk of populism is always present if political representatives are allowed to play with the negative fears and biases of the country at large.

A deeper issue surfaces here, and it is what European political leaders are failing to grasp: what happened in Paris with *Charlie Hebdo* is not only about religion. It is first and foremost about alienation of people not belonging to the mainstream society. Politicians right and left would like to isolate the threat of extremist religion or at least circumscribe it.[54] They believe that one part of Islam leads to violent extremism, but completely fail to examine the responsibilities of national states. France and the UK have been failing their people in numerous ways. They have entrenched harsh economic inequalities throughout the society and they have pursued illiberal policies which trample individual rights and privacy. The rise of extremism is a symptom of the crisis of the state.[55]

Alienation of young individuals goes hand-in-hand with a loss of faith in liberal democracies: it is also about the status of immigrants in a society that is not capable of offering opportunities to disenfranchised individuals.[56] Many have failed to notice what should be obvious. The first people to pay the price for economic decadence are the minorities in a society.

Ethical secularism asks national states to be conscious of what kind of paths lead to radicalization. Schools, workplaces, and social media: alienation and estrangement from the mainstream society happen there, and the state should be aware of it. When individuals are looking for answers, and the state and society are not providing them, strong religion may step in. In some cases, this may lead to individuals becoming radicalized.

The ECtHR has no power to tackle systematic biases arising from substantive inequalities, but it can ask national states to reflect on their shortcomings. Indeed, ethical secularism asks European institutions to address the underlying causes of religious strife, and does not simply offer a quick solution to discrete religious conflicts. The ECtHR has a responsibility that it cannot renounce: it must bring nation states to reflect on their own policies that entrench a double standard between the majority and the minority. When France excluded young Muslim girls from French

[53] Brems, 'The Experience of Face Veil Wearers in Europe and the Law' (n. 19).

[54] David Cameron's speech on religious extremism in Birmingham delivered on 20 July 2015, available at http://www.independent.co.uk/news/uk/politics/david-cameron-extremism-speech-read-the-transcript-in-full-10401948.html (last visited 28 August 2018).

[55] Zucca, 'The Crisis of the Secular State: A Reply to Professor Sajo', 7 *International Journal of Constitutional Law* (2009) 494.

[56] See, e.g., Obama's take on the European situation, available at http://foreignpolicy.com/2015/01/16/obama-slaps-europe-for-failing-to-integrate-muslims (last visited 28 August 2018).

public schools for wearing the veil, it contributed to disenfranchisement.[57] French public education is an instrument by means of which individuals are trained to become citizens of the republic. They cannot be expected to be citizens prior to entering school. Living together is a practice that can be facilitated by the state in major social institutions, such as schools. Living together cannot be used as a reason to criminalize the behaviour of people who are alienated from society. The ECtHR should not have accepted such a weak justification on the part of France in *S.A.S.* It should have challenged it and asked France to reconsider its position.

4. Conclusion

Europe needs to rethink secularism. It is often assumed that Europe is already secular, but that needs to be reassessed. I have tried to show that Europe is committed to negative secularism, which is the product of past struggles but which is not in touch with the present. Negative secularism thrives because of the existence of an enemy: fundamentalist religion. In this struggle, Europe has everything to lose. Negative secularism empowers the most aggressive religious minorities by putting them in the position of martyrs. Repression of religion provokes a strong backlash and alienates moderate religious people. Europe's long secular and religious heritage needs to be pulled apart and reimagined.

This chapter has suggested that ethical secularism should be at the centre of a European secular manifesto. Ethical secularism's central message is that diversity is superior to homogeneity. In order to thrive, diversity of all kinds requires a stable unitary framework, the marketplace of religions. Ethical secularism is an affirmation of the secular age, rather than a negation of religion. Ethical secularism attempts to free itself from inbuilt biases against religious minorities to become a fully independent worldview of worldviews. The illustration used in this chapter is the negative attitude towards European Muslims and towards Islam more generally which is so often seen in Europe. It is hard to deny that the ECtHR, for example, treats Islamic symbols and practices in a discriminatory fashion, even if it starts with the recognition of freedom of religion for all.

European courts will be successful if they address the inbuilt biases that make religious minorities aliens in a society, while entrenching the beliefs and symbols of religious majorities. Living together means developing an ethical secular framework within which all political and religious ideologies can find their place. So what if those ideologies clash? Clashes are part and parcel of dynamic societies. The burden of ethical secularism is to remove buried assumptions from the table that only lull us into believing that liberal institutions can find compromises at little cost. It will thus make sure that clashes can be channelled into moments of genuine exchange, which include actual debate about subjects such as the place of the crucifix in the classroom or the prohibition of the full-face veil in the streets. Genuine exchange will not

[57] For a full account of more than 20 years of debates, see C. Laborde, *Critical Republicanism and the Hijab* (2011).

produce agreement. Lines will have to be drawn. But I have suggested that lines drawn from a position of genuine openness, coupled with a clear instrumental framework such as the marketplace of religions, will be preferable over lines drawn from a position of inbuilt biases and illusions about overlapping consensus.

Secularism is being questioned in Europe, but the real question is not whether or not we want secularism; rather it is about which conception of secularism we want. The question we have to ask is: what do we want Europe to be like? Do we want it to be a racist place that discriminates against those people that do not fit the rather narrow profile shaped by the European Christian past? Or do we want it to be an open place that is confident about its secularism and its achievements and for that reason can afford a great amount of genuine diversity without falling apart? I opt for the second.

Index

The manufacturer's authorised representative in the EU for product safety is Oxford University Press España S.A. of el Parque Empresarial San Fernando de Henares, Avenida de Castilla, 2 – 28830 Madrid (www.oup.es/en or product.safety@oup.com). OUP España S.A. also acts as importer into Spain of products made by the manufacturer.

www.ingramcontent.com/pod-product-compliance
Lightning Source LLC
LaVergne TN
LVHW011804200926
848484LV00003B/779
* 9 7 8 0 1 9 8 8 1 2 0 6 7 *